THE END OF STRIFE

THE END OF STRIFE

Papers selected from the proceedings of the Colloquium of the Commission Internationale d'Histoire Ecclésiastique Comparée held at the University of Durham 2 to 9 September 1981

Edited by
DAVID LOADES

on behalf of the British Sub-Commission of C.I.H.E.C.

T. & T. CLARK
36 GEORGE STREET, EDINBURGH

Copyright © David Loades and Contributors, 1984

Set by C. R. Barber and Partners, Fort William
Printed by Billings, Worcester
for
T. & T. CLARK LTD., EDINBURGH

Index prepared by Fiona Carmichael and Margo Taylor of the USGS Index
Project, 21 Buccleuch Place, Edinburgh.

ISBN: 0 567 09347 6

FIRST PRINTED 1984

THE CONTRIBUTORS

Positions held at the time of the Colloquium.

The Reverend Robert Atwell	Chaplain and Fellow of Trinity College, Cambridge.
Professor Jonathan Riley-Smith	Professor of History, Royal Holloway College, London.
Dr. Georg Scheibelreiter	University Lecturer in Theology, Vienna.
Professor Klaus Guth	Professor für Volkskunde und Historische Landeskunde, Bamberg.
Dr. Claire Cross	Reader in History, University of York.
Robert Favre	Maitre-Assistant, Institut d'études politiques, Lyon II.
Professor Gerhard Müller	Professor of Ecclesiastical History, University of Erlangen.
Professor Marcel Pacaut	Directeur, Institut d'études politiques, Université de Lyon II.
Professor G. H. M. Posthumus Meyjes	Professor of Church History, University of Leiden.
Professor A. H. Bredero	Professor of Ecclesiastical History, Free University of Amsterdam.
Professor Kurt Schäferdiek	Professor of Ecclesiastical History, University of Bonn.
Dr. Clyde Binfield	Senior Lecturer in History, University of Sheffield.
Dr. Brian Aspinwall	Lecturer in History, University of Glasgow.
The Rev. Dr. Ian Hazlett	Lecturer in Ecclesiastical History, University of Glasgow.

EDITOR'S PREFACE

The papers appearing in this volume are a representative selection of those read at the colloquium of the Commission Internationale d'Histoire Ecclésiastique Comparée (C.I.H.E.C.) held at the University of Durham from 2 to 9 September 1981. The objective of the British Sub-Commission, which organised the colloquium, in entrusting me with the editorial responsibility for these proceedings was to produce a volume of academic distinction which should do justice both to the complexity and the coherence of a week of intensive work. Whether I have succeeded or not, the reader shall judge. The task has not been an easy one. Between seventy and eighty papers, *rapports* and communications were read to the different sections of the colloquium, relating to five distinct major themes, and every period from the patristic to the contemporary. Of these, forty-one were offered for inclusion in this collection; a fully representative group, but not coherent in any sense. Faced with this situation, even the establishment of criteria presented great difficulties, since the great majority of the work submitted was fully worthy, in the academic sense, of being published. It was clear from the start that considerations of cost would limit the size of the volume to approximately what has now been realised, and that consequently a selection which was primarily representative would have no coherence beyond the very general consideration that it would be 'all about' ecclesiastical history. Since this was felt to be unacceptable for a number of reasons, it was eventually decided to choose three related themes from among those which had been used at the colloquium, and under those headings of Death, Reconciliation, and Spirituality, to group a selection of papers which should be representative of different approaches and periods. Some consideration was also given to representing the rich mixture of nationalities which had participated in the colloquium, although it was not possible to make more than a gesture in that direction.

Partly as a result of these difficulties, this book has been much longer in gestation than it should have been, and my main debt of gratitude is to all those who offered their work for inclusion, and who have been so patient and understanding about the selection process. Many excellent pieces had, perforce, to be rejected, and I am happy to say that several have appeared, or will shortly be appearing, in a variety of journals. Those whose work is included have had to be even more patient, and I can only thank them and hope that they will be pleased with the result. My second debt of gratitude is to the other members of the British Sub-Commission, who have given me valuable advice in those numerous areas in which my own academic expertise has been faulty or non-existent. Most particularly, all our thanks are due to Professor Michael Wilks, without whose skill and experience the volume would not have appeared at all.

As far as possible each paper appears exactly in the form in which it was finally submitted. Editorial interference has been kept to a minimum, particularly in the cases of the two papers appearing in French, and one in German. Papers appearing in English have been subjected to a certain amount of standardisation, particularly in the presentation of footnotes and the expanding of esoteric contractions. Finally, my thanks are due to Mrs. June Hughes for preparing the final typescript, and to Dr. Geoffrey Green of T. & T. Clark for steering it through the press.

U.C.N.W.   David Loades
30 December 1982

TABLE OF CONTENTS

ix

SECTION I: DEATH

ASPECTS IN ST. AUGUSTINE OF HIPPO'S THOUGHT AND SPIRITUALITY CONCERNING THE STATE OF THE FAITHFUL DEPARTED, 354–430

Robert Attwell

Examination of St. Augustine's writings reveals the extent to which his mother's death exercised a formative influence upon his understanding of life after death. Here in the intensity of the pain of bereavement we encounter the quintessence of his thought, and discover something of the quality of his faith and spirituality as the shock of death moves him to prayer and reflection.

In his *Confessions* Augustine recalls how, as death approached his mother, Monica, she momentarily recovered consciousness, announcing to her sons: 'Lay this body anywhere. Let no care of it disturb you: this only I ask of you, that you should remember me at the Altar of the Lord wherever you may be.'[1] With that she fell silent and, as Augustine goes on to record, her 'devout and holy soul was released from the body.' Apparently, it was Augustine himself who closed her eyes, and in a moving passage he describes the terrible grief he experienced, though at the time he shed no tear. In his own words, he felt that 'it was not fitting that her funeral should be solemnized with moaning and weeping and lamentation, for so it is normal to weep when death is seen as sheer misery or as complete extinction.'[2] After the chanting of several psalms, the corpse was taken out for burial and, as was customary, prayers and 'the sacrifice of our redemption was offered for her' at the graveside. Augustine did not reveal the depth of his grief until he wrote his *Confessions* some ten years later, and in them, it is interesting to note not only the maturity of his reflections, but also sentiments of a different kind being expressed: 'Now that my heart is

---

[1] *Confessions* (trans. F. J. Sheed, London, 1944), IX, II.
[2] *Ibid.*, 12.

3

healed of that wound, I pour forth to Thee O our God, tears of a very different sort for thy handmaid'.[3]

Nothing of his spontaneous confidence in the face of death has been lost, a confidence congruent with an authentic expression of Christian hope. The atmosphere of the passage is triumphant, for the death of Monica was not 'sheer misery', neither was it 'complete extinction'. The positive thrust of his prayer for his mother, and the simplicity of his petition that she should 'rest in peace' leaves us in no doubt as to his trust in her blissful state, as one who was already saved and whose pardon was sealed. And yet, for all this, it is equally apparent that within his general confidence there is a distinct awareness of human frailty with particular emphasis being laid upon the removal of sin in the afterlife.

Augustine admits that this thought had *not* been foremost in his mind at the time of his mother's death; but upon reflection, he concludes that though 'she had been made alive in Christ' and had led a virtuous life, yet she was not free from sin: 'I dare not say that from the moment of her regeneration in baptism no word issued from her mouth contrary to Thy command.'[4] He therefore feels moved to pray to God for his mother's sins, beseeching God's forgiveness for 'such trespasses as she may have been guilty of in all the years since her baptism.' The offering of the Eucharist for her repose takes on a similar nuance as well; with that which was initially offered in thanksgiving for a virtuous life now being pleaded as a means to the removal of sin. Doubtless Monica's name would have been inscribed upon the diptychs of her church (presumably her home church in North Africa), and it is not improbable that by his frequent references to her remembrance 'at the altar', Augustine is thinking not simply of her commemoration in the Sunday Eucharist, but her specific commemoration on certain days, notably her year's mind.

A pattern of eucharistic commemoration of the departed can be traced back with certainty to the second century and to the church of Tertullian's day.[5] The practice, it would appear, was engendered by the natural wish of those left behind to maintain their union with their departed relations and friends, and of this union, the eucharistic fellowship was the deepest expression. Prayers for 'repose', 'refreshment', 'light' and 'peace' and also (but to a lesser extent) for cleansing, forgiveness and sanctification, find their places throughout the liturgies of the early church, both East and West.[6] With Augustine, however, and here he is typical of the view that

---

[3] *Ibid.*, 13.

[4] *Ibid.*

[5] See Tertullian, *de Anima* 51; *de Monogamia* 10; *de Corona* III.

[6] See e.g. Tertullian (as above); *Anaphora of SS Adai and Mari*; *Didascalia Apostolorum*; N.B. It has been argued by Daniélou (*The Origins of Latin Christianity*, ET, London 1977, p. 26) that the theme of rest is *not* concerned with the repose of the soul after death, but refers to the rest of the seventh day, the sabbath rest, and is therefore synonymous not with quiet repose but with festivity.

had come to prevail in the West during the fourth century, while expressing the belief that the dead are aided by the prayers of the Church and the 'saving sacrifice', we find a conception of the eucharistic sacrifice as propitiary.[7] This, combined with the growing tendency in the West to ascribe a place for punishment in the life after death for the faithful, betrays the gradual re-orientation of thought in the Church, which as developed later by Gregory the Great, was to help foster the belief – so prevalent in the medieval period – that masses for the dead are specially beneficial in winning for the departed remission of sin or alleviation of suffering. Such a crude development, however, is not ascribable to Augustine. As we have seen, he merely testifies to the fact that his mother 'had bound her soul by the bond of faith to the sacrament of our redemption' and therefore he feels confident to assert that though 'she will not answer that she owes nothing, lest she should be contradicted and confuted by that cunning accuser, yet she will answer that her debts have been remitted by Him, to whom no-one can hand back the price He paid for us, though He owed it not'.[8]

Augustine's very personal testimony in all this, indicates something of the wide backcloth of related theological, liturgical and pastoral matters that impinged upon his thought about the state of the departed. Prayer for the dead, the propriety of eucharistic commemoration, the implications of a vocabulary and theology of merit, the complex of problems associated with post-baptismal sin and the application of the categories of a penitential system to the hereafter, not to mention the pastoral policy he developed during his episcopate, in the face of what can only be termed a 'pen-umbra' of Christian devotion to the dead (including the cult of the *refrigeria*), all qualify for analysis. Each strand is worthy of attention because each elucidates the rich tapestry of Augustine's thought about life after death. Time, however, permits the exploration of only one such thread: namely, the way in which Augustine's spirituality illuminates the context and presuppositions of his thought by revealing to us the interior of his praying mind.

As a preliminary to our discussion, it should be stated that there is not a little ambiguity in Augustine's writings concerning questions relating to the dead, an ambiguity which in the past has catered for divergent interpretations of his thought. Even Portalié, who elsewhere exhibits a remarkable felicity for transforming tentative opinions into definitive statements, is forced to admit 'a certain vagueness in the ideas of St. Augustine' at this point.[9] Augustine's reticence on some issues was due as much to a natural refusal to dogmatize in an area where, to quote Baillie,

---

[7] *de Anima et Origine*, II, xv, 21; *Enchiridion*, XXIX, 110; *de Sermone Domini*, 172, 2. Similar thought is to be found in the east, e.g. Cyril of Jerusalem – *Cachetesis Mystagogicae*, V, 9.

[8] *Confessions*, IX, 13.

[9] F. Portalié, *A Guide to the Thought of St. Augustine*, (ET, London, 1960), p. 291.

'agnosticism is assuredly the better part of wisdom',[10] as to a confluence of various theological ideas in his mind, not the least of which was the tension resulting from the interaction of a rigid predestinarianism and a belief that there may be those who, though saved, yet require refining from all taint of sin.

Broadly, it may be said that from the very first, Augustine seems to have envisaged some sort of separation in the state of the departed with the just enjoying bliss and happiness, and the damned suffering in torture and anguish.[11] It was his opinion that immediately after death the eternal destiny of each soul is fixed irrevocably, but that the respective joys and sufferings of the righteous and the impious are only preliminary manifestations of their ultimate destiny at the Last Day. Thus, even the great martyrs, Perpetua and Felicity, are not thought of as enjoying the *full* blessedness of the vision of God which is their eventual glory![12] Augustine's opinion here, it should be said, was prompted not out of any disregard for the status of the martyrs, but rather as a logical consequence of certain theological presuppositions which he held about the relationship of the soul to the body and all that that entailed for his understanding of the attainment of the beatific vision and sensibility to suffering and joy. Yet it is interesting to note that at the end of his life, as is clear from the *Retractions*, he was clearly unwilling utterly to deny to such souls the possibility of enjoying something that might be described as contemplation of the Love of God.[13] Indeed, in his discourse on the psalms he can say:

> Not such a place is that home of ours, Jerusalem, where all are good ... There all the just and holy enjoy the Word of God without reading ... For what is written for us in books they perceive through the face of God! O Great home of ours![14]

It is most probable, therefore, that when Augustine refers the retribution of man's works to the Last Judgement, he is not, as might appear, contradicting himself, or denying what he asserts of an individual judgement immediately after death, but rather designating the day of resurrection as a more solemn, public, and more complete retribution whereby the preliminary differentiation in the state of the departed, with its attendant joys or pains, is ratified and consummated for eternity.

It is within these firm boundaries that Augustine promotes his view concerning the purification of certain souls in the after-life. It was his opinion that most Christians were neither so transparently good or so

---

[10] J. Baillie, *And the Life Everlasting* (London 1934), p. 198.
[11] *Enchiridion* (trs. E. Evans, London, 1953) XXIX, 109.
[12] *de Sermone Domini*, 280, 5.
[13] *Retractions*, I, 14, 2.
[14] *Enarrationes in Psalmos*, 119, 6.

transparently believing, that they could be said unequivocally to be destined for heaven; nor, on the other hand, were most Christians so clearly evil that they were destined for hell. A doctrine of an intermediate state, however, which incorporated the possibility for growth and purification corresponded, at least at the level of experience, more exactly with the way men lived than an absolute alternative. Evidently the stark alternative of heaven and hell failed to satisfy either Augustine's conception of God's goodness, or his opinion of man's deserts! Indeed, it was precisely within this category that Augustine had ventured to place his own saintly mother. Not surprisingly, therefore, we find Augustine's thought in this matter to be both highly complex and highly personalised, proceeding as it did out of inner ferment and a mind often preoccupied with his own past errors.

It seemed inevitable to Augustine that suffering would play its part in man's complete sanctification in the life to come because, for him, deeper penitence necessarily brought its measure of suffering. Such a notion was not original to Augustine. It had a long lineage traceable from Clement of Alexandria. What is original to Augustine, however, is the way in which he analyses and integrates this inherited thought, associating it very closely with his understanding of prayer, and combining both with his own insights from biblical exegesis; and in doing so, providing what was to become the substance of the medieval synthesis.

For example, commenting on the Pauline words saved 'yet so as by fire' (I Cor. 3.11–15), Augustine offers us a beautifully measured statement:

> Whether, therefore, men undergo such sufferings in this life only, or whether some such judgements follow also after this life, I do not think this view of the passage to conflict with truth and reason.[15]

In essence, this is the Augustinian position. Suffering is seen as the means to purgation, the inevitable consequence and penalty of sin. The purpose of life is viewed as nothing less than the attainment of the vision of God, and the penitential process whereby a man becomes fit to stand in the presence of God, *if not already begun this side of death, must surely occur after it.* In his commentary on the Psalms he endorses this view, praying God so to purify him in this life that he would not have to suffer after death the purifying fire.[16] Indeed, during his terminal illness, we find Augustine undertaking a voluntary ten-day period of penance in solitude, in order to prepare himself to meet his Maker. Evidently, it is the prayer of the publican, 'God be merciful to me a sinner' that accompanies the saint to the gates of heaven.

But what was this fire, this *ignis emendatorius*, this *ignis purgatorius*, of which Augustine speaks? It is not my intention to attempt a summary of

---

[15] *de Fide et Operibus*, XVI, 29.
[16] *Enar. in Ps.*, 37, 3.

Augustine's thought concerning the nature of the purgatorial fire, an excellent analysis of which already exists in the work of Joseph Ntedika.[17] However, it would be true to say that Augustine never really ventured to commit himself on the subject. And here, Ntedika is surely mistaken in his attempt to construct a case for a development in Augustine's thought. It is Ntedika's opinion[18] that, in the early stages of his career, Augustine upheld the location of the fire of purgation at the end of the period between death and resurrection, identifying it with the fire of judgement – as did many patristic commentators – but that, towards the end of his life, Augustine changed his view, transferring the fire more specifically to the intermediate period between death and resurrection, which henceforth achieve an equivalence and, ultimately, an identity. The state of purgation ends at the Last Judgement because the final sentence recognises only the elect and the reprobate.

Such a development, which might be seen as exemplifying the transition from patristic thought to the more formalised pattern of later medieval theology, while attractive in some of its aspects, is surely too simplistic a view of the evidence. Ntedika himself, for example, is forced to admit that at least two of Augustine's statements in *de Civitate Dei* (XX.16; XXI.16), being completed towards the end of his career, would tell against his hypothesis. Furthermore, as Portalié is forced to point out,[19] Augustine would not be loath to admit with other of the Fathers – St. Hilary, for example – the purification of certain souls at the very momemt of judgement in accordance with the sayings of Malachi 3.1–6 and Isaiah 4.4. To quote Augustine: 'It seems more clear that some souls in that judgement shall suffer some kind of cleansing punishments'.[20]

Statements such as these go against Ntedika and, instead, serve to underline Augustine's reticence in this area of discourse. For similar reasons one should be equally apprehensive about accepting the verdict of Portalié who, without the slightest hesitation, can assert that Augustine was 'absolutely certain' about the existence of Purgatory.[21] Such a dogmatic statement does little justice to the bishop's academic caution, and moreover, applies later terminology in a somewhat arbitrary fashion. At no time was Augustine overtaken by the western preoccupation with theological formulation which might have led him into defining *places* rather than widely differing *conditions* in the life beyond. Still less was he tempted to apportion detailed awards and punishments to the good and bad in the intermediate state as later medieval theologians were wont to do. Augustine was rather satisfied with grounds for hoping whatever

---

[17] *L'Evolution de la Doctrine du Purgatoiure chez Saint Augustine* (Paris, 1966).
[18] *L'Evolution*, p. 45 f.
[19] *A Guide*, p. 297.
[20] *de Civitate Dei* (Everyman edition), XX, 25.
[21] *A Guide*, p. 295.

knowledge of God, trust in God, love of God lies in our character at death, will be fully developed in ways which, though probably not without cost to ourselves, are nevertheless ways not yet wholly foreseeable.

Indeed, it is precisely here, in his conception of the purpose of the spiritual life, that the true context of his thought emerges. All too frequently in discussions of Augustine's understanding of the rôle of purgative suffering in the after-life, interest becomes rivetted upon his understanding of the relationship between sin and punishment and the penitential system almost to the exclusion of any appreciation of his spirituality.

Augustine believed that it is through the life of moral activity that men become fit for the contemplation of God which for him alone constituted man's *summum bonum*.[22] Indeed, it would be true to say that, for Augustine, all human activity has to be directed towards the possession of God. Man's quest is not to be for intellectual enlightenment (*scientia*), but rather for that knowledge which is born only out of the personal contact of life with life (*sapientia*).[23] Thus in *de Civitate Dei* (XIX.13) he can give a summary of the ideal of peace to which the Christian life is tending, as one in which not only the rebellion of man has ceased towards his Creator, but also one in which there is a positive acceptance of harmonious relationships that fulfil God's intention. All this is involved in the pursuit of perfection, whereby man's life, understanding and love are perpetually renewed and deepened by grace. In a sermon on the healing of the man born blind, Augustine says:

> Our whole business in this life is to heal the heart's eye by which God is seen. For this the holy mysteries are celebrated, for this the word of God is preached; this end is served by the Church's moral exhortations, touching the correction of conduct, the amendment of carnal desires; the renouncing of this world not with our lips only but by a changed life; this end is served by all Holy Scriptures: that the inner man be be purged from that which hinders us from looking upon God.[24]

The specifically Christian ethic (as distinct from that of the Neo-Platonist) in this process of healing, which is here seen to involve variously correction, mortification, renunciation and purgation, is one based on the Incarnation.[25] For, as Augustine writes in his *Treatise on the Trinity*, 'there

[22] *de Trinitate*, I, 31.
[23] The distinction is discussed in books XII to XIV of the *de Trinitate*. See also Rowan Williams, *The Wound of Knowledge* (London 1979), p. 74; and John Burnaby, *Amor Dei: A Study of the Religion of St. Augustine* (London 1938), pp. 60–73.
[24] *de Sermone*, 88, 5.
[25] *Confessions*, VII, 13.

are some who think that they can be purified for the contemplation of God
and for union with Him by their own virtue – whose pride is itself the
deepest stain upon them; for there is no fault to which the law of God is
more contrary'.[26] Against such notions, Augustine repeatedly stressed the
fact that the apprehension of God is a gift, not an achievement,[27] and the
gift of God is at once the gift of his healing love and the gift of his
unmerited forgiveness, as found in the person of Jesus Christ. Both these
aspects are to be found in his theology of the spiritual life, and as a result
they become the lenses through which Augustine could focus his thoughts
about the nature and purpose of an intermediate state between death and
final resurrection.

Thus, for example, throughout his writings one finds testimony to the
drawing power of the love of God as that which is crucial for the growth of
man in holiness and for the exercise of his true freedom. 'My weight is my
love. By it I am carried wherever I am carried. By thy gift, we are
enkindled and are carried upward. We burn inwardly, and move forward
. . . we go forward because we go up to the peace of Jerusalem'.[28]
Moreover, for Augustine, the love that gives freedom to man's will is
enkindled within him as he participates in the dying and rising of Christ, so
that when he speaks of the imitation of Christ and of the Christian
pilgrimage as one of following and participating in the sufferings of Christ,
he is describing a dynamic movement in which man is caught up into love
by the love of God. The spiritual life on this understanding becomes a
positive movement, one not necessarily without a measure of pain, but
certainly one in which 'we are renewed'.[29] It is a process which Augustine
envisaged as necessarily extending beyond death as it seeks ultimate
fulfilment in the perfection of love in the contemplation of God.
Reflection upon heaven can, therefore, never be a futile or even
dangerously misleading activity for Augustine. For what is involved is a
perception of oneself as being formed by the attractive power of the love of
God.

In a similar way, Augustine can also view the spiritual life in terms of
repentance, forgiveness and purgation. Since the apprehension of God is a
gift, not an achievement, it follows that sin, which is the only barrier
between man and God, and which debilitates him in his search for his
creator, can also only be purged by an act of God.[30] The one purgation for
iniquity and pride is in 'the blood of the Righteous and the humility of
God'.[31] Thus, although the soul's cleansing is a journey – a journey which

---

[26] de Trinitate, IV, 15, 20.
[27] de Civitate Dei, X, 29.
[28] Confessions, XIII, 9.
[29] Enar. in Ps., 37, 27.
[30] de Civitate Dei, X, 22.
[31] de Trinitate, IV, 2, 4.

involves the elimination of imperfections and which ultimately leads through mortification to union with God – it is a journey which we could not make, had not the Way itself come down to us in the person of Jesus Christ,[32] Augustine identifies the symptoms of man's malaise as follows:

> What is evil is the will's aversion from the changeless Good and its conversion to the goods that are changing; and this aversion and conversion, being voluntary, and not compelled, is followed by the fit and just punishment of misery.[33]

In this definition is disclosed one of the presuppositions of Augustinian spirituality, for his view of the nature of man's sin is seen to be the direct corollary of his view of the *summum bonum*. At one level it is the failure to love God. At another level it is the inevitable transference of love to objects which, though good in themselves, being God's creatures, are nevertheless goods less than the highest which, for Augustine, can only be the contemplation of the unchangeable, and to human eyes invisible, substance of God.[34] It is a definition which in part reflects the influence of Neo-Platonism; but it also betrays the influence of the penitential system, with suffering, either now or hereafter, being seen as the inevitable consequence and penalty of sin.

These two aspects of Augustine's spirituality achieve a deeper synthesis in his theology of prayer where the various notions of attraction, illumination, purgation, mortification and contemplation receive expression.[35] Here Augustine provides us with the fulcrum of his spirituality, but more importantly for our purposes, an authentic mirror with which to view his understanding of the state of the departed in relation to the totality of the Christian life.

In his treatise *de Quantitate Animae*, written shortly after his baptism, Augustine distinguishes seven grades or degrees (*gradus*) in the functions or operations of the soul, which he sees as the principle of life, sensation, intelligence and morality. The precise numeration of these degrees in prayer is immaterial. Suffice it to say that in the early stages of prayer Augustine envisages there being a longing for God, for something not clearly known or yet understood. This longing, this thirst for God, will become more clearly differentiated as the destruction of vices in the soul and the elimination of imperfections take place. Thus the fifth grade is characterised by Augustine as '*tranquillitas*', the calming of the passions; and the sixth as '*ingressio*', the approach to contemplation, which itself constitutes the seventh and final stage. In essence (though not in detail) this

---

[32] *de Doctrina Christiani*, I, 10.
[33] *de Libero Arbitrio*, II, 200.
[34] *de Trinitate*, I, 31. *De Gen. at Litt.*, XII, 35, 38.
[35] See on this: F. Cayre, *La Contemplation Augustinienne* (Paris 1945).

thought reflects much of the earlier thought of Origen on the subject though the last three stages which Augustine mentions correspond in idea, though not in nomenclature, more to the division which later writers were to make in terms of the purgative, illuminative and unitive ways of prayer. Augustine himself reserves the actual word 'purgation' for the fourth grade, which he regards as a necessary preliminary to further growth. In the fifth stage God reforms the soul, in the sixth he leads it, and in the seventh he feeds it and perfects it in love; because Augustine claims, 'it is one thing to purify the soul, and another to keep it pure; one thing to restore it when sullied, another not to suffer it to become sullied again'.[36] More than once, Augustine insists upon the truth that not until this purification of the soul has been effected, not until it has been 'cleansed and healed', can it proceed to the contemplation of God which is the 'highest reward of the saints'.[37]

It should not be thought from this delineation of degrees in prayer that Augustine envisaged some sort of arbitrary division in the spiritual life into neat compartments whereby an individual might progress from one stage to another on completion of a course of treatment! Nor should it be imagined that Augustine thought within the confines of a temporal framework whereby, for example, stages one to four might be completed in this life, and the rest hereafter. No such structure was in his mind. It was rather Augustine's wish to testify to that diversity of experience which was the common possession of all Christians who persevered in the life of prayer and to give it some cohesion and significance. It was his opinion that although the spiritual life was in its essence a deepening of one's love of God, and consequently a 'progression', it was not a process open to simple evaluation. For example, like Origen before him, Augustine held that while penitence is to be seen as the beginning of the spiritual life, this is not equivalent to saying that it is a stage to be left behind. On the contrary, as we have seen, it is not a stage at all for Augustine, but a condition that must in some sense continue permanently, both now at the point of death, and after death, as the constant attitude of all who truly aspire to be united with God in love. Similarly, it is apparent that although Augustine asserted contemplation to be the ultimate reward of the saints in heaven and, therefore, something that really belongs to the next life, he yet held it possible for some beginnings of it to occur in this life, some passing glimpses or intuitions of divine things.[38]

In this way, therefore, Augustine was equally as capable of interpreting the spiritual life in terms of a cyclic movement as he was of describing it within the more conventional categories pertaining to a linear progression. The soul acquires that which it already possesses in order to effect a deeper surrender. Contemplation is as much a present possession to be deepened

[36] *de Quantitate Animae*, 79, 80.
[37] *de Trinitate*, XII, 22.
[38] *Tractatus in Ioanem*, CXXIV, 5.

and renewed, as a distant goal to which we travel. Augustine's thought
about the spiritual life is perpetually caught within the tension that exists
between these polarities, born as it is out of the paradox that love contains
within itself the promise and reality of its own fulfilment, and that God will
not fail to 'crown His gifts'.

> It is He whom we long to receive, who makes us ask. He whom we
> desire to find, who makes us seek ... And when He has been
> received, He still works in us an asking and a seeking, that He may be
> received more abundantly.[39]

In this context, the text 'Seek His face evermore' was one that Augustine
loved to ponder. God always comes to meet the seeker, and the search is
continuously rewarding, but it discloses only an infinite perspective
beyond our attainment.[40] Does such seeking belong to this life only?
questions Augustine, an existence in which 'faith already finds Him, hope
still seeks Him, and love finds Him through faith, yet seeks to possess Him
through sight?' Augustine is not sure; but he begins to wrestle with the
implications of what communion with God might hold, projecting from
his experience of life and his awareness of a potential for growth at once
conditioned by, yet, independent of, the constraints of our present
existence (and, for that matter, of the limitations of our probable future
time), a notion of 'life' surpassing man's imagination. It may well be, says
Augustine, that even after death, even at the Last Day when we will see
God as He is, He will yet be *sine fine quaerendus quia sine fine amandus*: for if
there is no end to love's increase, love's seeking, the deepening of its
apprehension, it may be that the ultimate realisation of the contemplation
of God will itself yield an infinite perspective for growth.[41] This is the focal
point to which Augustine's spirituality converges, the centre around which
it pivots. Appropriately enough, it is no static conceit but a living, dynamic
conception, the still point which itself yields the principle of movement
that unites and vitalises Augustine's whole thought about life, death and the
hereafter. As with so many other doctrines, it was Augustine who set the
seal on western teaching regarding the state of the faithful departed. A
familiar cliché describes him as 'a man living on the frontiers of two
worlds, the ancient world which was passing away, and the medieval
world which was coming into being.' As has been seen, this description is
not entirely without foundation. But in this examination of Augustine's
spirituality, I have tried to explore a dimension of his thought not usually
associated with his theology of the state of the departed, for it is my
contention that here is to be discovered both the crystallisation point for his
theology and a germination point for our understanding of it.

[39] *Enar. in Ps.*, 118, XIV, 2.
[40] *de Trinitate*, XV, 2.
[41] *Enar. in Ps.*, 104, 3.

DEATH ON THE FIRST CRUSADE

Jonathan Riley-Smith

Although preached by the pope and accompanied, and to a limited extent controlled, by the clergy, the first crusade was predominantly a lay enterprise. Pope Urban II made this clear to the monks of the congregation of Vallombrosa, some of whom had wanted to participate.

> We have stimulated the minds of knights to go on this expedition . . .
> We do not want those who have abandoned the world and have
> vowed themselves to spiritual warfare either to bear arms or to go on
> this journey; we go so far as to forbid them to do so.[1]

It was the duty of knights, not churchmen, to fight and this distinction of functions was stressed by the contemporary writer Baldric of Bourgueil, who put into Urban's mouth at the Council of Clermont words comparing the responsibilities of *oratores* with those of *pugnatores*, with a reference to Moses' outstretched arms during the battle of Raphidim (in Exodus xvii, 11–12).

> Our duty is to pray. Yours must be to fight against the Amalekites.
> We will hold out tireless hands like Moses, praying to heaven; you
> must draw and brandish your swords, you fearless warriors against
> Amalek.[2]

Baldric saw the crusade, in fact, as an expression of that right relationship between the spiritual and temporal orders about which the eleventh-century reformers were so insistent.

[1] W. Wiederhold, 'Papsturkunden in Florenz', *Nachrichten von der Gesellschaft der Wissenshaften zu Göttingen*. Phil.-hist. Kl. (Göttingen, 1901), p. 313.

[2] Baldric of Bourgueil, 'Historia Jerosolimitana', *Recueil des historiens des croisades. Historiens occidentaux*, iv, p. 15.

See the *sacerdotium* and the *regnum*. The clerical order and the lay are in agreement in sharing the leadership of the army of God. Bishop (Adhémar of Le Puy) and Count (Raymond of Toulouse) are before us in the guises of Moses and Aaron.[3]

The crusade was the culminating event of a period in which the reformers had laid down a role for laymen as defenders of the church, but as defenders subject to the church. Guibert of Nogent, the most intelligent commentator on the crusade, emphasized this in a famous passage of his *Gesta*.

> God has instituted in our time holy wars, so that the order of knights and the crowd running in their wake, who following the example of the ancient pagans have been engaged in slaughtering one another, might find a new way of gaining salvation. And so they are not forced to abandon secular affairs completely by choosing the monastic life or any religious profession, as used to be the custom, but can attain in some measure God's grace while pursuing their own careers, with the liberty and in the dress to which they are accustomed.[4]

The conviction that the crusade provided laymen with a positive role through which they could gain grace without changing their way of life was also expressed in the comparisons between old reprobate warriors and new knights of Christ that were a feature of crusade propaganda.[5]

It was typical of popular theology then, and indeed at any time in Christian history, that it was not good enough for preachers to refer in general terms to service of this kind being meritorious; they had to specify in what way an action could lead to salvation. For crusaders there was the enjoyment of the conviction that their dead were martyrs. With regard to the indulgence there is a revealing description by Ralph of Caen of the state of mind of Tancred, who was to be one of the leaders of the crusade, when he took the cross.

> Frequently he burned with anxiety, because the warfare he engaged in as a knight seemed to be contrary to the Lord's commands. The Lord, in fact, ordered him to offer the cheek that had been struck

[3] Baldric of Bourgueil, p. 16.
[4] Guibert of Nogent, 'Historia quae dicitur Gesta Dei per Francos', *Recueil des historiens des croisades. Historiens occidentaux*, iv, p. 124.
[5] Fulcher of Chartres, *Historia Hierosolymitana*, ed. H. Hagenmeyer (Heidelberg, 1913), pp. 136–7; Robert of Rheims, 'Historia Iherosolimitana', *Recueil des historiens des croisades. Historiens occidentaux*, iii, pp. 728, 748; Guibert of Nogent, p. 138; Baldric of Bourgueil, pp. 14–15; William of Malmesbury, *De gestis regum Anglorum libri quinque*, ed. W. Stubbs, ii (London, 1889), p. 394.

together with his other cheek to the striker; but secular knighthood did not spare the blood of relatives. The Lord urged him to give his tunic and his cloak as well to the man who would take them away; the needs of war impelled him to take from a man already despoiled of both whatever remained to him. And so, if ever that wise man could give himself up to repose, these contradictions deprived him of courage. But after the judgement of Pope Urban granted remission of all their sins to all Christians going out to fight the gentiles, then at last, as if previously asleep, his vigour was aroused, his powers grew, his eyes opened, his courage was born. For before ... his mind was divided, uncertain whether to follow in the footsteps of the Gospel or the world. But after the call to arms in the service of Christ, the two-fold reason for fighting inflamed him beyond belief.

Tacred's burden of guilt was lightened when he heard of the indulgence offered to crusaders in 1095 and it is clear that what mattered to him was the fact that the privilege confirmed that the crusade was a war he could fight without endangering his soul; more than that, he no longer had any need to choose between religion and the world, for he could find salvation in the world.[6] The importance of the indulgence, in other words, was that it was a privilege confirming in concrete terms that waging war could lead to salvation.

To Tancred it came as a surprise. Indulgences were not common, but they were not novelties by the late eleventh century; what had been very rare were indulgences for fighting.[7] It has been suggested recently (on the basis of what seems to be contradictory phrases describing the crusade indulgence on the one hand merely as a relaxation of penance imposed in confession and on the other as a remission of sins, involving the cancellation of all temporal punishments which would have been imposed by God for past sins) that the preachers of the cross went further than Pope Urban had intended when he granted the indulgence or even that the pope himself was confused, since in his letters he referred both to release from penances and to remission of sins.[8] But there is no hint in the sources that contemporaries felt confused or saw any conflict between what was granted and what was

---

[6] Ralph of Caen, 'Gesta Tancredi', Recueil des historiens des croisades. Historiens occidentaux, iii, pp. 605–6.

[7] See N. Paulus, Geschichte des Ablasses im Mittelalter, i (Paderborn, 1922), pp. 1–97 passim.

[8] See H. E. Mayer, The Crusades (Oxford, 1972), pp. 25–40; J. S. C. Riley-Smith, What were the crusades? (London, 1977), pp. 57–9. The pope's references to indulgences are to be found in R. Somerville, The Councils of Urban II.1. Decreta Claromontensia (Annuarium Historiae Conciliorum. Suppl. 1 Amsterdam, 1972), p. 74; H. Hagenmeyer, Die Kreuzzugsbriefe aus den Jahren 1088-1100 (Innsbruck, 1901), pp. 136, 137; P. Kehr, Papsturkunden in Spanien i. Katalonien (Berlin, 1926), pp. 287–8.

preached. In the eleventh century the reconciliation of the sinner was occurring before the performance of the enjoined penance and there were growing doubts about the sufficiency of any penance, but it seems to have been accepted that the crusade, which as a pilgrimage to Jerusalem would anyway have ranked in the minds of most contemporaries as adequate penitential satisfaction for a serious sin, was so rigorous, painful and dangerous an exercise that it would purge the participants of their past crimes. Accounts of the crusade contained references to the crusaders being 'cleansed of their sins',[9] 'purged and reconciled to God'[10] and 'reborn through confession and the penance which you undergo daily in hard labour'.[11] It is clear that release from penance was granted by the pope for the very good reason that the crusade itself was a severely penitential act and he promised remission of sins because each crusader would perform adequate satisfaction by risking his life or even by dying for his brothers in the faith.[12] Release from penance and remission of sins were two aspects of the same idea and effectively meant the same thing.[13] This is precisely how Orderic Vitalis, writing four decades later, saw the grant of the indulgence in 1095.

> (Pope Urban) absolved on God's authority all the penitent from all their sins from the hour they took the Lord's cross and he lovingly released them from all hardships, whether fasting or other mortifications of the flesh.

The pope had done this, Orderic went on, because he had considered that the crusaders would suffer almost constant dangers and be tormented by changes of fortune, through which they would be cleansed from the guilt of all their sins.[14] It is not surprising that a full release from temporal punishment for past sins was expected by the crusaders,[15] a release that was

---

[9] Fulcher of Chartres, pp. 226–7.

[10] Robert of Rheims, p. 829. See also Albert of Aachen, 'Historia Hierosolymitana', *Recueil des historiens des croisades. Historiens occidentaux*, iv, p. 487; Orderic Vitalis, *Historia aecclesiastica*, ed. M. Chibnall, v (Oxford, 1975), pp. 747–8.

[11] Robert of Rheims, pp. 747–8.

[12] See Kehr, *Papsturkunden*, pp. 287–8; Fulcher of Chartres, p. 135.

[13] So I accept the view of B. Poschmann, *Der Ablass im Licht der Bussgeschichte* (Bonn, 1948), pp. 54–7, although on rather different grounds from him.

[14] Orderic Vitalis, v, pp. 16–18; see also *ibid.*, p. 26. For the association of the two elements, see also the bull of Alexander II in S. Löwenfeld, *Epistolae pontificum Romanorum ineditae* (Leipzig, 1885), p. 43; and 'De reliquiis Sanctissimae Crucis et Dominici Sepulchri, Scaphusam allatis', *Recueil des historiens des croisades. Historiens occidentaux*, v, p. 336.

[15] B. E. C. Guérard, *Cartulaire de l'abbaye de Saint-Père de Chartres*, ii (Paris, 1840), p. 428; Guibert of Nogent, p. 200.

treated at the same time as a reward and as a way to salvation,[16] or that the usual way of referring to the indulgence of 1095 was as a *remissio peccatorum*.[17] There was no contradiction in the pope's mind, nor should any distinction be made between what he intended and what the faithful believed.

Although historians, who have been concerned to demonstrate the developing idea of meritorious warfare, have tended to treat the indulgence and martyrdom together, it should be understood that they are strictly speaking different things. The fact is that, being a free gift of God issued on his behalf by the pope and absolving a sinner from the temporal punishments imposed for sin, the indulgence operates on a different level to martyrdom which, involving the voluntary acceptance of death for the sake of the faith and reflecting the death of Christ, is the supreme act of love of which a Christian is capable and is the perfect example of a Christian death. The effect of an indulgence, of course, is also to open the gates of paradise to a man who dies enjoying it, because the time he would have had to spend in purgatory is remitted. It was believed, at least by the French archbishop Baldric of Bourgueil, to be operative from the moment a man took the cross and not simply after the completion of the crusade: 'God distributes his own penny, at the first and at the eleventh hour',[17a] although in the thirteenth century men were still worrying whether they would

---

[16] Hagenmeyer, *Die Kreuzzugsbriefe*, p. 142; *Gesta Francorum et aliorum Hierosolimitanorum*, ed. R. Hill (London, 1962), p. 2; Peter Tudebode, *Historia de Hierosolymitano itinere*, ed. J. H. and L. L. Hill (Paris, 1977), p. 32; Fulcher of Chartres, pp. 136–7, 142–3; Guibert of Nogent, pp. 225, 250; Baldric of Bourgueil, p. 15; Hugh of St. Maria, 'Itineris Hierosolymitani compendium', *Recueil des historiens des croisades, Historiens occidentaux*, v, p. 363; 'Historia peregrinorum euntium Jerusolymam', *Recueil des historiens des croisades. Historiens occidentaux*, iii, p. 173; Albert of Aachen, p. 402; Caffaro di Caschifellone, 'De liberatione civitatum orientis', *Annali Genovesi*, ed. L. T. Belgrano, i (Genoa, 1890), p. 102.

[17] Hagenmeyer, *Die Kreuzzugsbriefe*, pp. 173, 175; A. Bernard and A. Bruel, *Recueil des chartes de l'abbaye de Cluny*, v (Paris, 1894), p. 59; Fulcher of Chartres, pp. 135, 140; Bernold 'Chronicon', *Monumenta Germaniae Historica. Scriptores*, v, p. 464; Robert of Rheims, p. 729; Bartolf of Nangis, 'Gesta Francorum expugnantium Iherusalem', *Recueil des historiens des croisades. Historiens occidentaux*, iii, p. 492; Ralph of Caen, p. 606; Ekkehard of Aura, 'Hierosolymita', *Recueil des historiens des croisades. Historiens occidentaux*, v, p. 15; 'Historia peregrinorum', p. 169; Caffaro di Caschifellone, pp. 100–1, 106. There are also references to absolution in William of Malmesbury, ii, p. 396 and Orderic Vitalis, pp. 16–18; and to pardon (*venia*) in Baldric of Bourgueil, p. 15. A most interesting distinction is made in 'Historia de translatione sanctorum magni Nicolai ... ejusdem avunculi, alterius Nicolai, Theodorique ...' (*Recueil des historiens des croisades. Historiens occidentaux*, v, p. 274) in which Christ gives 'de praeteritis peccatis ... vobis remissionem et indulgentiam, de praesentibus absolutionem et veniam, de futuris gratiae sua custodiam.'

[17a] Baldric of Bourgueil, p. 15.

enjoy the indulgence if they failed to reach Jerusalem, or died before departure.[18] But whereas an indulgence was a gift of God, martyrdom was the martyr's gift to God of his own life. It was so great an act of merit that it justified the martyr immediately in God's sight. Witnessing to his faith and grace, it was made possible by his intention and resolution and he had no need of an indulgence for his justification. Writing of dead crusaders, Guibert of Nogent expressed this clearly.

> If there was any need to suffer penalties for their sins, the spilling of their blood alone was a most powerful means of expiating all offences.[19]

In this paper I will concentrate on martyrdom, arguing that the conviction that some crusaders were martyrs emerged only in the course of the expedition and that, in an age in which the religious life was regarded as superior to the secular, it had a powerful influence on a changing attitude on the part of churchmen towards the laity.

The martyrs of the first crusade can be divided into three classes.[20] The first consists of those who died of disease. This group includes the knight Enguerrand of St. Pol, who was later seen in heaven in a vision,[21] and the papal legate Adhémar of Le Puy who died, probably of typhoid, on 1 August 1098. All the narrators of accounts of the crusade believed that he had gone to heaven, although one, to whom I will refer later, made him suffer temporarily in the afterlife for his scepticism about the relic of the Holy Lance. They tended to stress the sanctity of his life rather than his martyrdom,[22] but in a letter written late in 1099 the archbishop of Rheims included him and the bishop of Orange, who had fallen ill and died on c. 20 December 1098, among those 'who have died in peace, crowned with glorious martyrdom.'[23] The ranks of martyrs, therefore, included all those

---

[18] See for example James of Vitry, 'Sermones vulgares', ed. J. B. Pitra, *Analecta novissima*, ii (Paris, 1888), p. 427; St. Thomas Aquinas, 'Quodlibetum 2.16', *Opera*, ix (Parma, 1859), pp. 484–5.

[19] Guibert of Nogent, p. 179.

[20] There is also one example of the term martyrdom used of a man's suffering, although he himself survived. Technically, of course, he was a confessor, not a martyr. Orderic Vitalis, v, p. 352.

[21] See below, p. 24. For his death, see H. Hagenmeyer, *Chronologie de la première croisade (1094-1100)* (Paris, 1902), p. 201.

[22] *Gesta Francorum*, p. 74; Raymond of Aguilers, *Liber*, ed. J. H. and L. L. Hill (Paris, 1969), p. 84; Fulcher of Chartres, p. 258; Peter Tudebode, pp. 116–17; Robert of Rheims, p. 839; Guibert of Nogent, p. 210; Baldric of Bourgueil, p. 82; Bartolf of Nangis, p. 506; Ralph of Caen, p. 673; 'Historia peregrinorum', p. 207. Cf. Hagenmeyer, *Die Kreuzzugsbriefe*, p. 164. See below pp. 23–4.

[23] Hagenmeyer, *Die Kreuzzugsbriefe*, p. 176. For the mere fact of dying on the crusade ranking as martyrdom, see Albert of Aachen, p. 416.

who died good deaths, for whatever reason, on the crusade. In the second category are priests and laymen who were conventional martyrs in that they died passively, being killed when they were non-combatants or were unarmed or because they refused to renounce the Christian faith after being captured by the Muslims. A good example is Raynald Porchet, a Norman knight from southern Italy, who was captured by the Muslims on 6 March 1098. The story as told by an eyewitness of the crusade was that, paraded on *c.* 3 April by his captors on the city walls of Antioch to plead for ransom, he defiantly refused to do so and encouraged the Christian leaders to persist in the siege of the city, informing them that the Muslim garrison was weakened. He was taken down from the walls and brought before the Muslim commander, who offered him whatever he wanted in return for his apostasy. Raynald asked for time to think, but spent it praying that God might receive him into heaven. When told by an interpreter that Raynald was in fact denying Islam, the enraged commander ordered him to be beheaded and had all other captured crusaders brought before him and burnt in a great pyre.[24] Although only one of the earliest surviving histories of the crusade contains a description of Raynald's martyrdom, his cultus seems to have become widespread: an elaborated and to some extent altered account was included in the *Chanson d'Antioche* and in *c.* 1130 he was referred to as a saint.[25]

The third category of martyrs consists of those who died in battle, for instance Roger of Barneville, a famous Norman knight, who was universally loved, was killed on 4 June 1098 and was buried in the narthex of the cathedral of Antioch.[26] The idea that a man could achieve martyrdom at a time when he himself was perpetrating violence was not new; in the fourth century a cult had even developed of the martyrdom of

---

[24] Peter Tudebode, pp. 79–81.

[25] *La Chanson d'Antioche*, ed. S. Duparc-Quioc (Paris, 1976–8), i, pp. 205, 212–33, ii, pp. 198–9, 212–14; 'Historia peregrinorum', p. 194. For other martyrs in this category, see *Gesta Francorum*, p. 4; Peter Tudebode, pp. 35–6, 138; Robert of Rheims, pp. 734, 795; Guibert of Nogent, pp. 145, 146, 183–4; Baldric of Bourgueil, pp. 19–20; 'Historia peregrinorum', p. 175; Albert of Aachen, p. 288; Orderic Vitalis, v, pp. 38–40. See also Hagenmeyer, *Die Kreuzzugsbriefe*, p. 159; Guibert of Nogent, p. 252.

[26] Raymond of Aguilers, p. 66; Robert of Rheims, pp. 808–9; Gilo, 'Historia de via Hierosolymitana', *Recueil des historiens des croisades. Historiens occidentaux*, v, pp. 769–70; 'Historia peregrinorum', p. 198; Orderic Vitalis, v, p. 102. See also Hagenmeyer, *Die Kreuzzugsbriefe*, p. 159; Albert of Aachen, pp. 407–8. For other martyrs of this type, see Hagenmeyer, *Die Kreuzzugsbriefe*, pp. 150, 153, 154, 176; *Gesta Francorum*, pp. 4, 17, 40, 85; Raymond of Aguilers, pp. 108–9, 119; Peter Tudebode, pp. 75, 131; Robert of Rheims, pp. 735, 857; Guibert of Nogent, pp. 218–19; Baldric of Bourgueil, p. 93; Ralph of Caen, pp. 680–1; 'Historia peregrinorum', pp. 192, 211, 215; Albert of Aachen, p. 288; 'Auctarium Aquicienense Continuatio Sigeberti', *Monumenta Germaniae Historica. Scriptores*, vi, pp. 394–5; and see below notes 47, 58–64, 67.

virgins who had turned violence on themselves, committing suicide rather than face defilement by Roman soldiers.[27] But the first clear evidence for martyrdom in battle that has been found in western Christian history concerned the Frankish count Gerold, who was killed fighting the Avars in 799.[28] A letter from Pope Leo IV in 853 to the Franks promised heavenly rewards to those who died fighting for the faith, the salvation of their souls and the defence of the *patria*;[29] another letter from Pope John VIII in 878, in answer to a query from the Frankish bishops, assured those who died fighting pagans and infidels of eternal life[30] and the anonymous author of a remarkable treatise of *c.* 900 wrote much the same.[31] Before the battle of Civitate in 1053 Pope Leo IX promised his soldiers that if they died they would be martyrs; apparently he proved this to be the case, which suggests that he referred to Pope Leo IV's letter, and, although some reformers like Peter Damian disapproved of his involvement in warfare, there developed, with his encouragement, a cultus of the dead in battle.[32] In 1074 Pope Gregory VII wrote of eternal rewards for those who would take part in the expedition he was planning to the East[33] and at about the same time the idea of martyrdom in battle was a theme in Manegold of Lautenbach's treatment of the death of St. Oswald of Northumbria.[34] Leo IV's letter was included by the canonist Ivo of Chartres in his *Decretum* and *Panormia*, compiled just before the preaching of the first crusade.[35] The idea of

---

[27] St. Augustine, *de civitate Dei*, i, 26.

[28] The material on Gerold's death was collected by S. Abel and B. Simson, *Jahrbücher des frankischen Reiches unter Karl dem Grossen*, ii (Leipzig, 1883), pp. 189–94. For references to martyrdom in battle before 1095, I have relied on A. Gottlob, *Kreuzablass und Almosenablass* (Stuttgart, 1906), pp. 1–62; Paulus, *Geschichte des Ablasses*, pp. 1–211; C. Erdmann, *The Origin of the Idea of Crusade* (Princeton, 1977), *passim*; E. H. Kantorowicz, *The King's Two Bodies* (Princeton, 1957), pp. 232–42; A. Noth, *Heiliger Krieg und Heiliger Kampf in Islam und Christentum* (Bonn, 1966), pp. 95–109.

[29] *Monumenta Germaniae Historica. Epistolae Karolini aevi*, iii, p. 601.

[30] *Monumenta Germaniae Historica. Epistolae Karolini aevi*, iv, pp. 126–7.

[31] 'Epistola consolatoria ad pergentes in bellum', ed. W. Schmitz, *Neues Archiv*, xv (1890), pp. 605–7. The statement at the Council of Limoges in 1031 (*Patrologia Latina*, cxlii, col. 1400) that death for one's feudal lord was in its loyalty martyrdom for God, of which much has been made, may not have been meant seriously.

[32] Wibert of Toul, 'Vita Leonis IX', ed. I. M. Watterich, *Pontificum Romanorum vitae*, i (Leipzig, 1862), p. 165; Bruno of Segni, 'Libellus de Symoniacis', *Monumenta Germaniae Historica. Libelli de lite*, ii, pp. 550–1 ; Erdmann, *The Origin*, pp. 122–3, 145.

[33] Gregory VII, *Register*, ed. E. Casper, 2nd ed. ii (Berlin, 1955), p. 173.

[34] Manegold of Lautenbach, 'Liber ad Gebehardum', *Monumenta Germaniae Historica. Libelli de lite*, i, p. 399. See I. S. Robinson, *Authority and Resistance in the Investiture Contest* (Manchester, 1978), pp. 118–19.

[35] Ivo of Chartres, 'Decretum', x, 87; 'Panormia', viii, 30 (*Patrologia Latina*, clxi, cols. 719–20, 1311).

martyrdom in battle was obviously becoming more prominent in the eleventh century, but the evidence for a belief in warrior-martyrs before 1095 is still not plentiful and even supposing that a few more references remain to be discovered, it is only with the sources for the first crusade that a mass of material on the subject appears. It is hard to avoid concluding that at the time the crusade was preached the classification of warriors in the same category as those gentle souls who passively accepted violence perpetrated against themselves was still startling and was not universally acceptable. Even a century later the author of a dialogue on the religious life could write

> Read all the lives and passions of the holy martyrs and you will not find any martyr who wished to kill his persecutor. It is a new kind of martyr who wishes to kill another.[36]

There is another way of showing that in 1095 it was not by any means universally held that a warrior who died when engaged in holy war achieved martyrdom. It is hard to know exactly what Pope Urban II said in his speeches at Clermont that launched the crusade. Of the near contemporary accounts of them, all of which were written after the crusade had been successful, only two, one written by a man who had heard the pope, the other by a man who almost certainly had not, suggested that he had spoken of martyrdom.[37] There were no clear and unambiguous references to martyrdom in the letters written by crusaders as they travelled east until March 1098,[38] by which time they had reached Antioch, although statements that crusaders were dying that they might live, and dying for Christ who had died for them, began to appear in the previous January.[39] So the conviction that dead crusaders achieved martyrdom seems only to have dawned gradually on the participants once Asia Minor had been crossed. Exactly the same process of thought is to be found with regard to the idea that God was actively helping them, which seems only to have become a certainty in their minds when Antioch was reached.[40] As they

---

[36] 'Liber de poenitentia et tentationibus religiosorum', *Patrologia Latina*, ccxiii, col. 893.

[37] Baldric of Bourgueil, p. 15; Guibert of Nogent, p. 138. For a later reference, see William of Malmesbury, ii, p. 396.

[38] Hagenmeyer, *Die Kreuzzugsbriefe*, p. 150; and see the later letters on pp. 153, 154, 176. For references to death with no attribution of martyrdom, see *ibid.*, pp. 139, 145 (June and November 1097) and pp. 158, 159, 166 (July and October 1098).

[39] Hagenmeyer, *Die Kreuzzugsbriefe*, pp. 148, 151. Note the promise made by Christ in a vision experienced by the Greek Patriarch of Jerusalem that labourers on the crusade would be crowned on the last day. This was described in a letter of 18 October 1097. *Ibid.*, p. 142; and see also. p. 148.

[40] J. S. C. Riley-Smith, 'An Approach to Crusading Ethics', *Reading Medieval studies*, vi (1980), pp. 11–12.

became aware of the greatness of their achievement, so they became convinced that the hand of an omnipotent God was guiding and protecting them and that their enterprise was truly sacred.

It is understandable that it was at that time that individuals in the army began to experience visions, among which were appearances of the ghosts of dead crusaders, who admonished and counselled them and even physically helped the crusade: a heavenly army bearing white standards and led by Greek soldier saints which was supposed to have come to its aid during the battle of Antioch on 28 June 1098 was believed to have been made up partly of the recently dead.[41] Adhémar of Le Puy was reported making appearances immediately after his death on 1 August 1098. He was reported to have made in all seven visitations to four persons, all of them in the service of Count Raymond of Toulouse. The only record of these visions is the account of Raymond of Aguilers, Count Raymond's chaplain and a fervent believer in the authenticity of the relic of the Holy Lance, discovered in the cathedral of Antioch on instructions supposedly passed by St. Andrew to a visionary in the count's service and regarded with open scepticism by Adhémar before his death. It is not surprising that in five of his appearances, some of them to the visionary who had discovered the Holy Lance, Adhémar was concerned to show that he now knew that the Lance was genuine and that he had suffered for his doubts: he had been sent temporarily to hell, he had been whipped, his face had been burned and his beard singed, although a candle offered for his soul by his friends and a small oblation he had made to the Lance had saved him.[42] Adhémar also delivered other messages. The dead would help the crusaders and he himself would appear to offer counsel. One of his cloaks should be given to the church of St. Andrew in Antioch, presumably as a peace-offering for having disbelieved the messages of the saint.[43] He reproved the crusaders for ignoring his orders and those of Our Lady. His cross, which appears to have been a relic of the True Cross, must be carried in the vanguard of the army.[44] In early July 1099, when the crusade was running into difficulties during the siege of Jerusalem, he again appeared with instructions on how to propitiate God which included fasting and processing barefooted round the city and he prophesied that Jerusalem would fall in nine days.[45] When the city was taken on 15 July he was seen by

---

[41] Peter Tudebode, p. 100; Raymond of Aguilers, p. 78; Bartolf of Nangis, p. 502. See Robert of Rheims, p. 796.

[42] Raymond of Aguilers, pp. 84–6, 116–17, 119, 123–4, 127–8. He reported that Adhémar appeared to Peter Bartholomew, Bertrand of Le Puy, Stephen of Valence and Peter Desiderius. For Adhémar's scepticism, see Riley-Smith, 'An Approach to Crusading Ethics', pp. 14–15.

[43] Raymond of Aguilers, pp. 84–6.

[44] Ibid., pp. 127–8.

[45] Ibid., pp. 143–4.

many scrambling over the walls at the head of the assault.[46]

In one of these appearances Adhémar was accompanied by his standard-bearer Heraclius, the brother of the viscount of Polignac, who had been severely wounded in the battle of Antioch on 28 June 1098 and had died soon afterwards. Heraclius still bore on his face his mortal wound and told the visionary who saw him that Christ had granted him the privilege of bearing for eternity the open wounds from which he had died.[47]

Probably the best-known vision of this kind – since two separate but closely related versions of it survive – was experienced by Anselm of Ribemont either the night or the siesta time before he died on c. 25 February 1099. In the first version, reported by Raymond of Aguilers, he saw the young knight Enguerrand of St. Pol, who had died about two months before. Enguerrand appeared to be exceptionally handsome and, assuring Anselm that 'of course those who end their lives in the service of Christ are not dead', took him to heaven and showed him his house, beautiful beyond compare. He told Anselm that a far more beautiful mansion was being prepared for him on the morrow.[48] In the second, transmitted by Arnulf of Chocques, chaplain to the duke of Normandy the first Latin Patriarch of Jerusalem, who claimed to have been told it by Anselm himself, Anselm found himself standing on a pile of filth, from whence he looked up towards a splendid palace. He saw innumerable fine-looking persons, barely recognizable to him so changed were they, passing through the door. One of them, a man recently lost and presumably Enguerrand of St. Pol, turned to him and told him that these were crusaders who were now crowned as martyrs. He informed Anselm that he would be the next to join them.[49]

These visions reflected and at the same time substantiated the growing conviction of the crusaders that their confrères who died in battle went straight to paradise. But the notion was inchoate and the precedents for it were rare, as we have seen. It badly needed justifying in terms of the traditional theology of martyrdom. That was precisely what was done in the narrative accounts of the crusade, many of them written by senior churchmen in the west who had not taken part but had the education and intelligence to seize on elements provided by the eye-witnesses and to express them in ways that provided them with firm intellectual and theological foundations. By the 1130s there had emerged a coherent theory, based, as was so much in crusading thought, on the premise that crusaders expressed in their actions love of God and love of their neighbours. I have considered the general subject of crusading charity

---

[46] *Ibid.*, p. 151.
[47] *Ibid.*, pp. 119–20.
[48] *Ibid.*, pp. 108–9.
[49] Ralph of Caen, pp. 680–1; 'Historia peregrinorum', p. 215.

elsewhere;[50] here I want only to stress that the loving quality of participating in the first crusade is an important theme in the sources. It was believed that men took the cross out of love for God or Christ:[51] in fact they literally fulfilled Christ's precept 'If any man will come after me, let him deny himself and take up his cross and follow me' (Luke ix, 23 or Matt. xvi, 24)[52] and his statement that 'every one that hath left house or brethren or sisters or father or mother or wife or children or lands, for my name's sake, shall receive an hundredfold and shall possess life everlasting'. (Matt. xix, 29):[53] a recurring image in writings on the crusade was that of exile.[54] They also loved their neighbours, literally carrying out Christ's maxim, 'Greater love than this no man hath, that a man lay down his life for his friends' (John xv, 13) or, as they put it more often, brothers,[55] to whose aid they went and for whom they fought, endangering their lives.[56] They were described moreover, as being united with one another in Christian charity.[57] Their martyrdom was to be seen against this background of Christian love: indeed it was an expression of that love for God or Christ[58]

[50] J. S. C. Riley-Smith, 'Crusading as an act of love', History, lxv (1980), pp. 177–92.

[51] Hagenmeyer, Die Kreuzzugsbriefe, p. 137; Gesta Francorum, p. 74; Fulcher of Chartres, pp. 117, 203, 212: Peter Tudebode, pp. 46, 116; Robert of Rheims, pp. 782, 850; 'Historia peregrinorum', pp. 169, 171, 179; Albert of Aachen, pp. 291, 418; Orderic Vitalis, v, p. 32.

[52] Hagenmeyer, Die Kreuzzugsbriefe, p. 164; Gesta Francorum, p. 1; Peter Tudebode, p. 31; Robert of Rheims, pp. 730, 850; Baldric of Bourgueil, p. 16; Ekkehard of Aura, pp. 15, 34; Ralph of Caen, p. 674; 'Historia de translatione', p. 257; 'Historia peregrinorum', pp. 172, 173.

[53] Hagenmeyer, Die Kreuzzugsbriefe, pp. 178–9; Fulcher of Chartres, pp. 115–16, 163; Raymond of Aguilers, p. 117; Robert of Rheims, pp. 728, 747; Guibert of Nogent, pp. 161, 201, 221; Baldric of Bourgueil, p. 9; Ekkehard of Aura, pp. 12, 34; Gaufridus, 'Dictamen de primordiis ecclesiae Castaliensis', Recueil des historiens des croisades. Historiens occidentaux, v, p. 349; Henry of Huntingdon, 'De captione Antiochiae a Christianis', Recueil des historiens des croisades. Historiens occidentaux, v, p. 374; Albert of Aachen, pp. 271, 320, 382, 501; 'Historia peregrinorum', pp. 172, 173; Orderic Vitalis, v, p. 16, 34, 48, 184–6. See also Albert of Aachen, pp. 401–2.

[54] Hagenmeyer, Die Kreuzzugsbriefe, p. 179; Guibert of Nogent, pp. 124, 141, 148–9, 199; Ekkehard of Aura, pp. 33, 40; William of Malmesbury, ii, p. 398; Albert of Aachen, pp. 271, 348, 408, 416; Orderic Vitalis, v, pp. 34, 70.

[55] Hagenmeyer, Die Kreuzzugsbriefe, pp. 137, 179; Fulcher of Chartres, p. 203; Baldric of Bourgueil, pp. 15, 44, 46; 'Narratio Floriacensis de captis Antiochia et Hierosolyma', Recueil des historiens des croisades. Historiens occidentaux, v, p. 357; William of Malmesbury, ii, pp. 394, 398; Albert of Aachen, p. 402.

[56] See for instance Baldric of Bourgueil, pp. 12–13, 28; Hugh of St. Maria, p. 363.

[57] Fulcher of Chartres, p. 203; Baldric of Bourgueil, p. 95; Ekkehard of Aura, p. 16; William of Malmesbury, ii, p. 399; Orderic Vitalis, v, p. 154. See also Peter Tudebode, p. 122.

[58] Fulcher of Chartres, p. 117; Peter Tudebode, pp. 80, 81; Guibert of Nogent, p. 221; Albert of Aachen, pp. 382, 402, 415.

and also for their brothers, their fellow Christians.[59] It was a voluntary act[60] by which they exchanged temporal for external life.[61] They died for Christ, who had died for them[62] – indeed bearing the cross they echoed in their own torments Christ's crucifixion[63] – and for the faith, of which they were witnesses.[64] The writers on the first crusade collectively presented a picture of martyrdom in the course of battle which survived for centuries, a late example of it being a martyrology of the knights of Malta, published in 1643, which contained lists of those killed in wars with the Muslims.[65]

Among the martyrs there were men whose lives were regarded as being almost as admirable as their deaths. Adhémar of Le Puy was one of these, but two laymen are of more interest to us. The first was a knight called Matthew, who at some point on the crusade was captured by the Muslims and was beheaded by them because he would not renounce his faith. He is known to us only because the writer Guibert of Nogent devoted a passage in his Gesta to him. Guibert and Matthew, in fact, had grown up together: Matthew's parents and then Matthew himself had held a fief in Guibert's family lordship. What Guibert stressed in his account was Matthew's goodness. He was nobly born and a good knight, but Guibert considered that he was entirely immune from the vice of wantonness. In the imperial palace at Constantinople he was well-known for his care in following the religious observances of the pilgrimage. He was prayerful, 'frequenting Mass more often than I have seen a knight or even a bishop.' Devout and generous in alms-giving, he was saintly in intention and deserved nothing better than martyrdom. Guibert used Matthew's life to illustrate what to him was an important point: that the crusading martyrs were

> not only priests nor simply lettered men, but military men, some of them common people. There had been no previous hope that these would bear witness to their faith.[66]

[59] Baldric of Bourgueil, pp. 30, 44; William of Malmesbury, ii, p. 398; Orderic Vitalis, v, p. 56.

[60] Fulcher of Chartres, pp. 226–7. See Robert of Rheims, p. 740; Guibert of Nogent, p. 221; Gilo, p. 745; William of Malmesbury, ii, p. 397; Albert of Aachen, p. 381.

[61] Robert of Rheims, pp. 829–30; Guibert of Nogent, p. 161; Albert of Aachen, pp. 402, 492.

[62] Raymond of Aguilers, p. 113; Baldric of Bourgueil, pp. 15, 101. See Peter Tudebode, p. 36; Ralph of Caen, p. 667; 'Narratio Floriacensis', pp. 357–8; 'Historia peregrinorum', p. 192.

[63] Ekkehard of Aura, p. 39.

[64] Guibert of Nogent, p. 179. On the other hand a note of uncertainty may perhaps be detected occasionally. Gesta Francorum, p. 74; Guibert of Nogent, p. 205.

[65] M. de Goussancourt, Le Martyrologe des Chevaliers de St. Iean de Hierusalem, dits de Malte, 2 vols. (Paris, 1643), passim.

[66] Guibert of Nogent, pp. 183–4.

His story demonstrated how a layman could achieve salvation in his own way.

The second was Anselm of Ribemont, who was killed in battle on *c.* 25 February 1099 after experiencing the vision which has already been described. He was a remarkable man, much admired by his contemporaries for his wisdom as well as his military skills. Guibert of Nogent, who probably knew him personally, wrote of his liberality, sagacity and faith and Ralph of Caen, who certainly knew those who had been familiar with him, wrote of his probity, honesty and fame.[67] He was a pious layman, the founder of the monastery of Ribemont and a benefactor of the houses of St. Amand and Anchin,[68] who had a devotion to St. Quentin, the patron of the region in which he lived,[69] and was a friend of the archbishop of Rheims.[70] In other words he had that churchiness which was becoming a feature of European knights. Accounts of his martyrdom – he was struck on the head by a stone thrown by a petrary while fighting the Muslims – stressed that he had made confession and taken communion before the battle.[71] A tradition at Anchin credited him with crying out three times on his deathbed, 'God help me'.[72] He was also supposed to have been responsible for the arrival at Anchin of the relic of the arm of St. George, brought to the monastery from Lydda (which was not occupied by the crusaders until after his death) by count Robert of Flanders.[73]

Anselm, like Matthew, was a devout layman who was also martyred. More typical of the crusading dead were brave paladins like Raynald Porchet or Roger of Barneville, about whose past it was unnecessary to speak in the light of their martyrdoms. But the treatment of all these men demonstrates that in the eyes of churchmen, which was what nearly all the writers of narrative accounts of the crusades were, the laity was coming into its own and it is not surprising that after the crusade the idea of

---

[67] Guibert of Nogent, pp. 218–19; Ralph of Caen, p. 680. See also Robert of Rheims, p. 857; Gilo, p. 788; Hagenmeyer, *Die Kreuzzugsbriefe*, pp. 63–6.

[68] Hagenmeyer, *Die Kreuzzugsbriefe*, p. 64; *Recueil des historiens des croisades. Historiens occidentaux*, iii, p. lviii; 'Monumenta Aquicinctina', *Monumenta Germaniae Historica. Scriptores*, xiv, pp. 580–1, 585; 'Auctarium Aquicinense', p. 394; Robert of Rheims, p. 857.

[69] Guibert of Nogent, p. 219; 'Auctarium Ursicampinum, Continuatio Sigeberti', *Monumenta Germaniae Historica. Scriptores*, vi, p. 471.

[70] Hagenmeyer, *Die Kreuzzugsbriefe*, pp. 144–6, 156–60. See Guibert of Nogent, pp. 219, 251.

[71] Raymond of Aguilers, pp. 108–9; Ralph of Caen, pp. 680–1: 'Historia peregrinorum', pp. 211, 215. See Hagenmeyer, *Die Kreuzzugsbriefe*, p. 176; *Gesta Francorum*, p. 85; Peter Tudebode, p. 131; Fulcher of Chartres, p. 270; Robert of Rheims, p. 857; Guibert of Nogent, pp. 218–19; Baldric of Bourgueil, p. 93; Gilo, p. 788; Albert of Aachen, p. 452; Henry of Huntingdon, p. 379; Orderic Vitalis, v, p. 150.

[72] 'Auctarium Aquicinense', pp. 394–5.

[73] 'Monumenta Aquicinctina', p. 586.

martyrdom in war very quickly spread: perhaps to the compilers of the
Song of Roland; certainly to the writers of works like the Millstätter
Exodus and even to Geoffrey of Monmouth in his treatment of Arthur's
defence of Britain.[74] Recent work on the reform movement, in which,
incidentally, the crusade has never been considered, has shown that a new
and positive role for laymen in the church came to be generally accepted in
the light of an evangelical awakening and a return to the gospels, by-
passing existing institutions, which was a feature of the thought of the
time.[75] Others besides Guibert of Nogent were coming to recognize that
secular callings could contribute to salvation. But there is more to be said. If
there was a feature of eleventh- and twelfth-century devotional writings it
was an emphasis on the importance of the cross to Christians. The
summons to take up that cross had been one that had led inevitably to the
adoption of that monastic habit, to the acceptance of a life of mortification
in which one died to the world.[76] But now the cross was applied to what
had always been preeminently a lay activity, even if it was one that was
now linked to pilgrimage.[77] We have already seen that crusaders were
believed to be literally denying themselves and taking up Christ's cross; and
they believed this of themselves, for the leaders of the expedition referred
to it in a letter they wrote to the pope from Antioch in September 1098.[78]
To the narrators of the history of the crusade the crusaders, fortified and
sanctified by the cross[79] which they bore on their hearts and in their mind as
well as on their bodies,[80] fought for its victory.[81] Ekkehard of Aura drew a
parallel between their veneration for the cross and the Emperor
Constantine's and he stated that, true martyrs in their passions, they
followed the way of the cross with Simon of Cyrene.[82] Baldric of
Bourgueil compared their liberation of Jerusalem to Joseph of Arimathea
taking Christ down from the cross.[83] The strength of the image of the cross
to crusaders and to their contemporaries was demonstrated not only by the

[74] Kantorowicz, pp. 230–1; Noth, p. 107; D. H. Green, The Millstätter Exodus
(Cambridge, 1966), passim.

[75] M.-D. Chenu, Nature, Man and Society in the Twelfth Century (Chicago, 1968),
pp. 219–30.

[76] J. Pelikan, The Christian Tradition. 3. The Growth of Medieval Theology (600–
1300) (Chicago, 1978), pp. 126–7; and see pp. 131–4 for the cult of the cross.

[77] For the cross and pilgrimage, see, for instance, Orderic Vitalis, v, p. 230, in
which the cross is taken 'more peregrini'.

[78] Hagenmeyer, Die Kreuzzugsbriefe, p. 164.

[79] Gesta Francorum, pp. 15, 31, 37, 40, 68, 70, 83; Fulcher of Chartres, pp. 140–1;
Peter Tudebode, pp. 72, 111, 112, 129; Baldric of Bourgueil, pp. 16, 47; Albert of
Aachen, p. 492; 'Historia peregrinorum', pp. 191, 205, 207, 210; Orderic Vitalis, v,
p. 78.

[80] Guibert of Nogent, pp. 171, 216.

[81] Gesta Francorum, pp. 19–20; Robert of Rheims, p. 874; Ralph of Caen, p. 668.

[82] Ekkehard of Aura, pp. 16, 39. See 'Historia peregrinorum', p. 174.

[83] Baldric of Bourgueil, p. 101.

fact that all crusaders wore crosses sewn to their clothes, but also in the way the cross became almost a synonym for crusading: northern Europeans arriving in France on their way to the east and unable to make themselves understood would make the sign of the cross with their hands to signify that they were crusaders.[84] A hysteria seems to have developed with individuals, sincere and insincere, branding or tatooing crosses on their bodies.[85]

In fact the way of the cross was becoming a path to salvation for laymen as well as for religious. The revolutionary consequence of this was the transfer to crusading thought of phrases and concepts which had previously been applied solely to monasticism. The best known of these, the literal use of the phrase *militia Christi*, had already occurred a decade or two before 1095, although it was only with the first crusade that it was systematically transferred to warfare.[86] The others appear with extraordinary suddenness. In contemporary monastic devotional writings one finds the image of the heavenly Jerusalem as the true goal of the religious life, more important, as St. Anselm of Canterbury stressed, than the earthly Jerusalem; to reach the heavenly Jerusalem required an interior journey, a true conversion.[87] But while the armies were still on the march the goal of the heavenly Jerusalem was also associated with the crusade: in September 1098 the leaders called on the pope to come out and 'open for us the gates of both Jerusalems'.[88] This was taken up by contemporary historians. Jerusalem

> both prefigures and simulates that heavenly city. You can see that visible enemies oppose us here. Invisible enemies, moreover, hem in the roads coming to her, against whom a spiritual conflict remains. And it is more important for us to struggle *against the spirits of wickedness in the high places* than *against flesh and blood* (Ephesians vi, 12) which we see. . . . We will be altogether unfitted and ineffectual in the spiritual struggle if we do not take a stand against these weak dogs.[89]

Some years later there was a tradition in Lorraine that before the crusade one of Godfrey of Bouillon's attendants had dreamt of him climbing a

[84] Guibert of Nogent, p. 125.

[85] Fulcher of Chartres, pp. 169–70; Raymond of Aguilers, p. 102; Guibert of Nogent, pp. 182–3; 250–1; Baldric of Bourgueil, p. 17; Bernold, p. 464; 'Historia de translatione', p. 255; Orderic Vitalis, v, p. 30.

[86] I. S. Robinson, 'Gregory VII and the Soldiers of Christ', *History* viii (1973), pp. 177–9. See also my forthcoming article 'The First Crusade and St. Peter' in *Outremer*, ed. R. C. Smail, H. E. Mayer and B. Z. Kedar.

[87] St. Anselm of Canterbury, *Opera omnia*, ed. F. S. Schmitt, iii (Edinburgh, 1946), p. 254 (ep. 117).

[88] Hagenmeyer, *Die Kreuzzugsbriefe*, p. 164.

[89] Baldric of Bourgueil, p. 101. See also Baldric of Bourgueil, p. 100; Robert of Rheims, pp. 881–2; 'De reliquiis', p. 336; Orderic Vitalis, v, p. 164.

golden ladder to a hall in which was laid a banquet and Albert of Aachen
interpreted the ladder as being the way to Jerusalem, 'which is the gate of
the heavenly kingdom', only attainable with a pure heart and perfect
humility.[90] These references to the spiritual Jerusalem suggest that the
crusaders were believed to be making an internal as well as an external
pilgrimage; Albert of Aachen, interpreting another dream supposed to be
connected with the crusade, implied this when he wrote that in 1099 only
those who merited Jerusalem reached her, purified by their sufferings.[91] It is
not surprising that, in spite of Urban II's statement to the monks of
Vallombrosa,[92] the crusade was sometimes seen as a spiritual, not a carnal,
war, better, Guibert of Nogent put it, than those carnal wars fought by the
Israelites 'to fill their bellies'.[93] As with *militia Christi* we find here the
application of imagery previously associated with monastic life to a lay
enterprise.

Even more remarkable was the use of the image of the early church. It
has been written that

> the religious life of the primitive Church became an ideal, indeed a
> sort of mystique that engaged the productive energies of men.[94]

In the eleventh century the reformers had aimed to impose the common
life on all churchmen, following the example of the early church:
conversion and the *vita communis* were marks of the *vita apostolica*.[95] It has
often been shown how this was applied to and envigorated the religious
life, but it has never been noticed that it was also applied to the crusade.
Baldric of Bourgueil, in a sentence especially startling coming from an
archbishop, wrote that 'nearly all things were held in common, just as in
the primitive church'.[96] Elsewhere he used the terms *sanctum collegium* and
congregatio Christianorum of the army.[97] That he was not alone in making
this comparison is suggested by phrases used by other writers on the
crusade: *peregrina ecclesia Francorum*[98] and *sacra societas fidelium Dei*.[99]

It is clear that contemporaries, whether themselves crusaders or not,

---

[90] Albert of Aachen, pp. 481–2.

[91] *Ibid.*, p. 487.

[92] See above p. 14.

[93] Guibert of Nogent, pp. 221, 225; *Gesta Francorum*, p. 37; Robert of Rheims,
p. 829; 'Historia de translatione', p. 255.

[94] Chenu, pp. 239–40.

[95] *Ibid.*, pp. 207, 211.

[96] Baldric of Bourgueil, p. 28.

[97] Baldric of Bourgueil, p. 67. See Orderic Vitalis, v, p. 100.

[98] Raymond of Aguilers, p. 83. For crusaders compared to the apostles, see
Raymond of Aguilers, pp. 87, 93; and for crusaders compared to Christ's disciples,
see Ekkehard of Aura, p. 21.

[99] Robert of Rheims, p. 781.

were prepared to treat crusading almost as an apostolic activity. The crusaders, denying themselves and leaving all things for Christ's sake, expressed in their actions love of God and their fellow-men and, if they died, were treated as martyrs; the war they fought could be said to be spiritual, not merely temporal, and their life on the march could even be seen as echoing that of the early church. The conviction that the crusade's dead were martyrs never gained such ground as to become generally accepted as a cause for canonization – I know of no crusader canonized by virtue of his martyrdom alone, although a search through local calendars might reveal some – but it was the first crusade as much as anything else that presented laymen with the hope of salvation and a means of doing good, which explains the attraction of crusading for them until well into the fourteenth century.

THE DEATH OF THE BISHOP IN THE EARLY MIDDLE AGES

Georg Scheibelreiter

Among the passages of a *Vita* which are most difficult to interpret are those describing the death of the hero. It is nowhere else that the author of the description has to keep so close to the model of the ideal Christian. In general we can say that no other part of a *Vita* offers less for historical insight.

Moreover in many cases the death of the saint marks the beginning of miraculous events. All this is followed by the usual catalogue of wonders.[1] The author must present certain phenomena there. But it is not our task to reflect on the death of the saint; it is the bishop who is going to be the centre of this paper. Here we do not only meet ideal representatives of a Christian way of life. The description of the death and what it meant to contemporaries are important correctives for the historian since the authors of *Vitae* were restricted to a standard way of writing.[2] Therefore a style simple and devoid of ornament is hardly to be found among the lives of saints. The death of the 'true' bishop is the climax of his life as the shepherd of his flock, as a constant fighter for personal perfection. His death is a

[1] According to Friedrich Lotter, 'Methodisches zur Gewinnung historischer Erkenntnisse aus hagiographischen Quellen', *Historisches Zeitschrift*, 229 (1979), pp. 312 and 322 sq., the part of the *vita* dealing with the period from the birth to his climax is richest in 'topos', or hagiographical convention. Death as the crowning end of a bishop's life is not taken into consideration at all by Lotter.

[2] Today hagiography is seen in a more differentiated way. We can distinguish between several types of *Vitae* especially with regard to their origins as well as to their further efficacy. Some of them belong more or less to other literary genres, some are excluded from traditional hagiography. Martin Heinzelmann, 'Neue Aspekte der biographischen und hagiographischen Literatur in der lateinischen Welt (1–6 Jahrhundert)', *Francia*, 1 (1973), pp. 27–44, and Lotter op. cit., pp. 307 sqq.

mighty final chord after a victorious life. This fact must not be simply stated: it has to reflect the model life of the holy bishop in a way worthy of him. In some respects the description has to show a bishop worthy on his deathbed of the delights of the paradise he is going to enjoy; at any rate his dying is a proof of the benevolence of God.

Brief notes about the death of the bishop are restricted to sources which compress the events into a few sentences and in the same way tell about the life of a person. The words used by the author are rather undramatic (e.g. 'obire, migrare, transire'), so that we cannot draw conclusions from them about the specific circumstances of the death.[3] Whereas the use of 'topos' for the description of the death is essential in *Vitae*, the same matter is treated in Annals, Chronicles and Gesta in a rather simple style. When they state the mere fact of the death they rarely use phrases that can tell us anything about the authority of the deceased, about the moral worth of his person or about his merits and faults.[4] So we may say – without simplifying things – that we hardly find a realistic description of a bishop's death in the period we are dealing with. In some ways Gregory of Tours may be regarded as an exception but examining this matter more exactly would lead us too far.

An 'ordinary way of dying', i.e. a description of a death for natural reasons is only to be found with 'second rate' bishops, who cross the way of the hero in some way or other. The bishop who ranks among the leading personalities of his time and who is the subject of a *Vita* must die according to his 'ordo' if he is not to be regarded as a bad representative of his office.[5] The description of this 'ordo' is full of 'topos'; it is from here that we must draw our conclusions; those that are significant in general as well as those that are of particular interest.

God distinguishes the saint by telling him the day of his recall from the Vale of Tears. This knowledge is one of the most infallible signs that the bishop has found the Lord's mercy. Most of the *Vitae* refer to this fact. But

---

[3] A study on the 'transitus', its special meaning and its connection with the 'pascha' is to be published by Alf Härdelin (Uppsala).

[4] The death of the deposed Raginfrid (bishop of Rouen and abbot of St.-Wandrille) is described only very briefly in the *Gesta sanctorum patrum Fontanellensis coenobii* (eds F. Lohier and J. Laporte, 1936), VIII, 2, pp. 62 sq. From that – together with other passages about him – we can see that he must have appeared in a very negative light to his contemporaries. As opposed to it the plain note of the death of bishop Erkenbod of Thérouanne (abbot of St.-Bertin as well) in the *Gesta abbatum sancti Bertini Sithiensium* of Folcwin (ed. O. Holder-Egger 1881) *Monumenta Germaniae Historica, Scriptores* 13, XXIV, *Monumenta Germaniae Historica*, pp. 611 sq. may be interpreted in a positive way. The same is true with the bishops Magnard and Dodo of Toul; *Gesta episcoporum Tullensium* (ed. G. Waitz 1848) *Mon. Germ. Hist. Script.* 8, XIX sq., p. 636.

[5] Bishops like these die in a different way! But 'topos' is very important to them, too, even if this is not always obvious.

hardly a bishop was found worthy of such a solemn preparation for his death as Nicetius of Trier. He had been visited in his dreams by St. Paul and St. John Baptist who announced to him his imminent assumption.[6] The fact that two eminent saints appear to Nicetius may be regarded as a sign of his authority as well as indicating his merits for the expansion of Christianity in the area of the Moselle.

Another source tells us that Gallus of Clermont was told by an angel that he need not be afraid of the plague, which was raging in the country since he would not die for another eight years.[7] Without doubt this is a prophecy *ex post facto*, but another source tells us that when Gallus was confined to bed by an illness, he was told by the Lord that he would only live another three days.[8] Though both events are reported by Gregory of Tours, one report is not to be seen in relation to the other. Gregory describes Gallus' illness in detail[9] and it is obvious that the severe illness of the seventy-year-old bishop makes it possible to predict his imminent death. But in describing the demise of his saintlike relative Gregory is not satisfied with the natural facts. He has to fix the exact day of death, as that is the way in which another has to describe the decease of a bishop.

Salvius of Albi and Betharius of Chartres were informed about their imminent death just in time to prepare for it.[10] Salvius was said to have been a strict and ideal bishop. In connection with him Gregory uses the phrase 'in my opinion' when he refers to the 'Revelatio Domini'. This restriction seems to be interesting. Especially with this prelate an intervention of God was to be expected because Salvius was said to have been allowed a visit to the other world.[11]

With Caesarius of Arles realistic features meet with a 'topos' structure[12]; 'per spiritum' he realized that he was going to die. So he enquired after the date of St. Augustine's day (28 August). When he learned that that day was not far off, he hoped that God would let him die 'non longe' before or after it, since he had always worshipped the great bishop of Hippo especially. Indeed, Caesarius died on 27 August. Of course we have to admit that the authors of the *Vita*, who were his pupils and bishops themselves, were interested to show how much their master pleased the Lord and how much he himself resembled St. Augustine. Nevertheless their report is likely to be

---

[6] Gregory of Tours, *Liber vitae patrum* (ed. B. Krusch 1885) *Mon. Germ. Hist. Script. rer. Merov.* 1, XVII, 6, p. 733.

[7] Gregory of Tours, *Historia Francorum* IV, 5, p. 138.

[8] Gregory of Tours, *Liber vitae patrum*, VI, 7, p. 685.

[9] While the term 'interna febris' says little, the loss of hair even from the bishop's beard, was an obvious sign of illness.

[10] Gregory of Tours, *Hist. Franc.* VII, 1, 326 and *Vita Betharii episcopi Carnotensis* (ed. B. Krusch 1896) *Mon. Germ. Hist. Script. rer. Merov.* 3, XVI, p. 619.

[11] Gregory of Tours, *Hist. Franc.* VII, 1, pp. 324 sq.

[12] *Vita Caesarii episcopi Arelatensis* (ed. B. Krusch 1896), *Mon. Germ. Hist. Script. rer. Merov.* 3, II, pp. 46, 499 sq.

true in some respects if we take into consideration the severe illness of the bishop together with his desire.

The preparations the bishops made when they felt their end approach were usually these: they sought to secure their succession; they made efforts to placate God and they looked for a suitable burial place. A man like Salvius of Albi is an extraordinary personality among the Merovingian bishops. When he felt his end approach he procured his own coffin, he washed, put on a shroud and then he died. His modesty is rather that of the Martinian bishop, an ascetic attitude which may be regarded as an anachronism in the late sixth century. It is characteristic of this outstanding bishop that he lacks any feeling for celebrating his decease with pomp and glory.[13]

When the bishop had to secure his succession he had to respect first of all the pretensions of his relatives or the wish for designation of one of his pupils. Aeonius of Arles would not resign until he could be sure that Caesarius his relative and pupil, was going to be his successor ('securus de successore . . . migravit ad Dominum').[14] With the help of the Holy Spirit, 'ecclesia concordante' Avitus of Clermont succeeded in securing this position for his brother Bonitus.[15] In Utrecht the clergy and the people were waiting for Alberich, since his uncle, the Abbot-Bishop Gregory, had been confined to bed because of a severe illness. It had been agreed upon long before that Alberich should be the successor but just then he was in Italy on a royal mission. It was to be feared that the nephew would not meet his uncle alive. But Gregory set his clergy at ease with a show of divine certainty.[16]

As mentioned above, all had been planned long before; yet the *Vitae* present the matter thus, as if the question of the succession could not be decided before the bishop was lying on his deathbed. The true shepherd has to think of the welfare of his flock; this is how the dying bishop has to be imagined. We may also assume that – when lying on his deathbed – the bishop asked for the clergy's approval of his designee, and we must not underrate the psychological effect of such a promise.

Bishop Gallus of Clermont was said to have known that he was to live

[13] It is significant that we have no *Vita* of Salvius. Though he was a member of a noble family he did not satisfy the expectations of his contemporaries who expected him to lead a splendid life; cf. Karl Friedrich Stroheker, *Der senatorische Adel im spätantiken Gallien* (1948), p. 346, and Martin Heinzelmann, 'Bischofsherrschaft in Gallien', *Beihefte der Francia*, 5 (1976) 112.

[14] *Vita Caesarii*, I, 13, pp. 461 sq.

[15] *Vita Boniti episcopi Arverni* (ed. B. Krusch 1913) *Mon. Germ. Hist. Script.* 6, IV, p. 121.

[16] He exclaimed: 'Noli timere! Non transibo antequem ipse veniat!' *Liudgeri Vita Gregorii abbatis Traeiectensis* (ed. O. Holder-Eggar 1887) *Mon. Germ. Hist. Script.* 15, XV, p. 79. He sought to prevent the clergy from turning towards another candidate at the last moment.

only another three days. Therefore he summoned the 'populus' and
dispensed the communion 'sancta ac pia voluntate'.[17] We may see the
doings of the bishop in two ways: as a pious action or a semi-political act. It
depends on the way in which we interpret the term 'populus': either as
people in general or as the urban ruling class. If we take the latter for
granted questions of the common welfare were certainly discussed in that
meeting also, although we must not doubt the bishop's religious sincerity.

Before his death Apollinaris of Valence was induced by a vision to go
and see his relatives in Provence. Above all he wanted to reach the 'limina
Sancti Genesii martyris' in Arles. We have an exact report of this journey
he had undertaken to see his influential relatives who held the highest
positions in the administration.[18] This fact is connected with a number of
miraculous events that show the bishop as an exorcist. The author of the
Vita wants to tell us how the devil tried to lead away the saintly man from
his firm Christian belief shortly before his death.

Another unavoidable problem for the bishop who is going to die is to
get the burial place he wants. Usually a church is chosen which the bishop
has founded himself but the idea of 'sociare cum sanctis' is also of great
importance.[19] Again and again the exiled bishop Ansbert of Rouen sent
messengers to the Mayor of the Palace, Pipin II, to ask his permission to be
buried in Fontanelle-St. Wandrille where he had been abbot.[20] Hrodbert of
Worms-Salzburg convoked his pupils to Salzburg and then went back to
his 'propria sedes', because he knew that the day of his recall was near.[21]
Here we meet an idea which is of non-Christian provenance. Even in death
the bishop wanted to be connected with his kin. It was only the ascetic
bishops who did not bother about their last resting place; they died on their

---

[17] Gregory of Tours, *Lib. vitae patr.*, VI, 7, p. 685.

[18] *Vita Apollinaris episcopi Valentinensis* (ed. B. Krusch 1896) *Mon. Germ. Hist.
Script. rer. Merov.* 3, VII sq., pp. 200 sq.

[19] Gregory of Langres wanted to be buried in Dijon; Gregory of Tours, *Lib. vitae
patr.* VII, 3, p. 688. Betharius of Chartres 'in pagum Blesianum ad cellam quam
olim aedificaverat ob memoriam sui,' (*Vita* loc. cit. XVI 619); Vinditianus of
Cambrai 'in basilica, in loco . . . qui dicitur Mons sancti Eligii', (*Gesta episcoporum
Cameracensium*, ed. L. Bethmann 1846, *Mon. Germ. Hist. Script.* 7, XXVIII, p. 413);
Korbinian of Freising made exact arrangements for his burial place next to that of
Saint Valentine in Mais (Southern Tyrol); (*Arbeonis episcopi Frisingensis Vita
Corbiniani episcopi Baiuvariorum*, (ed. B. Krusch 1920), *Mon. Germ. Hist. Script. rer.
German. in us. schol.* XXXIII, p. 224). Godo of Toul wanted to be buried 'in ecclesia
cuiusdam sui praedii nomine Castellum' (*Gesta epp. Tull.*, XXI, p. 636).

[20] *Vita Ansberti episcopi Rotomagensis* (ed. W. Levison 1910) *Mon. Germ. Hist.
Script. rer. Merov.* 5, XXIV, p. 635.

[21] *Conversio Bagoariorum et Carantanorum* (ed. Herwig Wolfram 1979), I, p. 128.
See also Helmut Beumann, 'Zur vita Ruperti', *Mitteilungen der Gesellschaft für
Salzburger Landeskunde*, 115 (1975), pp. 81 sq. and Heinz Löwe, 'Salzburg als
Zentrum literarischen Schaffens im 8. Jahrhundert', loc. cit. pp. 108 sq.

'peregrinatio' and were buried where it pleased God. Even on their deathbeds they remained individuals without links to the world. The other bishops, however, either opted for the burial place of their family or for the community of the other bishops of their bishopric. It some cases, especially in the south of Gaul, both conditions could be met.

The description of the day and hour of the bishop's death is bound to be most conventional. But when the author relates extraordinary events this is not only a means of edification for the listener, it is also to make him understand the worship after the bishop's death. The dying of the bishop – as described traditionally – is some sort of Christian ritual.[22] The solemn ceremonies that accompany his last doings, the preparations, even his gestures are part of a certain 'ordo' of dying which meets the requirements of a Christian and a nobleman.[23] We must be careful not to see merely practical 'topos' in the death scenes of the *Vitae*, which is far from reality. The firm conventional structure is also the structure of the real dying 'ordo'. Heavenly sweet scent, supernatural voices and lights, phenomena which we cannot interpret here on the other hand to be mere 'topos'. We don't find them with all bishops but they are used often enough without any connection to the events told.

Generally speaking the last day of a bishop appears to us as follows: the bishop, who knows about the hour of his death, summons the clergy of the cathedral (or, if he is on a journey, the clergy accompanying him), and admonishes them to keep up a firm belief in God and to do what is right. Then the bishop dispenses and takes the communion and expires while he is praying and singing psalms.[24] The static scene showing us the bishop on his deathbed surrounded by the clergy resembles the death of a king or at least the decease of the head of a family.

So much of its representative character, which was to be expressed even more clearly when the bishop was a political leader in addition to his office (e.g. *comes* or *defensor civitatis*). This was especially clear with Caesarius of Arles, who held an extraordinary position in the church of Gaul and who was *de facto* leader of the town. When he died several other bishops were present.[25]

[22] František Graus, *Volk, Herrscher und Heiliger im Reich der Merowinger*, (1965), p. 65.

[23] The raising of hands and eyes towards heaven in an impressive way, sighing and crying loudly – these were essential components of this way of mourning. Other examples can be found in *Vita Apollinaris* loc. cit. XIII, p. 202; *Vita Boniti* loc. cit. XXX, p. 134; *Vita Audomari* (ed. W. Levison 1910) *Mon. Germ. Hist. Script. rer. Merov.* 5, XIV, p. 762; *Vita Hugberti episcopi Traiectensis* (ed. W. Levison 1913) *Mon. Germ. Hist. Script. rer. Merov.* 6, XII, p. 490 and XIV, p. 491.

[24] This type is to be found again and again. It is not necessary to give examples; but it was a little different with Gallus of Clermont; Gregory of Tours, *Lib. vitae patr.* VI, 7, p. 685.

[25] *Vita Caesarii*, II, 48, p. 500.

38 THE END OF STRIFE

Great emphasis is put on the matter of weeping. It is mostly the bishop who has to comfort those who surround him. Tears are shed by the clergy and the poor. The dying bishop himself often weeps as it is characteristic of the piety of the time. The situation – though welcomed by the bishop with joy – demands a stream of tears.[26] As long as this was not the expression of (sinful) hopelessness, but a 'moderatus moeror' it was also becoming to a man and the bishop remained a model Christian showing this emotional attitude.[27]

After the bishop's death he was dressed in his pontifical vestments and the exequies began. When Caesarius of Arles died clergy and vergers had great trouble to restrain the people. With pious violence they tore pieces from the clothes of their deceased shepherd in order to take them home as relics.[28] Sometimes the poor distinguished themselves in a special way. After the burial of Bishop Sulpicius II of Bourges they occupied the church, 'iacebant ut cadavera', and made the celebration of the mass impossible.[29]

When the bishop died away from his 'civitas' he had to be brought back to the cathedral of his see. His transport resembled a triumphal procession but for the fact that it was accompanied by mourning people. According to the chroniclers towns were almost deserted, nobody wanted to stay at home. Everybody went to meet the bishop and showed his grief in public with a lot of noise.[30] We have a detailed description of the funeral procession of Bishop Ansbert of Rouen, who had died in exile in Haumont monastery and was transferred to Fontanelle-St. Wandrille. The abbot of Haumont was the leader of the procession. Members of the clergy with flags showing the Holy Cross, candles and lanterns followed, joined by a 'plebs innumera'. All the time hymns and 'carmina canticorum divinorum ... dulci modulatione' were sung. In Venette, a royal 'villa', the abbot passed over the responsibility to the 'episcopi conprovinciales' of the deceased Ansbert. They accompanied him with the same ceremonies and finally buried him in Fontanelle, after the procession had been on its way for 13 days.[31] Of course we are told of a number of miracles in connection with this funeral procession. Many of the places which the dead bishop had to pass wanted to take advantage of the glory and sanctity of the great man.

[26] See above, footnote 23.
[27] Heinrich Fichtenau. 'Askese und Laster in der Anschauung des Mittelalters'. *Beiträge zur Mediävistik*, 1 (1975), pp. 45, 83 sq.
[28] *Vita Caesarii*, II, 49, p. 500.
[29] *Vita Sulpicii episcopi Biturigi* (ed. B. Krusch 1902) *Mon. Germ. Hist. Script. rer. Merov.* 4, VII, p. 378. (Version A and B). Possibly they were not only 'matricularii', for they are reported to have been a great number of people.
[30] Cf. the *Vita Desiderii Cadurcae urbis episcopi* (ed. B. Krusch 1902) *Mon. Germ. Hist. Script. rer. Merov.* 4, XXXVII, p. 593 '... nullus monachus domi resedit, qui non obviam pastori procederet'. *Vita Hugberti* loc. cit. XV, p. 492 (a very detailed description).
[31] *Vita Ansberti* loc. cit. XXVIII sq., pp. 637 sq.

In this respect the *Vita* of Landbert of Maastricht is almost schematic: a miracle (mostly the healing of the sick) is said to have taken place wherever the bier came to a halt.[32]

When the corpse had reached the town, people of rank competed for the privilege of carrying the bier on their shoulders.[33] Sometimes we find even 'principes' among them[34] as was the case with the funeral of Bishop Eligius of Noyon. Queen Balthild came to Noyon with her sons and took part in the procession to the cathedral. She did not mind accompanying her former adviser though she had to walk and the path was covered with mud and snow.[35]

The funeral procession of Bishop Audoin of Rouen in 684 was a great event. King Theuderich III, Queen Chrodhild, Waratto, the Mayor of the Palace, and all 'proceres palatii' took part in the procession to Pontoise. There the vigils were celebrated and the night was spent at the bier of the deceased. Then the royal couple returned and senior clergy were responsible for the further transport which took them to Rouen.[36] The ceremonies for Audoin were celebrated in a way appropriate to a state funeral.

A bishop set out on his final way as a man of rank and a Christian miracle worker. The way his funeral ceremonies were held corresponded with the ideas which his contemporaries had about him. Moreover they fulfilled the requirements of his status. The 'topos' in these reports remains a frame which is necessary for the presentation, but we can distinguish it from the real ceremonies.

In spite of all the cruelties that were common in the Frankish kingdom, people were aware of the justice of God. They regarded the circumstances of a person's death as excellent evidence of whether he had pleased or displeased the Lord. This was especially important for the bishops. They might have committed crimes while on earth – the way in which they died demonstrated how God had valued their deeds.[37] Generally speaking we

---

[32] *Vita Landiberti episcopi Traeiectensis vetustissima* (ed. B. Krusch 1913) *Mon. Germ. Hist. Script. rer. Merov.* 6, XXVI sq., pp. 381 sq.

[33] *Vita Boniti* loc. cit. XXXIX, p. 138; *Vita Audoini episcopi Rotomagensis* (ed. W. Levison 1910) *Mon. Germ. Hist. Script. rer. Merov.* XVI, p. 564.

[34] From Ratisbon the 'princeps terrae cum satrapibus et sacerdotibus, deferentes patibula cum turabulis' went to meet the funeral procession of Haimhramn; *Arbeonis episcopi Frisingensis vita vel Passio Haimhrammi episcopi et martyris Ratisbonensis* (ed. B. Krusch 1920) *Mon. Germ. Hist. Script. rer. German. in us. schol.* XXIV, pp. 76 sq.

[35] *Vita Eligii episcopi Noviomagensis* (ed. B. Krusch 1902) *Mon. Germ. Hist. Script. rer. Merov.* 4, II, pp. 37 and 38, 721 sqq.

[36] *Vita Audoini* loc. cit. XVI sq., pp. 564 sq.

[37] Sagittarius of Gap and Salonius of Embrun were kept prisoners for a while in a monastery but – though they had changed for the better – after a short time they began their vicious lives again. At the suppression of the Gundovald rebellion

can say that sudden death was regarded as a sign of God's disapproval. But it is not only a sign of punishment for a wicked and unrepentant life (or at least a life which does not become a bishop), it is also a sign that the divine system of the world has been endangered by human insolence and must be restored again. If a newly installed bishop died soon or suddenly this was regarded as a sign that he was not worthy. Garivald of Clermont died 40 days after his instalment because he was in the way of Praeiectus the later 'martyr'.[38] Here an accidental event is interrelated with Providence. According to a prophecy at his birth Praeiectus was to become bishop which – on the other hand – is the presupposition for his death as a martyr. Without hesitation the author of the Vita involves God in the quarrels of the leading families in Clermont. It is of no use to Garivald to be legally entitled and no disadvantage that Praeiectus is false to his word; he is predestined to be the bishop of Clermont. When Garivald sees that he cannot make good his pretensions without being supported by the urban leaders, God intervenes and causes the death of the 'usurpator indignus'. To contemporaries this must have seemed a judgement; God does not allow the man he has elected to be slighted. The author of the Passio could rely upon the effect of the sudden death of Garivald, so he was not afraid of describing the circumstances that made Praeiectus a bishop; the dubious machinations of his party as well as the sound claims of the archdean Garivald. The latter's sudden death was proof enough that he was not worthy and thus all objections could be annihilated.

Even more striking is sudden death in addition to disgraceful circumstances of dying. Here a strong feeling of hatred is expressed together with satisfaction about the fall of the villain. Thus the author of the Vita et miracula St. Galli relates the death of Bishop Sidonius of Constance with apparent joy. The bishop died from dysentery and the chronicler takes pleasure in describing the disgusting details, reminding us of the death of Arius.[39] Thus – though he could not reproach Sidonius with a deviation from orthodoxy – the author could show how much he disapproved of him.

We may consider unexpected sudden death to be the clear opposite of a

Sagittarius was decapitated when he tried to flee; Salonius is never heard of again. The murder of the bishop of Gap is reported by Gregory without the slightest sign of regret; we might get the impression that the end of Sagittarius is a sort of 'moral'. At any rate it differs distinctly from the way the assassinations of other bishops are described.

[38] Passio Preiecti episcopi et martyris Arverni (ed. B. Krusch 1910) Mon. Germ. Hist. Script. rer. Merov. 5, XIII, p. 323.

[39] Vita et miracula sancti Galli (ed. G. Meyer von Knonau 1870) – Mitteilungen zur vaterländischen Geschichte, 12, LVIII, pp. 80 sq. The antagonism between the monastery of St. Gall and the bishops of Constance (who often were abbots of Reicenau, the rival monastery to St. Gall) seems to have reached a climax with Sidonius. But we must not doubt the way in which he was said to have died.

death that has been announced in a dream or a vision. From the Christian point of view it is a horrible idea to have to die without being given a chance to repent one's sins. Moreover a sudden death brought great disadvantages for the bishop who came from a noble family: he had to dispense with the solemn staging of his death, as was required by his rank. Apart from the negative sensation which was caused by a sudden death, this was the way in which ordinary people died. Disgraceful circumstances surrounding a bishop's death meant a great disadvantage for his family too.

Finally we are going to talk about the violent death of a bishop. Since the middle of the seventh century when quarrels broke out in the Merovingian kingdom this had been no unusual way to die. In the eighth century we meet highly secularized bishops who were repeatedly involved in military actions. A bishop of that kind need not necessarily appear in a negative light. Gerold of Mayence who fell in battle against the Saxons in 743 is not blamed for that. Nobody saw a judgement in his way of dying.[40] But of Gerold the same thing is true as it was of Bishop Hildgar of Cologne ten years later. He was killed by the Saxons, too[41] and it would have been easy to regard him a martyr since the Saxons were heathens. But no such description is to be found. The bishop who has died in battle is neither a martyr nor a sinner rejected by God.

It is different with Savaricus of Auxerre, who was struck by lightning while he was besieging Lyon.[42] He went beyond the possibilities that had been given to the 'new bishop' as he had existed since the decline of the Merovingian power. Savaricus preferred being a warrior to being a bishop and made his see the centre of his actions of conquest. Therefore his sudden and striking death must have had an important symbolical value and certainly was regarded as a judgement 'divino fulmine percussus'.

---

[40] Everybody understood why blood revenge was taken by Gewilib, Gerold's son and successor in Mayence. Yet Bonifatius initiated the deposition of Gewilib in 745. The bishop appealed to the pope, which shows us how deeply he was rooted in the ideas of his class, and how much bishops of his kind regarded the actions of Bonifatius as threatening to their existence. A nobleman simply had to take part in battles and to practise hunting. See Georg W. Sante, *Bonifatius, der Staat und die Kirche*. St. Bonifatius (1954), pp. 224 sq. and Theodor Schieffer, *Winfrid-Bonifatius* (1954), pp. 230 sqq. In the sixth century Gregory of Tours does not blame Siagrius, the son of Bishop Desideratus of Verdun, for having slain Sirivult, the greatest enemy of his father; *Hist. Franc.* III, 34 and 35, pp. 129 sq.

[41] He fell in a battle near the fortress of Iuberg (Westphalia) in 753. The report of the bishop's death in the battle can be found in some sources: *Annales Laureshamenses* (e.g. G. H. Pertz, 1826) *Mon. Germ. Hist. Script.* 1, p 26; *Chronicon Laurissense breve* (ed. H. Schnorr von Carolsfeld) NA 36 (1911), p. 28; *Annales sancti Amandi continuatio*, 10 and *Annales Petaviani continuatio*, 11 (ed. G. H. Pertz) loc. cit.; *Annales regni Francorum* (ed. F. Kurze 1895) *Mon. Germ. Hist. rer. German. in us. schol.* 10.

[42] *Gesta episcoporum Autissidorensium* (ed. G. Waitz 1881) *Mon. Germ. Hist.* 13, XXVI, p. 394.

Attitudes differ about bishops who died in the course of internecine strifes. It is interesting to see what conditions were regarded as essential to make the deceased a martyr. Let us think of the deaths of Leodegar of Autun, Landbert of Maastricht, Praeiectus of Clermont and Desiderius of Vienne. All of them suffered death in ways resembling in some respect the deaths of great saints, like St. Stephen or Christ himself. But this was not sufficient to qualify them as martyrs. Their contemporaries certainly knew about the political background and the real causes of their deaths. It was up to the families of the deceased to intervene; their kin had to be given advantages in the quarrels in the course of which the bishops had lost their lives. *Vitae* had to be written, places of worship had to be erected. It is a characteristic sign that we have a *Vita* for each of the four bishops. Apparently the *Vitae* were written in a hurry and therefore could not reconcile the difference between policital reality and the Christian ideal they were aiming at. This is noticeable in Landbert's *Vita vetustissima*. Here the archaic warrior is to be seen clearly behind the pious bishop. As regards Leodegar he seems to have been an important religious personality so that his reckless appearance in the internecine strifes was no hindrance to his glorification. Yet the fact that a man like him, who came from a powerful family, did not escape from his imprisonment but was ready to bear torture and death, might have appeared as martyrdom to his contemporaries although they knew the political situation.[43]

Praeiectus owes his position as a martyr to his family. His *Passio* is full of 'topos'. His life was of little importance and therefore it needed all the more a description conforming to the traditional pattern.

With Desiderius it is not so much his family who made him a martyr as the fact that he was killed by order of Queen Brunhild. Having opposed that 'Jezebel' the executed bishop was held in honour officially after her fall.

Looking at the four examples mentioned above we see that all of these events have taken place in the seventh century. It seems to be very typical of this century of crisis in the Merovingian kingdom that a bishop who had died in a fight for political power could be presented as a martyr. When Praetextatus of Rouen was slain during a holy service in 588 the circumstances were not necessarily to be stylized in a *Vita*. But that event was of no consequence in our sense. Praetextatus had been a protagonist against the anticlerical policy of King Chilperich, but his aims were of no political significance. Before the beginning of the great fights in the seventh century the outstanding families do not seem to have put great emphasis upon the propaganda effect of such an event. But maybe Praetextatus had not been a member of an outstanding family. While in the sixth century the mere external circumstances of a person's death were not yet enough to qualify him as a martyr, by the eighth century they were no longer

---

[43] Lotter, 317 simplifies the case of Leodegar thinking that the political murder was taken as a martyrdom 'ex post', in a time that lacked true martyrdom.

sufficient, even for members of a leading family. To Ainmar of Auxerre, who escaped from imprisonment and was killed in 731 by order of Charles Martell it was of no avail to have received the mortal hit while he was spreading his arms in a crosslike way; thus praising God. He was buried where he had died and was regarded a rebel. Describing his death in the way he does, the author tries to characterise him as a martyr, but because of the negative attitude of his contemporaries his attempt may be compared to a single flash of lightning amidst darkness. The reasons why he is treated in a way different from that of the seventh century (see Leodegar or Landbert) are the following: on the one hand people had got used to the type of the martial bishop, on the other hand they could hardly make an enemy of the powerful Carolingian maiordomus into a saint.

WILLS AS EVIDENCE OF POPULAR PIETY IN THE REFORMATION PERIOD: LEEDS AND HULL, 1540–1640

Claire Cross

In his monumental work recently published in English as *The Hour of our Death* Philippe Ariès states that when wills began once more to be made systematically in the twelfth century they were no longer seen primarily as a means of transmitting property, as they had been in classical antiquity, but as essentially religious documents. At the end of their lives the church expected Christians to make a confession of faith, and acknowledgement of their sins and atonement in the form of a bequest to pious uses. He did, however, introduce a note of caution. By the sixteenth century, a time of accelerating theological conflict when testators might have been expected to have wanted to leave an unambiguous statement of doctrinal orthodoxy, wills had become the exclusive responsibility of the notary.[1] M. Ariès has drawn most of his material from France: the situation may have been rather different in England. For some decades now historians have used will preambles to try to assess the degree of religious change in certain regions in the reigns of Henry VIII, Edward VI, Mary and Elizabeth. While always stressing that these preambles could do no more than indicate a trend and that they should in no sense be regarded as a means of scientific measurement, they nevertheless have generally been inclined to consider them as at least to some extent the personal professions of the testator's belief.[2] How far the composition of wills in England had also by

---

[1] P. Ariès, *The Hour of our Death* (London, 1981), pp. 188–90.

[2] A. G. Dickens, *Lollards and Protestants in the Diocese of York 1509–1558* (London, 1959), pp. 214–8; A. G. Dickens, *English Reformation* (London, 1964), pp. 191–2; D. M. Palliser, *The Reformation in York 1534–1553* (Borthwick Papers no. 40, York, 1971), pp. 19–21, 27–32; M. Spufford, *Contrasting Communities* (Cambridge, 1974), pp. 320–44; R. C. Richardson, 'Wills and will-makers in the sixteenth and

the early sixteenth century fallen into the hands of lawyers and their associates, and so should as in France be more properly classed as documents as formalised as, for example, land conveyances, needs further probing. An examination of around two thousand registered wills for the borough of Kingston upon Hull and the urbanised parish of Leeds from between 1520 and 1640 can yield a little additional information on this apparently somewhat hackneyed subject.[3]

In the nine years before the summoning of the Reformation Parliament and during the religious revolution of the second half of the reign of Henry VIII the wills of the inhabitants of Leeds and Hull reveal a very similar pattern. Almost without exception testators bequeathed their souls to 'God Almighty, St. Mary and to all the saints in heaven'. They rarely named these saints, referring to them collectively as the celestial court of the whole company of heaven. Until 1540 many individuals left money for masses for their souls after death. Since the local clergy featured frequently as witnesses and sometimes as supervisors this is all very much what might be anticipated. In the last years of Henry VIII occasional preambles in both Leeds and Hull omit any request for the intercession of the Virgin. On the accession of Edward VI an abbreviation took place in the preambles with testators consigning their souls merely to 'Almighty God, my maker and redeemer' or, even more briefly as at Hull, solely to 'God Almighty', though in some wills St. Mary is still mentioned. In line with the catholic restoration of Mary Tudor Leeds testators quickly readopted the old formulae, and once more left their souls to 'God Almighty, and to our blessed Lady, St. Mary, and to all the saints in heaven'. Matters differed slightly, however, in Hull where the Virgin returned in only a minority of the wills. The usual Hull bequest of the soul between 1553 and 1558 is 'to God Almighty, to be accompanied with all his saints in heaven', and this could just be a sign of clandestine protestantism the existence of which in the town is known pretty conclusively from other sources.[4] On Mary's death the will preambles changed again, though considerably more quickly in Hull than in Leeds where the intervention of the Virgin continued to be sought during the first four of five years of the new reign. Then in Leeds a plan formula emerged which went on being used well into

seventeenth centuries: some Lancashire evidence', *Local Population Studies*, 9, 1972, pp. 33–42; M. L. Zell, 'The use of religious preambles as a measure of religious belief in the sixteenth century', *Bulletin of the Institute of Historical Research*, 50, 1977, pp. 246–9; P. Clark, *English Provincial Society from the Reformation to the Revolution* (Hassocks, 1977), pp. 58–9, 76–7.

[3] These wills, 1091 for Hull, 875 for Leeds, are housed in the Borthwick Institute for Historical Research, York, the majority being registered copies in the probate registers, but from 1635 when there is a gap in the registers, original wills survive.

[4] C. Cross, 'Parochial structure and the dissemination of protestantism in sixteenth century England: a tale of two cities', in D. Baker, ed., *Studies in Church History*, 16, 1979, pp. 273–4.

the 1590s: testators gave their soul simply 'to Almighty God, my maker and redeemer'. Only very slowly in the 1590s did some Leeds inhabitants begin to choose a preamble which indicated a more fervent commitment to protestantism, and gradually what could be called a standard Leeds Trinitarian formula developed as testator after testator gave their souls to

> Almighty God, my maker, and to Jesus Christ his only son, my saviour and redeemer, verily trusting that through his blessed passion and glorious resurrection my soul shall be saved and be partaker of his heavenly kingdom at the last day, and to the Holy Ghost the comforter of the weak in all tribulations.[5]

In Hull the picture seems rather different. There more elaborate and much more explicitly protestant formulae emerged earlier until by the 1580s a distinctive Hull preamble with emphasis upon Christ as the lamb of God came to the fore and Hull citizens surrendered their souls into

> the hands of Almighty God, my only maker, saviour and sanctifier, trusting that the same my soul shall be saved by the free mercy of God through the death and passion of that immaculate, unspotted and eternal lamb, Christ Jesus, my only lord and saviour, and by none other means.[6]

As the century progressed the clergy of the two towns figured less and less in the wills. On the rather unusual occasions after 1559 when a cleric did witness a will he seems to have been acting more as a personal friend than as the testator's religious mentor. These wills do appear to confirm Ariès view that the making of wills had ceased to be a prerogative of the clergy, certainly by 1600 and perhaps even as early as 1560, though this seems to have happened rather more slowly in Hull and Leeds than in those parts of the continent where he worked.

So far these findings have a certain predictability and apart perhaps from the preferred local formulae do no more than echo other English regional studies. What demands further investigation is the degree to which the preamble of a will can be assumed to reflect the individual belief of a testator, and here the Leeds and Hull wills in conjunction offer a salutary warning. In March 1566 when his contemporaries were cautiously giving their souls to 'Almighty God' a Leeds chapman, Henry Runtwhayte, had drawn up a very long and apparently very personal will. First he made over

> into the hands of our Lord, my God, my soul, which he of his fatherly goodness gave me when he fashioned this my body in my

---

[5] Borthwick Institute Prob. Reg. 30 f 127 r–v.
[6] Borthwick Institute Prob. Reg. 22, pt. I f 204 r–v.

mother's womb, making me a living creature, nothing doubting but my Lord God, for his mercy's sake, set forth in the precious blood of his dearly beloved Son, Christ Jesus, our only saviour and redeemer will receive my soul into his glory, and place it in the company of his blessed mother, St. Mary, and all the saints in heaven.

He then went on to bestow his body

unto the earth whereof it came, trusting according to the articles of our faith that at the great day of the general resurrection, when we shall appear before the judgement seat of Christ, I shall receive it again by the mighty power of God, wherewith he is able to subdue all things unto himself, not [a] corruptible, mortal, weak or vile body as it is now, but uncorruptible, immortal, strong, perfect and in all points like unto the glorious body of my Lord and Saviour Christ Jesu.

Lastly, and very unusually, he pronounced in highly commendatory terms upon the estate of matrimony, alluding to his wife 'with whom I coupled myself in the fear of God, and refusing all other women, I linked myself unto her, living hitherto with her in the blessed state of honourable wedlock . . .' To her he left his house and various leases for life. In contrast with the prolix preamble, the body of the will is concise, though detailed enough to detract from the pious impression conveyed in the opening section by disclosing that Runtwhayte had sired a bastard son.[7]

This disjuction between the preamble and the content of the will provides a significant clue. In fact the preamble is standard form and, given the mention of the Virgin Mary, almost certainly originally taken from a catholic formularly. It fulfils Ariès definition in all respects, being an explicit though highly formalised confession of faith. One other will like it has survived from Leeds, and one from Hull, In 1607 Nicholas Gatonbe of Hull, describing himself merely as an 'unprofitable servant of God', produced a virtually identical preamble, consigning his soul to God in exactly the same words (apart from excising the reference to the Virgin Mary), his body to the earth in the same hope of resurrection and making exactly the same profession regarding the sanctity of marriage.[8] Nearly two decades later in Leeds a yeoman, Matthew Cooper, for the third time used the same formula both as regards his soul (again omitting any reference to the Virgin) and his body, though as a widower he understandably did not retain the clause in praise of matrimony.[9]

The probable source for both Gatonbe's and Cooper's wills can be

[7] Borthwick Institute Prob. Reg. 17, pt. II, f 540 r–v.
[8] Borthwick Institute Prob. Reg. 32 f 681 v–682 r.
[9] Borthwick Institute Prob. Reg. 37 f 368 v–371 v.

discovered in William West's *Symbolaeography* ... *or the Paterne of Praesidents, for the Notarie or Scrivener* first published in 1590 which proved immensely popular, running into many editions in the early seventeenth century. In 'a very perfect form of a will' West set out how an 'unprofitable servant of God' should bequeath his soul and body and how he should allude to marriage. In typical Elizabethan fashion West did not acknowledge the legal handbooks upon which his compendium was based, but there can be little doubt that he derived his pattern wills from earlier Elizabethan formularies which, taking into account Runtwhayte's appeal to the Virgin, are likely to go back at least to Mary's reign, if not earlier. In all West provided three specimen wills ranging from the highly elaborate model selected by Cooper and Gatonbe, through 'another form of a will' where the preamble reads much more simply 'I commend my soul into the hands of God my maker, hoping assuredly through the only merits of Jesus Christ, my saviour, to be made partaker of live everlasting' to 'a good president for a testament' which leaves the soul merely 'unto Almighty God, my maker and redeemer'.[10] This last and simplest exemplar parallels very closely the only model will included in the anonymous *A newe Boke of Presidents*, first published in 1543 which went through constant reprintings in the sixteenth century.[11] The wide circulation of these Tudor legal formularies would suggest that lawyers and scriveners were in England exercising considerably more influence upon the composition of wills than has previously been recognised. They also pose the question as to whether any will preambles, however individualistic they may sound, can in fact any longer be presumed to be a personal statement of faith. Perhaps a sixteenth or seventeenth century testator may normally have done no more than choose a pious preamble from several offered to him by his will maker. (West implied that he intended the lengthy preamble for the higher ranks of society, the more concise ones for merchants.) Even more nihilistically, perhaps many testators may have abandoned the whole business of the preamble to those acquainted with the formulae and have concerned themselves with what really interested them, the transmission of property and personal estate. A detailed analysis of the legal handbooks used by West on the lines of that carried out by Professor Derrett for Henry Swinburne, West's civil law contemporary, might go far to solve this problem.[12] In the meanwhile, total scepticism concerning the possibility of linking confessions of faith in wills and the actual beliefs of the testator would not yet seem to be altogether warranted.

In the first place, the question of personal beliefs has in one sense only moved up one level from the testator to the will writer, attorney, notary

---

[10] W. West, *Symbolaeography* ... (London, 1597), sections 642, 643, 645.

[11] *A Book of Presidents*, London [1583], f cx.

[12] J. D. M. Derrett, *Henry Swinburne (?1551–1624), Civil Lawyer of York* (Borthwick Papers no. 44, York, 1973), pp. 35–50.

public, scrivener, schoolmaster or whoever he may have been. Why, as was the case in both Hull and Leeds, though at a rather different pace, should the writers of wills have been putting before their clients increasingly emphatic protestant formulae as the century advanced? The answer seems to be that despite their traditional reputation for conservatism some lawyers and their associates at least positively supported the change in religious allegiance. The personal commitment of one such will maker can certainly be documented in Hull. In many of the Hull wills which contained explicit protestant preambles stressing salvation through the merits of Christ alone the name of John Lynne appeared either as witness or, much less often, as supervisor. In 1597 the scrivener made his own will:

> Renouncing utterly all man's merits and what devices soever have been dreamed for salvation of mankind by our ancestors, being contrary to the word of God, I do commit my sinful soul unto the holy protection of Almighty God, being most merciful, which God I do profess to be divided into three persons, that is to wit, God the Father, who hath made all mankind of nothing, and the Son who at the time appointed by his Father in his wisdom came down from the heavens to take upon him our human nature to the end to redeem all those that faithfully trust in him, and God the Holy Spirit, who is the sanctifier of all God's elected, and in his faith I will by the grace of God. And I commit my body to the earth from whence it came, trusting that at the last day with these mine eyes I shall see the Lord my saviour and with no other. And I utterly here profess to detest all popery as the seed of Satan, being assured that the same doctrine is illusive and devised by shavelings for the malevolence, not of the glory of God, but of their own bellies, as it pleaseth the Almighty of his secret wisdom to appoint the same.[13]

Here surely speaks the authentic voice of a man who in his turn guided his clients in the drafting of their wills, and it seems very likely that there was a succession of professional will writers in both Hull and Leeds who thought and acted as he did in the latter part of the sixteenth and in the early seventeenth century.

The second reason for not abandoning preambles entirely as indicators of personal religious beliefs lies in the fact that very occasionally testators did indeed make their own wills. A Hull merchant, William Jackson, wrote his will with his own hand in 1566, and produced a fairly long, but not particularly distinctive Trinitarian preamble.[14] John Hartcastle of Hull, in 1583 also wrote a will which could well be his own composition. He bequeathed his soul

[13] Borthwick Institute Prob. Reg. 27, pt. I f 129 v–131 r.
[14] Borthwick Institute Prob. Reg. 17, pt. II f 612 v–613 r.

into the hands of my good and gracious God, the creator, saviour, redeemer, preserver, instructor and sanctifier of all his good and holy workmanship, believing most constantly and assuredly to be an elect vessel to eternal salvation, and that only by the free grace and mercy of God in that he did send down his only Son and our sweet saviour and redeemer, Jesus Christ, so that he is the only propitiation and full satisfaction for the sins of so many as truly do believe, and that was and is his only office, so that as that holy prophet David saith in the psalm, 'No man may redeem his brother nor pay ransom for his soul', for it cost more than that, even the holy and precious heart blood of that immaculate lamb our only saviour and redeemer, Jesus Christ.[15]

One final example, although he did not expressly say so, must also have included the actual beliefs of the testator, a third Hull merchant, Robert Coldcoollie: it was made in 1640.

First and before all things I commit myself soul and body to Almighty God and to his mercy in Christ Jesus, hoping asuredly without any doubt or mistrust that by God's grace and the merits of Jesus Christ and by virtue of his passion and resurrection I shall have remission of sins and resurrection body and soul, for I am sure that my redeemer liveth, and that I shall rise out of the earth at the last day, and shall be covered again with my skin, and though worms destroy this body I shall see God in my flesh (Job 19). This my hope is laid up in my bosom . . .

He next professed his belief in 'one mediator . . . betwixt God and me . . ., Christ Jesus', and proceeded at considerable length acknowledging God's providential correction with his visitation of the plague (quoting Hebrews chapter 12, 'Whom the Lord loveth he chasteneth'), being prompted to set his estate in order by the command of Isaiah to King Hezekiah, and desiring with St. Paul 'to be dissolved and to be with Christ "which is best of all".'[16]

So in the end biblical eloquence and expertise triumphs over scepticism. The wills of Hull and Leeds made between 1520 and 1640 do not admit of any statistical treatment, they cannot be counted to show how many citizens had come to a reasoned acceptance of protestantism at the time of their deaths but taken together with other evidence, presentations in ecclesiastical courts, bequests to endow and supplement preaching posts, the fairly widespread circulation of bibles and other religious books, they can be used with caution to indicate a trend towards a more commited form of protestantism. In the past when studying preambles not enough

[15] Borthwick Institute Prob. Reg. 23, pt. I f 394 v.
[16] Borthwick Institute Original wills May 1640.

emphasis has been placed upon the opinions of the will writers as opposed to those of the testators and more investigation is needed into the will formularies in existence at least from the early part of the sixteenth century. Particular care must be taken before a preamble can be assumed to reflect the actual beliefs of a testator, but amid what was increasingly becoming a stereotyped form some authentic confessions of faith can still be found in wills.

L'ÉVOLUTION DES PREPARATIONS À LA MORT EN FRANCE DU XVIIe AU XVIIIe SIÈCLE

Robert Favre

Que sont devenues les Préparations à la mort pendant la période où leur publication en langue française subit apparemment une inéluctable régresssion? Coment ce genre, qui s'était si largement épanoui au long du XVIIe siècle, a-t-il résisté à la montée des critiques que lançaient les hommes des Lumières contre l'Eglise catholique, contre la foi chrétienne, ou même contre toute attitude religieuse?

A côté d'autres historiens français de la mort, Daniel Roche avait particulièrement étudié un large corpus de Préparations à la mort dans son important article: 'La Mémoire de la mort. Recherche sur la place des arts de mourir dans la librairie et la lecture en France aux XVIIe et XVIIIe siècles'. Il a paru dans *Annales, Economie. Sociétés. Civilisations* en février 1976, le mois òu je soutenais ma thèse sur *La Mort dans la littérature et la pensée françaises au XVIIIe siècle*. Depuis lors, nous avons réuni nos efforts et nos découvertes, afin de tenter de constituer une bibliographie aussi complète que possible des Préparations à la mort. Je tiens à signaler dès l'abord cette collaboration si précieuse pour moi.

Le project principal de ma thèse était ailleurs. Je cherchais à découvrir les idées et les thèmes littéraires d'écrivains, 'philosophes' ou non, qui n'ont aucunement écarté la mort de leurs pensées et de leurs oeuvres, contrairement à ce que prétendaient les meilleurs spécialistes du siècle des Lumières. J'étais par là conduit à confronter ces oeuvres à des textes moins prestigieux où s'exprime la pensée traditionnelle sur la mort: recueils de sermons, traités de théologie morale, etc., et surtout arts de mourir publiés ou réédités à la fin du XVIIe et au XVIIIe siècles. Comment apprécier certains épisodes de *La Vie de Marianne*, chez Marivaux, de *La Religieuse*, chez Diderot, la mort de Julie dans *La Nouvelle Héloïse*, ou le dénouement de *Paul et Virginie*, sinon par référence aux leçons chrétiennes sur la mort? En outre, Voltaire, Buffon, Diderot, le baron d'Holbach montrent en maints endroits qu'ils connaissaient fort bien ces arts de mourir auxquels ils donnent la réplique.

En m'appuyant sur ces lectures et sur les travaux parallèles de D. Roche, j'ai acquis une quasi-certitude: aux XVIIIe siècle, et jusqu'à la Révolution française, le domaine de la Préparation à la mort ne se réduit pas brutalement, non seulement grâce aux rééditions, mais même par l'édition d'ouvrages nouveaux; son influence demeure étendue; mais le genre devient de plus en plus difficile à déterminer.

De toute évidence, il faut d'abord mettre à part les arts de mourir philosophiquement, qui sont d'esprit anti-chrétien ou anti-religieux. Parmi les premiers, à la suite des *Quatrains du déiste* (1622), citons les *Réflexions sur les grands hommes qui sont morts en plaisantant*, de Boureau-Deslandes, souvent rééditées depuis 1712, ainsi que les célèbres *Epîtres* de Voltaire *à Uranie* et, presque testamentaire, *à Horace* (1772); son court dialogue de *Sophronime et Adèlos* (1766) offre un excellent condensé de l'anti-Préparation à la mort, cependant qu'un obscur Glénat en décline platement des arguments analogues dans un traité *Contre les craintes de la mort* (1757). La leçon athéiste se trouve dans les *Réflexions contre les craintes de la mort* et dans les *Lettres à Eugénie*, attribuées au baron d'Holbach, qui la développe aussi dans une large part de son *Système de la Nature* (1771). N'oublions pas l'article 'Mort' de l'*Encyclopédie*, par le chevalier de Jaucourt. Ces textes, et d'autres encore, nous concernent indirectement. Car ils montrent que le genre de la Préparation à la mort a été capté par les adversaires du christianisme. Le prestige du genre se maintient paradoxalement à travers les textes qui visent à en détruire l'influence, jusque chez le marquis de Sade qui a fait dialoguer un moribond et un prêtre.

Remarquons en outre que l'enseignement traditionnel sur la mort a remporté une sorte de victoire morale sur ses ennemis, puisqu'ils conservèrent souvent les mêmes schémas de pensée que les auteurs chrétiens; comme eux, les 'philosophes' affirment: connaître la vérité sur la mort aide à l'affronter en paix, les derniers moments son décisifs, il faut se prémunir contre une défaillance ultime, il est bon que l'entourage apporte ses secours au mourant. Et des épisodes réels ou romanesque nous montrent en action ces sortes de confréries de la bonne mort philosophique.

Mais il est temps d'en venir aux Préparations à la mort proprement religieuses.

Dès le XVIIe siècle, D. Roche le sougligne au début de son article, ces arts de mourir ont acquis une grande diversité. A côté des exposés abstraits, des traités sur les quatre fins dernières, des recueils de sermons constitués en exercices de retraite, on a vu apparaître des dialogues, des exhortations, des récits de morts exemplaires, des testaments spirituels offerts eux aussi en modèle, des commentaires de textes sacrés, des méditations poétiques sur la Passion du Christ, ou sur notre condition éphémère ... Des traductions, surtout de l'italien, s'ajoutent aux originaux en langue française. Le P. Jean Brignon, s.j., grand traducteur de Préparations à la mort, propose en outre une relecture de l'*Introduction à la vie dévote* de saint François de Sales qui la transforme en art de bien mourir (1696; rééd.: 1752, 1758, 1766, 1768).

Une fois cet éventail largement ouvert au XVIIe siècle, on admire les auteurs qui ne cessent pas d'ajouter des titres nouveaux à la réédition de nombreux titres anciens durant presque un siècle encore. Après tout, beaucoup de genres littéraires ont connu une plus rapide décadence. Examinons l'évolution quantitative et qualitative de ce genre, qui va se perpétuer assez bien jusqu'à la veille de la Révolution, et qui va d'ailleurs avoir lui aussi sa 'Restauration'.

Je vais donc reprendre d'abord, aussi brièvement que possible, les observations chiffrées de D. Roche en 1976, avec les additifs dont il m'a fait amicalement profiter, et avec des compléments que j'ai pu moi-même y apporter (voir le tableau en appendice).

Ensuite, nous pourrons discuter de quelques réflexions sur les limites de genre. En explorant des zones frontalières, nous rencontrerons quelques cas assez nets, mais aussi d'autres cas dont il est difficile de dire avec assurance s'ils appartiennent ou non à notre domaine.

Que nous apportait l'étude de D. Roche?

Il avait dénombré 236 titres différents de Préparations à la mort entre 1600 et 1799. Leur nombre s'accroissait régulièrement durant tout le XVIIe siècle, passant de 26 pour les 25 premières années (1600–1624) à une soixantaine pour les 25 dernières (1675–1699). C'est alors le maximum. Pour les quatre quarts du XVIIIe siècle, on trouvait successivement 38 titres (1700–1724), 20 (1725–1749), puis seulement 6 (1750–1774) et 7 (1775–1799), au total 71 titres, soit 30%. Ce déclin, même compensé par 112 rééditions provinciales, confirmerait que le siècle des Lumières est bien une période de crise pour la foi, ou du moins une période de recherche d'une expression nouvelle pour cette foi.

Or, grâce à des recherches récentes, D. Roche a repéré 25 autres titres, surtout au XVIIe siècle, et j'en ajoute 57 autre, dont 38 pour le XVIIIe siècle. Parmi d'autre sources encore possibles, j'ai utilisé diverses bibliothèques de Lyon, dont celle de l'Hôtel-Dieu, des catalogues de libraires, et les nouvelles littéraires de périodiques du XVIIIe siècle, notamment les *Mémoires de Trévoux*. Nous voici donc passés de 236 à 318 titres, ce qui représente une considérable augmentation de plus d'un tiers (34%). D'autres découvertes restent possibles.

Ce corpus de 318 titres permet de proposer quelques observations. D'abord, est confirmé le mouvement de forte croissance au XVIIe siècle. Mais la répartition nouvelle par quarts de siècle (28-47-65-70) accentue encore la progression et montre que le triomphe des arts de mourir est établi dès les années 1650–1674.

Quant au XVIIIe siècle, que représente désormais 33.6% du total, il ne donne que 107 titres, et encore 33 d'entre eux datés de 1700 à 1715 pourraient-ils être rattachés au 'siècle de Louis XIV'. Par quarts de siècle globalement saisis, nous trouvons d'abord ici 51 titres (33 + 18), puis un recul net: 29, 14 et 14. Mais pour les années 1750 à 1799, ce n'est plus un effondrement. Nous voici non plus à 13, mais à 28 titres.

En réalité, ces décomptes par tranches de 25 ans sont trompeurs. Si une chute se manifeste, c'est parce que nous n'avons retrouvé aucune édition nouvelle dans deux périodes: entre 1752 et 1755, et surtout entre 1764 et 1770. De 1752 à 1755, on note en compensation 17 rééditions en quatre ans, ce qui est supérieur au rythme moyen des années voisines. De 1764 a 1770, au contraire, le rythme des rééditions – une ou deux par an – reste stable. L'effrondrement de l'édition de nouveaux arts de mourir en 1764 ne correspondrait-il pas à la crise née de l'expulsion des Jésuites de France? Ce n'est qu'une hypothèse. Mais quand on connaît la part importante que les auteurs jésuites ont occupée dans la rédaction des Préparations à la mort – 50% des auteurs identifiés, selon D. Roche[1], cette hypothèse prend une singulière consistance.

D'autres études complèteront sans doute un jour ces remarques et affineront cette analyse chronoligique encore sommaire. En ces lieux, je voudrais ajouter un mot sur les traductions, notables, mais tardives et assez rares, d'auteurs anglais en français. Ces traductions concernent d'abord William Sherlock pour ses deux ouvrages *De la Mort* (1696) et *Du Jugement* (1696), puis Stevens pour sa *Chaîne d'or* (1702), et plus tardivement John Bunyan, dont le *Pilgrim's Progress* n'est traduit à Rotterdam qu'en 1738. Ces textes publiés en Hollande visent un public protestant. Ils obtiennent tous des rééditions dans la seconde moitié du XVIIIe siècle: Sherlock en 1756, Stevens en 1758, et Bunyan à Paris même en 1772 et 1775. Le succès durable de Bunyan est attesté par seize rééditions de 1775 à 1854.

Mais pour mieux apprécier le rôle de la Prèparation à la mort durant le période de son reflux, il importe d'étudier l'évolution littéraire du genre, ce qui pose le problème de ses limites. Plusieurs oeuvres que je mentionnerai n'ont pas été prises en compte dans les calculs précédents, par prudence de méthode, mais la question reste ouverte.

Voice un 'art de bien vivre et de bien mourir'. Les conseils pour 'bien vivre' se relient-ils étroitement ou non à une pédagogie de la mort? La Préparation à la mort qui ouvre ou qui clôt un ouvrage en est-elle l'essentiel? Voilà un problème d'appréciation qui engage le lecteur. Un exemple: j'ai eu l'occasion d'opposer mon opinion à celle de M. Robert Mauzi à propos du *Traité du vrai mérite de l'homme* de Le Maître de Claville,[2] Ce livre publié en 1734 a obtenu un succès immédiat et durable. Diderot lui connaît une cinquantaine d'éditions, et je signale celles de 1759, 1777 et 1783. L'ouvrage, surtout si on ne le lit pas jusqu'au bout, peut passer pour l'expression d'un christianisme mondain, conciliant, invitant à vivre 'sans

---

[1] 'La Mémoire de la mort', *Annales, E.S.C.*, 31e année, no 1, février 1976, p. 94.
[2] On peut se reporter aux exposés des deux thèses: R. Mauzi, *L'Idée du bonheur . . . aux XVIIIe siècle*, (Paris, A. Colin, 1960), p. 202 notamment; R. Favre, *La Mort au siècle des Lumières*, (Lyon, Presses Universitaires de Lyon, 1978), pp. 137–139.

que les moyens du bonheur présent ruinent les espérances de l'avenir' (c'est-
à-dire du salut). Mais tout est orienté, finalement, vers une 'bonne mort'.
Après avoir fait gravir au lecteur les quatre degrés de la moralité: 'le galant
homme', 'l'homme de mérite', 'l'honnête homme' et 'l'homme de bien', le
Maître de Claville veut que ce lecteur fasse mourir en lui ces personnages et
se prépare au milieu même du monde à l'éternité: 'Toutes les minutes de la
vie d'un chrétien vont frapper à la porte de l'éternité.' sur près de 180 pages,
soit le dernier quart de ce *Traité*, il développe ses considérations sur une
bonne vie apte à procurer une bonne mort, disant: 'Apprenez donc une fois
par jour à bien mourir. On ne peut étudier assez tôt ni trop longtemps la
seule science qui peut servir toujours.' Comment ne pas discerner là un 'art
de bien vivre et de bien mourir' adapté à des lecteurs mondains qu'ils
importe de savoir persuader?

D'autres cas sont plus douteux. Certes la préparation à la retraite et la
méditation de la mort y jouent un rôle important, mais l'ensemble ne paraît
pas aussi nettement orienté. Ainsi, dans les *Entretiens d'une âme pénitente avec
son Créateur*, de Le Bret (1767; rééd.: 1771), une série de chapitres
conduisent à la méditation des fins dernières, en rappelant 'la difficulté
d'obtenir la rémission des péchés sur le lit de la mort'; mais ces chapitres
restent noyés dans les trois volumes. Au contraire, le chevalier de Lasne
d'Aiguebelle a composé de la façon suivante *La Religion de coeur* (1768;
rééd.: 1777, 1787; 7 rééd. de 1817 à 1851): le livre s'ouvre sur des soupirs de
désir mystique et sur un élan de gratitude envers la mort bienfaisante, puis
en vient aux fins dernières; après quelques autres considérations, une
soixante de pages concluent par un retour à la mort et au jugement; et le
dernier article est un 'Cantique à la louange de l'amour divin' avec ce
refrain: 'Languir, désirer et mourir'. Malgré la variété de son contenu, ce
livre de piété sentimentale s'inscrit bien dans l'axe des Préparations à la
mort, et il est fortement marqué par la spiritualité des 'saints désirs de la
mort' qu'au XVIIe siècle le P. Pierre Lallemant avait répandue en trois arts
de mourir, plusieurs fois réédites au XVIIIe.

Le genre de la Préparation à la mort tend donc à s'intégrer dans des
ensembles. On le retrouve dans maint livre de dévotion, en bonne place.
Par example, au sixième et dernier tome de *La Religion chrétienne méditée
dans le véritable espit de ses maximes* (1762-1763), les PP. Jard et de Bonnaire
consacrent sept jours à la mort et au jugement parmi leurs *Lectures de piété
pour tous les jour du mois*, y-compris bien sûr le dernier jour. Mais comment
prendre en compte tous ces textes?

Une autre variante possible apparaît avec la méditation sur des morts
édifiantes. Outre la Passion du Christ, on a très tôt offert d'autres 'exempla',
plus ou moins célèbres. Vers la fin du XVIIIe siècle, nous retrouvons cette
catégorie dans un ouvrage en deux volumes des abbés Sabatier de Castres et
Donzé de Verteuil, les *Derniers Sentiments des plus illustres personnages
condamnés à mort* (1775). Et voici encore plus remarquable la *Relation de la
conversion et de la mort de M. Bouguer, membre de l'Académie des sciences* par le

P. Laberthonie, o.p. (1784). J'ai introduit sans hésitation ces titres dans notre catalogue. Mais faudrait-il aussi y ajouter des ouvrages apparamment plus polémiques qu'édifiants, récits exposant à l'inverse la mort atroce des impies? Tel est le *Rituel des esprits forts*, de Gros de Besplats, publié en 1759, réédite en 1762 avec ce sous-titre: *ou le tableau des incrédules modernes au lit de la mort*. Tel est aussi, entre autres, le fameux et infâme pamphlet d'un capucin, le P. Elie Harel, *Voltaire, Recueil des particularités curieuses de sa vie et da sa mort* (1781). Ce sont bien là des éléments d'une Préparation a la mort. L'exposition répugnante de l'agonie d'un impie illustre appartient au même système de pédagogie de la mort que les tableaux du pécheur à l'agonie. Pourtant la polémique et la personnalisation de l'attaque nous empêchent aujourd'hui de voir là des invitations à pratiquer l'art de bien mourir. Sommes-nous devenus trop délicats? Ne devons-nous pas accepter d'enregistrer ces effets de 'terreur salutaire', tout comme nous acceptons les excès macabres d'un prédicateur?

Mort émouvante et grave du bon chrétien, mort atroce de l'impie, de telles scènes n'ont pas seulement leur place dans des retraites spirituelles et dans des arts de mourir. Deux abbés en font des images marquantes et des épisodes importants de leurs romans apologétiques: l'abbé Gérard dans trois longes scènes du *Comte de Valmont ou les Egarements de la raison* (1774; 6e ed.: 1781), et l'abbé de Crillon pour couronner la démonstration dans ses *Mémoires philosophiques du baron de* ^{xxx} *ramané à la religion catholique au moyen d'arguments et de preuves sans réplique* (1777; rééd.: 1779). Ce sont des Préparations à la mort à faible dose, administrées au lecteur presque par surprise.

La poésie permet mieux de mêler la leçon funèbre et l'action sur la sensibilité. Nous voici loin assurément de Chassignet, de Sponde ou de Drelincourt, poètes de la mort baroque. Mais des auteurs s'essayent à la poésie, en cette seconde moitié du XVIIIe siècle. Notons que Lasne d'Aiguebelle avait écrit sa *Religion du coeur* en prose rythmée, ponctuée d'alexandrins. Un curé admirateur de Voltaire poète, Cotterau du Coudrey, versifie les *Sentiments d'un vrai chrétien à l'heure de la mort* et les publie (Sens, 1761; rééd.: 1772). En juillet de le même année 1761, le *Journal ecclésiastique* présente à ses lecteurs 21 quatrains intitulés 'Sentiments de piété de Madame la marquise ^{xxx} à la vue d'une tête de mort en argent, dans laquelle on avait enchâssé une montre . . . ':

'A considérer cette tête
Je passe les nuits et les jours;
A mourir, quoique toujours prête,
Pour mieux mourir, je meurs toujours.

Oui, cette montre, mieux qu'un livre,
Depuis le matin jusqu'au soir,
Me marque comment je dois vivre,
Et me rappelle à mon devoir.'

Ne nous arrêtons pas à cette tête de mort qui prépare 'mieux qu'un livre'. Mais cet accessoire macabre nous entraîne vers la littérature dite 'préromantique' des cimetières, des ruines et de la nuit. Une partie de cette littérature peut parfois tenir un rôle de substitut des Préparations à la mort, notamment dans le courant issu en France de la poésie anglaise des cimetières, avec Young, Gray et Hervey.

Ducis, adaptateur des tragédies de Shakespeare, vers la fin du XVIIIe siècle, nous apprend que sa mère, chrétienne pieuse,

> '... dévora cent fois ces complaints célèbres
> Où l'amant de la nuit, l'ami des malheureux,
> Le trop sensible Young, sous des cyprès affreux,
> A chanté sa douleur, la mort et les ténèbres.'[3]

L'abbé Gérard, dans une note de son roman, se recommande de l'auteur d'une très orthodoxe Préparation à la mort, le *Tableau de la mort*, Louis-Antoine de Caraccioli; il se donne pour autres modèles 'l'illustre traducteur des *Nuits*', Letourneur, et le romancier Baculard d'Arnaud; ces trois écrivains ont en effet 'accoutumé de nos jours les esprits les plus difficiles en ce genre à la peinture des grandes et terribles vérités de la religion'.[4]

Le rapprochement de ces trois noms n'est pas arbitraire; il détermine assez bien une zone de contact entre la méditation de la mort et la création littéraire. Young, vous le savez, a été amplement traduit, adapté, imité. Retenons ici le nom de Mouslier de Moissy pour *Le Vertueux Mourant*, drame en trois actes et en prose inspiré d'un épisode des *Nuits*, et pour ses *Vérités philosophique tirées des Nuits d'Young et mises en vers libres*, publiés tous deux en 1770. Ce sont de véritables Préparations à la mort, selon moi, non moins que le livre de l'abbé Baudrand: *Esprit, maximes et pensées de Young, extraits de ses 'Nuits'* (1786), destiné à des lecteurs catholiques.

Quant à Baculard d'Arnaud, lorsqu'il publia sa pièce *Les Amants malheureux ou le Comte de Comminges* en 1764, il y joignit un Discours

---

[3] J.-Fr. Ducis, *Oeuvres*, (Paris, Nepveu, 1819), tome III, p. 64. Dans cette 'Epître à ma mère sur sa convalescence', l'auteur a dit que la malade n'a vu

> 'dans la mort que l'immortalité
> Et dans la tombeau qu'un asile.'

Il ajoute, évoquant le tombeau:

> 'Tu n'as point attendu qu'en cas moments funèbres
> Il te vînt, mais trop tard, révéler ses secrets.
> Tu dévoras cent fois ... '

[4] Gérard, *Le Comte de Valmont*, (nlle éd., Paris, Moutard, 1776) tome III, p. 224, note. *Le Tableau de la mort* eut trois éditions en 1761 et une réédition en 1767.

préliminaire où nous voyons se mêler littérature et religion de façon
inextricable: d'une part ses héros sont présentés comme d'authentiques
croyants et la religion comme la seule possibilité d'affronter la mort avec
joie; d'autre part il vante la religion pour ses effets 'terribles'. Ajoutons que
parmi ses modèles littéraires il cite 'L'Enfer de Dante, Le Paradis perdu de
Milton, les Nuits du docteur Young'.

Sans doute, certaines de ces méditations sur la mort semblent être des
prétextes, des occasions de développer des thèmes littéraires sur le régistre
d'une mélancolie tout humaine: thème de l'universelle destruction, thème
du néant de ce monde, thème du bonheur illusoire ou éphémère, thème de
la mort bienfaisante qui apporte la liberté ou la paix. Voilà ce que proposent
des poèmes comme Les Tombeaux (1755) et Les Ruines (1767) de Feutry, ou
Les Ruines (1768) de Coeuilhe. Chez Loaisel de Tréogate, dans 'Le Songe',
l'une des Soirées de mélancolie (1777), un jeune homme découvre la vanité de
l'amour et de la gloire, et il va méditer sur la tombe de son père; le conte
s'achève sur le voeu d'être enterré aupres de lui, et sur une prière à Dieu.

Or ces textes, et d'autres encore, n'expriment pas une mélancolie
purement profane. Le recours final à Dieu, seule permanence, y est
fréquent. Cette religiosité demeure vaguement déiste chex Coeuilhe et
Loaisel de Tréogate, et même chez Baculard d'Arnaud. Mais les références
et les connotations chrétiennes peuvent apparaître assez clairement, parfois.
Feutry, qui présentait une visite aux damnés dans son Temple de la mort
(1753), lui donnait pour épigraphe 'Mors piis non timenda'; et l'apocalypse
évoquée dans son Ode aux nations s'achevait sur une invitation au repentir.
Dans Le Vertueux Mourant, Moissy annonce que le moribond a reçu les
derniers sacrements (acte I, scène 1), il met en scène les interventions du curé
qui, à la fin, commente dans une exhortation très traditionnelle cette agonie
à l'intention des parents, amis et domestiques:

'O vous qui aviez part aux bontés de son âme, venez tous pour
vous instruire et vous consoler, venez apprendre à vivre et à mourir
. . .
Un lit de mort, c'est un lit de triomphe.
C'est ice que le flambeau de la vérité luit dans tout son éclat, la
vertu seule a de la majesté jusque dans les bras de la mort.'
(acte III, scène 8).

Permettez-mois d'esquisser maintenant un bilan encore provisoire.

Après l'essor des Préparations à la mort au XVIIe siècle, nous avons
constaté un net recul au XVIIIe; mais au regard de la production massive du
siècle précédent qui se continue par d'innombrables rééditions, les auteurs
du XVIIIe siècle ont eu un particulier mérite d'assurer la permanence du
genre, et cela d'autant plus qu'il avait très tôt acquis une remarquable
diversité.

De plus, la régression constatée n'est pas un effondrement brutal: les chiffres rectifiés de la seconde moitié du siècle le montrent. Cette production d'ouvrages nouveaux a plutôt subi des à-coups, dont le plus grave – entre 1764 et 1770 – peut trouver une explication dans un phénomène historique plus vaste qui ne tient pas au genre lui-même. D'ailleurs la courbe se redresse de façon notable entre 1770 et 1786. C'est en somme cette dernière date de 1786 qui pose désormais pour moi un problème.

L'atmosphère de polémique entre 'philosophes' et chrétiens favorise une forme particulière de la Préparation à la mort qui se fonde ou non sur des 'exempla': ainsi sont produits des texts relatant la bonne mort de pieuses personnes, et cela jusque dans des romans et des drames; ou bien l'on cherche des effets de 'terreur' par le récit de la mort atroce d'un impie, et notamment de Voltaire.

D'autre part, le genre peut à l'inverse se fondre dans des oeuvres plus amples, où la réflexion morale est orientée par la méditation de la mort, souvent présentée comme objet de 'désir'.

Les thèmes pessimistes imprègnent fortement la sensibilité religieuse de ce siècle. Ils se répandent dans des oeuvres littéraires destinées assurément à des lecteurs lettrés et mondains. Mais un assez large public a dû les accueillir, si l'on juge par les rééditions de certains titres. Le succès prolongé des oeuvres inspirées de Young est ici particulièrement remarquable. On ne peut le considérer comme un simple phénomène de mode littéraire ou d'anglomanie.

Ainsi, les frontières du genre tendent à s'estomper au XVIIIe siècle, surtout après 1750. Mais ne voyons-nous pas au même moment, ou plutôt durant tout le siècle, progresser la critique des genres strictement définis? L'âge classique, avec ses règles, ses distinctions nettes, est lui aussi sur le déclin. On redécouvre les merites de la complexité, du mélange; c'est le temps de la confusion entre vertu et sensibilité, et non pas seulement chez Jean-Jacques Rousseau. Nous découvrons, en fait de Préparation à la mort, l'existence d'un double courant, qui n'est peut-être contradictoire qu'en apparence. D'une part, des auteurs religieux – clercs et laïcs – cherchent dans la poésie, dans la fiction des supports nouveaux et plus aisément aptes à 'intéresser', à émouvoir, afin d'exposer la leçon chrétienne sur la mort. Cela peut être le signe nouveau d'une désaffection du public lettré, qu'il convient de flatter, de séduire. Mais après tout, cent ou cent cinquante ans plus tôt, à l'âge baroque, Chassignet, Drelincourt, d'autres moins connus avaient mis la poésie au service de l'art de mourir; et l'évêque Camus avait écrit des romans bien noirs dans cette même perspective. Cette évolution que nous avons observée à partir de 1750 n'est donc pas nécessairement une décadence, mais peut-être une résurgence du baroque.

D'autre part, dans un mouvement inverse mais concordant, on voit des écrivains profanes choisir de 'faire de la littérature' en exploitant la thématique du pessimisme chrétien sur la vie et en exaltant les bienfaits de la mort qui ouvre à l'âme inquiète les portes du seul bonheur possible. Que ces écrivains se contentent d'une vague religiosité ou qu'ils se situent dans un cadre spécifiquement chrétien, je dirai: peu importe! Le problème principal concerne l'accueil fait par les lecteurs plutôt que l'intention intime des auteurs. Or comment savoir quelle lecture – toute profane ou réellement spirituelle – à été faite de ces livres, de ces poèmes? Recherchait-on des chatouillements de la sensibilité, un aliment doux-amer pour sa mélancolie? ou bien a-t-on accédé, à travers Baculard d'Arnaud, Feutry ou Young, à une méditation sur les fins dernières? Nous souhaiterions trouver dans les mémoires et les correspondances beaucoup de témoignages comme celui de Ducis sur sa mère . . . Hélas! la récolte s'avère décevante.

Mais, finalement, n'est-ce pas une déformation récente et discutable qui nous porte à distinguer, voire opposer l'émotion esthétique et l'intérèt porté à la signification morale ou religieuse d'une oeuvre? Vous me permettrez de choisir une autre conception, plus conforme à la mentalité du XVIIIe siècle français, et de ne pas séparer l'art et la pensée, la sensibilité et la réflexion.

Mais peut-être pensera-t-on que j'en arrive à voir partout des Préparations à la mort[5].

APPENDIX

PREPARATIONS A LA MORT

écrites en langue francaises au XVIIe et XVIIIe siècles

		titres retrouves
XVIIe s.	1600–1624	28
	1625–1649	47
	1650–1674	65
	1675–1699	70
	Total	210
XVIIIe s.	1700–1724	51
	1725–1749	29
	1750–1774	14
	1775–1799*	14
	Total	108
	Total General	318

*En fait, 1793, a Lausanne.

[5] Une relecture des ouvrages suscités par le tremblement de terre de Lisbonne ne permettrait-elle pas de découvrir de nouvelles Préparations à la mort, sous des titres divers, en 1756–1757?

ÉVOLUTION DU NOMBRE DES TITRES

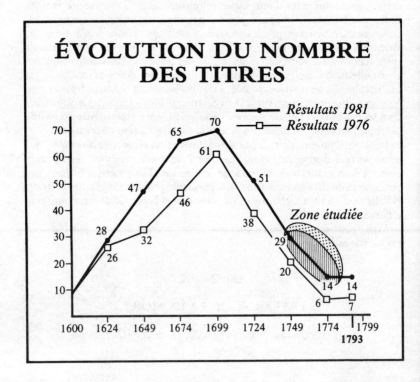

Daniel Roche
Robert Favre

SECTION II: RECONCILIATION

VOLKSKULTUR IN DER FRÜHMITTELALTERLICHEN KONTAKTZONE ZWISCHEN ISLAM UND CHRISTENTUM

Klaus Guth

1.0 DER HEILIG-LAND-BERICHT WILLIBALDS VON EICHSTÄTT (+ 787) PROBLEME DER HISTORISCHEN GATTUNG 'ITINERAR'

Der Bericht[1] über die Pilgerreise des angelsächsischen Mönches und späteren Missionsbischofs Willibald von Eichstätt (742–787)[2] in den

[1] A. Bauch (Hrsg.), *Quellen zur Geschichte der Diözese Eichstätt*, Bd. 1: Biographien der Gründungszeit. Texte, Übersetzung und Erläuterung von Andreas Bauch, hier: *Vita Willibaldi episcopi Eichstetensis*, (Eichstätt 1962) S. 22–122. Der lateinische Text richtet sich nach der Edition von O. Holder-Egger, *Vita Willibaldi*, in: MG SS XV, S. 86–106. A. Bauch, 'Der heilige Willibald, Bischof von Eistätt', in: G. Schwaiger (Hrsg.), *Bavaria Sancta*, Bd. 1, (Regensburg 1970) S. 148–167. K. Guth, *Studien zum Pilgerleben Willibalds von Eichtätt* (in Vorbereitung).

[2] Zum Kulturaustausch zwischen Irland und dem Kontinent in der vorausgehenden Phase der iro-schottischen Mission (7./8. Jahrhundert) vgl. besonders: A. Hauck, *Kirchengeschichte Deutschlands*, Bd. 1, 7. Aufl., (Berlin 1952) bes. S. 402–552. K. Bihlmeyer–H. Tüchle, *Kirchengeschichte*, 2. Teil: Mittelalter, (Paderborn² 1948) S. 1–27. G. Schreiber, *Irland im deutschen und abendländischen Sakralraum*, Köln 1956. F. Prinz, *Frühes Mönchtum im Frankenreich. Kultur und Gesselschaft in Gallien, den Rheinlanden und Bayern am Beispiel der monastischen Entwicklung (4.–8. Jahrhundert)*, (München 1965) bes. S. 263–445. H. Löwe, Pirmin, Willibrord und Bonifatius. Ihre Bedeutung für die Missionsgeschichte ihrer Zeit, in: K. Schäferdiek (Hrsg.), *Kirchengeschichte als Missionsgeschichte*, Bd. II, 1, (München 1978) S. 192–226. K. Schäferdiek, Die Grundlegung der angelsächsischen Kirche im Spannungsfeld insular-keltischen und kontinental-römischen Christentums, in: K. Schäferdiek (Hrsg.) *Kirchengeschichte als Missionsgeschichte*, Bd. II, 1, München 1978, S. 149–191.

Vorderen Orient, insonderheit in das Heilige Land, gehört, unter gattungsgeschichtlichen Aspekten betrachtet, in die lange Reihe christicher Heilig-Land-Führer oder Itinerarien. Sie haben die Aufgabe und den Zweck, den nie abreissenden Strom von Palästina-Pilgern aus dem mittelalterlichen Abendland über den Weg ihrer Pilgerfahrt zu informieren und die Organisation ihrer Reise durch Angabe von Etappen unterwegs zu erleichtern. Diese vordergründig funktionale Intention der Quellengattung[3] würde aber nur einen Teil, eine Seite dieser historischen Quelle beschreiben und definieren. Ebenso teilt sie auch etwas von der frommen Begeisterung des jeweiligen berichterstattenden Pilgers oder der die Heiligen Stätten beschreibenden Pilgerin mit und kann dadurch den Leser zu einer eigenen Pilger- oder Bussfahrt an heilige Stätten motivieren. So bilden finale wie funktionale Strukturen in den abendländischen Itinerarien des frühen und hohen Mittelalters noch eine innere Einheit. Sie regen zue einer persönlichen Pilgerreise in Wirklichkeit oder im geistigen Nachvollzug an und verweisen damit auf Stationen der Nachfolge[4] Wie fast alle grossen Pilgerberichte über Heilig-Land-Fahrten der antiken oder frühmittelalterlichen Kirche,[5] erinnert sei nur an die Heilig-Land-Reise der Pilgerin Aetheria (ca. 394), vermutlich aus Galicien[6] aufgebrochen, an das Itinerarium Burdigalense (Bordeaux) für Jerusalem (nach 335?), an die Pilgerreise der hl. Paula ins Heilige Land nach einem Brief des hl. Hieronymus[7] von 404, an das Pilgerbüchlein des Theodosius (um 500), an die Heilig-Land-Erinnerungen des sogenannten Anonymus von Piacenza (um 570), vermischt die Niederschrift über Willibalds Heilig-Land-Fahrt (778 begonnen) genaue Beobachtung der Heiligen Stätten auf der persönlich festgelegten Pilgerroute mit wenigen Anklängen an ältere Wege- und Ortsbeschreibungen aus christlicher Tradition. Nach den

---

[3] Zum Problem historischer Quellengattung vgl. F.-J. Schmale, Vorwort zur Neuausgabe: W. Wattenbach–R. Holtzmann. *Deutschlands Geschichtsquellen im Mittelalter*, 1. Teil, (Darmstadt 1967) bes. S. XV–XVII.

[4] B. Kötting, *Peregrinatio religiosa. Wallfahrten in der Antike und das Pilgerwesen der alten Kirche*, (Münster 1950) 351 f lässt die sachliche Unterscheidung in 'Itinerarien als Reisehandbücher und Itinerarien als Pilgererinnerungen' nur für die Zeit der Entstehung gelten. R. Plötz, Peregrini–Palmieri–Romei. Untersuchungen zum Pilgerbegriff der Zeit Dantes. In: *Jahrbuch für Volkskunde der Görresgesellschaft*, N.F. 2, 1979, S. 103–134 (mit ausfürlichen Quellen- und Literaturangaben zum Begriff 'Pilger' im Früh- und Hochmittelalter).

[5] Vgl. dazu: B. Kötting, *Peregrinatio religiosa* (wie Anm. 4), S. 343–367. P. Geyer, *Itinera Hierosolymitana saeculi IV–VIII* (CSEL 39), (Leipzig-Wien 1898) J. Zettinger, *Die Berichte über Rompilger aus dem Frankenreich*, Freiburg/Br. 1900 Tobler–A. Molinier, *Itinera Hierosolymitana et descriptiones terrae sanctae*, (Genf 1877-1890) G. Tellenbach, Zur Frühgeschichte abendländischer Reisebeschreibungen, in: *Historia integra. Festschrift für E. Hassinger*, Berlin 1977, S. 51–80.

[6] Hieronymus Ep. 108 (= CSEL 5), 306–351, B. Kötting, (wie Anm. 4). S. 358.

[7] B. Kötting (wie Anm. 4), S. 354 f.

Untersuchungen von A. Bauch lassen sich jedoch nur 'einige Parallelen im Pilgerbericht Arkulfs (um 670) und in dem Werke Bedas "De locis sanctis' (um 720)'[8] dazu finden. Insgesmat aber kann man dem Wort der Nonne Hugeburc[9] Glauben schenken, sie stütze sich nur auf das Diktat des Pilgers und späteren Bischofs Willibald: '. . . non ab alio reperta nisi ab ipso audita et ex illius ore dictata perscripsimus in monasterio Heidanheim, testibus mihi diaconis eius et aliis nonnullis iunioris eius'.[10]

2.0 CHRISTLICHE BRÄUCHE UND LEBENSFORMEN UNTER DER HERRSCHAFT DES ISLAM

Die frümittelalterliche Pilgerfahrt angelsächsischer Mönche kann unter verschiedenen Aspekten analysiert werden. Vom Standpunkt der Mönchspilger aus betrachtet erfüllte sich eine uralte religiöse Sehnsucht, den Spuren ihres Herrn und Meisters in buchstäblichem Sinn zu folgen (vgl. Mt 19, 27). Dabei wird in deren Pilgerschaft ohne Rückkehr in die Heimat auch der Gedanke der Busse und des Neubeginns in ihrem Leben nach aussen dokumentiert. Neue Eindrücke und Erfahrungen unterwegs, der Kontakt mit unterschiedlichen Kulturkreisen und Kulturzentren, wie Rom, Byzanz oder Damaskus und Jerusalem, gaben einer Pilgerfahrt von damals auch den Charakter einer Bildunsgreise. Wilibalds Bericht über seine Heilig-Land-Reise, der uns in der Niederschrift der Nonne Hugeburc im 'Willibald-Leben' vorliegt, spiegelt die religiöse Volkskultur[11] eines Landes in der Kontaktzone zwischen Christen und Moslem wider. Sie soll auf merkwürdige Bräuche und Lebensformen[12] hin im folgenden erstmals analysiert werden. Für eine vergleichende europäische Volkskunde kann dadurch zugleich auf eine bislang vernachlässigte mittelalterliche historische Quellengattung im Vorfeld der Fachgeschichte aufmerksam gemacht werden.[13]

[8] A. Bauch, *Biographien* (wie Anm. 1), S. 14.

[9] B. Bischof, Wer ist die Nonne von Heidenheim?, in: *Studien und Mitteilungen zur Geschichte des Benediktinerordens und seiner Zweige*, Neue Folge, Bd. 18 (1931), Heft IV.

[10] A. Bauch, *Biographien der Gründungszeit* (wie Anm. 1), S. 82. Das Kloster Heidenheim wurde 752 gegründet. Vgl. LThK Bd. 10, ² 1965, Sp. 1165.

[11] Vgl. zum Begriff Volkskultur: K. Guth, 'Volk. Versuch einer Begriffs- und Funkionsbestimmung in gegenwärtiger Volksforschung,' in: ders (Hrsg.), *Lebendige Volkskultur, Festschrift Elisabeth Roth*, (Bamberg 1980) S. 87–98.

[12] Vgl. zum Begriff Lebensform: K. Guth, 'Standesethos als Ausdruck hochmittelalterlicher Lebensform,' in: *Freiburger Zeitschrift für Philosophie und Theologie* 28, 1981, S. 111–132.

[13] Vgl. J. Weber–Kellermann, *Deutsche Volkskunde zwischen Germanistik und Sozialwissenschaften*, (Stuttgart 1969) S. 1–4, klammert diese Quellengattung (vielleicht aus technischen Gründen) in der Geschichte des Faches aus.

Willibalds Heilig-Land-Bericht (723–726/29) gliedert sich in mehrere Etappen:

in ein Vorspiel, in die Reise von Rom nach Griechenland und Kleinasien (723),
in einen mehrjährigen Palästina-Aufenthalt mit drei Reisen durch das Heilige Land (723–726),
in ein Nachspiel mit vorläufiger Bleibe als Eremit in Konstantinopel (727–729) und anschliessender Rückfahrt nach Italien.

Aus der Zeit seiner Palästina-Fahrt werden kulturelle Besonderheiten aus der Sicht eines angelsächsischen Pilgermönchs überliefert. Sie lassen sich um drei Themenbereichte gruppieren:

um Sonderformen frühmittelalterlichen Pilgerwesens,[14]
um volksfromme Bräuche im Umkreis der Heiligen- und Reliquienverehrung,[15]
um kulturhistorische Beobachtungen des Mönches.

Beginnen wir mit dem Aspekt abendländischer Jerusalemfahrten zu Beginn des 8. Jahrhunderts.

2.1 Strukturen der angelsächsischen Pilgerfahrt

Der Aufbruch in die Fremde, ins Heilige Land, wird von der adeligen Schicht angelsächsischer Pilgermönche mit fast gleichen Worten begründet: Verlassen der Heimat, d.h. Aufgabe der adeligen Klostergemeinschaft wie des in der Nähe des Klosters wohnenden Familienverbandes und Nachfolge ihres Herrn und Meisters im wörtlichen Sinn. Diese Nachfolge geschah in der Lebensform und nach der Regel des hl. Benedikt. Sie wurde auch als Einzelpilger oder Eremit beibehalten. Deren Strukturen sind:[16]

[14] Vgl. dazu die neuere Literatur, wie: F. Raphael u.a., *Les Pèlerinages de l'occident médiéval*, (Paris 1973) E. Mullins, *The Pilgrimage to Santiago*, (London 1974). J. Sumption, *Pilgrimage. An Image of Mediaeval Religion*, (London 1975). R. C. Finucane, *Miracles and Pilgrims. Popular Beliefs in Medieval England*, (London 1977). R. Oursel, *Pelerins du Moyen Age. Les hommes, les chemins, les sanctuaires*, (Paris 1978). Victor and Edith Turner, *Image and Pilgrimage in Christian Culture. Anthropological Perspectives.* (Oxford 1978), Jan van Herwaarden, *Opgelegde Bedevaarten . . . in de Nederlanden gedurende de late middeleeuwen (ca. 1330 – ca. 1550)*, (Amsterdam 1978).

[15] *Heilige in Geschichte, Legende, Kult. Beiträge zur Erforschung volkstümlicher Heiligenverehrung und zur Hagiographie*, hgg. v. Klaus Welker, (Karlsruhe 1979), bes.: F. Hensel, 'Frömmigkeit in Beharrung und Wandel. Überlegungen zum Verständnis religiös-volkskundlicher Forschung als theologischer Disziplin', in: *ebenda*, S. 3–23.

[16] Vgl. *Willibaldi* (wie Anm. 1), S. 36 (89, 30–33).

Aufgabe des Besitzes, Verlassen der Sippe, Eintritt in eine
Mönchgemeinschaft des Heimatlandes,
Verlassen der Mönchgemeinschaft, Verzicht auf
verwandtschaftlichen Schutz (clientela),[17] Wegzug aus der Heimat,
getrieben vom Grundmotiv der radikalen Nachfolge Jesu,
Stadium der Pilgerschaft (peregrinationis . . . telluram temptare)[18]
(Vorläufiger oder endgültiger) Aufenthalt in der Fremde an Hl.
Stätte[19] als Rekluse oder Eremit.

Die Motive für eine dergestalte Pilgerschaft, die einen *inneren* und
äusseren Aufbruch bedeuteten, fasste Willibald 720 in prägnanten Worten
zusammen: Abkehr von 'trügerischen Glücksgütern' und Hinwendung
zur rechten Lebensform im Dienste Gottes (. . . ad recte constitutionis
formam et ad caelestis militiae . . . servitium)[20] Eine ungestillte heilige
Sehnsucht trieb diese angelsächsischen Pilger in die Fremde. In der 'Vita
Wynnebaldi' wird diese beschrieben: '. . . et sic in externis barbarorum
finibus vitam ducere monachicalem magne mentis devotione cottidie
anhelando desiderabat, quod postea devotus adimplevit, d.h.: Und so
sehnte er sich danach, das Leben eines Mönches Tag für Tag mit grosser
Hingabe im Land der Barbaren (Germanien) zu führen. Das hat er später als
Geweihter auch getan'.[21]
Die Stationen der Pilgerfahrt Willibalds decken sich mit denen
frühchristlicher Pilger. Auch Aetheria, die berühmte Pilgerin aus dem 4.
Jahrhundert, hat vermutlich[22] auf dem Landweg über Konstantinopel und
Kleinasien das Heilige Land besucht. Von Jerusalem aus erkundete sie, im
Unterschied zu Willibald, noch Ägypten mit Alexandrien, bestieg den

[17] Vgl. ebda S. 36; *Vita Wynnibaldi* (wie Anm. 1), S. 136 (89, 31–34).
[18] Ebda S. 36 (89, 32–33). Vgl. dazu: H. von Campenhausen, *Die asketische Heimatlosigkeit im altkirchlichen und frühmittelalterlichen Mönchtum*, (Tübingen 1930). A. Angenendt, *Monachi peregrini. Studien zu Pirmin und den monastischen Vorstellungen des frühen Mittelalters*, (München 1972) (Münstersche Mittelalter-Schriften 6). J. Wollasch, *Mönchtum des Mittelalters zwischen Kirche und Welt*, (München 1973). B. de Gaffier, 'Pèlerinages et Culte des Saints', in: *Etudes Critiques d'Hagiographie et d'Iconologie par Baudoin de Gaiffier*, (Bruxelles 1967), S. 30–49 (Subsidia Hagiographica 43). F. Prinz, 'Peregrinatio, Mönchtum und Mission,' in: K. Schäferdiek (Hrsg.), *Kirchengeschichte als Missionsgeschichte*, Bd. II, 1, (München 1978), S. 445–465.
[19] Willibald blieb zwischen 727–729 in Konstantinopel, Wynnebald in Rom von 720 bis 727 und von ca. 730–739.
[20] Vgl. zu Wallfahrtsmotiven auch neuerdings: A. Bauch, *Quellen zur Geschichte der Diözese Eichstätt*, Bd. II: Ein bayerisches Mirakelbuch aus der Karolingerzeit. Die Monheimer Walpurgis-Wunder des Priester Wolfhard, (Regensburg 1979), S. 48–51.
[21] *Vita Willibaldi* (wie Anm. 1), S. 38 (90, 10–12).
[22] *Vita Wynnebaldi*: ebenda S. 136 (107, 17–20).

Berg Sinai und kehrte nach drei Jahren über Antiochien, Edessa, Tarsus nach Konstantinopen züruck.[23] Willibalds Pilgerfahrt vollzog sich in Armut und Entbehrung: Hunger und Durst,[24] die Kälte des Winters wie die Gefahren zur See[25] bedrängten ihn.[26] Mit seinen Gefährten, – sieben Landsleute hatten sich ihm angeschlossen –, wurde er in Emesa nordöstlich von Tripolis von den Sarazenen als Spion verhaftet und eingekerkert. Der Loskauf der Gefangen durch einen Kaufmann der Stadt wurde vom Statthalter des Kalifen Hischam (724–743) nicht gestattet. Dafür gewährte dieser den Pilgern eine lockere Isolierhaft. Mit Hilfe der Kaufmannsfamilie konnten sie zweimal in der Woche das Bad besuchen und Einkäufe am Markt tätigen, wenn der Sohn des Kaufmanns sie am Sonntag zur Kirche brachte. Auf die Fürsprache eines Spaniers beim 'König' der Sarazenen (= Kalifen von Bagdad) wurden sie schliesslich wieder auf freien Fuss gesetzt.[27] Sie pilgerten durch Syrien 'cum licentia' (mit offizieller Genehmigung) weiter und erreichten über Damaskus Palästina. Ihr Reisepass lief nämlich nach drei Jahren ab.[28]

Aus diesem Zwischenaufenthalt in Emesa wird deutlich, dass eine Pilgerfahrt im Herrschaftsbereich des Kalifen, in der Kontaktzone von Islam und Christentum, bereits in geregelten Bahnen velief. Greifbar wird die grosse Toleranz des Islam gegenüber abendländischen Pilgern aus frühmittelalterlicher Zeit. Der Besuch heiliger Stätten – so die 'Wallfahrt' nach Mekka und Medina – war ja auch in ihrer Religion eine heilige Pflicht. Im Brauch der Pilgerfahrt ins Heilige Land erfüllten Christen 'ihr Gesetz', wie es ein reicher alter Mann, ein islamischer Bewohner von Emesa formulierte: 'Oft sah ich Menschen kommen aus jenenen Gegenden der Erde (d.h. aus dem fernen Westen), Glaubensgenossen derselben. Sie wollen nichts Schlimmes, sondern begehren nur, ihr Gesetz zue erfüllen'.[29] Im Gegensatz zur späteren Epoche der Kreuzzüge lebte das christliche Pilgerwesen jener Zeit von der Toleranz durch die islamische Herrschaft. Der Kalif ging davon aus, dass in drei Jahren der religiosen Pflicht eines Christen in Palästina Genüge geleistet sein konnte. Dass dies auch möglich war, zeigen die drei Reisen Willibalds (von 723–726) durchs Heilige Land. Sie waren jeweils mit dem Besuch der Heiligen Stätten verbunden. Dazu kamen vier Aufenthalte in Jerusalem. Die Weiterreise nach Konstantinopel wurde in der Hafenstadt Tyrus im Spätherbst 726 (30. November) angetreten. Ein besonderer Schutzbrief des Statthalters von Emesa hatte

---

[23] B. Kötting, *Peregrinatio* (wie Anm. 4), S. 355.
[24] *Vita Willibaldi* (wie Anm. 1), S. 48 (93, 18–20).
[25] *Ebenda* S. 48.
[26] Sie waren jedoch wohlbekleidet, 'Männer von schöner Gestalt', *ebenda* S. 51 unten.
[27] *Vita Willibaldi* (wie Anm. 1), S. 50–52 (94, 21–34, 95, 1–14).
[28] Versuch der Erneuerung des Resepasses im Jahr 726: *ebenda* S. 66 (100, 10–12).
[29] *Vita Willibaldi* (wie Anm. 1), S. 51 (94, 19–21).

ihnen in Zweier-Gruppen die Pilgerreise durch Phönizien erleichtert.[30] Von Erleichterungen durch amtliche Vertreter der christlichen Kirche, die dem Pilgermönch mit seinen wechselnden Gefährten an heiligen Stätten hatten begegnen können, schweigt Willibalds Bericht. Anscheinend hatten sie auf Zypern die letzte feste (griechische) Kirchenorganisation für die nächsten Jahre der Pilgerreise verlassen. Zyperns zwölf griechisch-orthodoxe Bischofssitze lagen bereits in der neutralen Kontaktzone zwischen Islam und Christentum. Von Kirchen, Klöstern und Christen, die an heiligen Stätten lebten, spricht Willibalds Bericht immer wieder: in Tiberias, Bethsaida, Corozain, Cesarea, Galgala und besondern in Jerusalem. Von einer 'grossen Zahl von Christen' wird aus Cesarea, in dessen Nähe vom Johannes-Kloster mit 20 Mönchen berichtet.[31] Heute steht es, ähnlich dem 'monasterium magnum' im Tale Laura südlich von Bethlehem,[32] nur noch als Ruine. Ein Teil der Mönche lebte damals in Berhöhlen rings um das Tal, wo das Kloster des hl. Sabas[33] steht. Der Besuch der Stätte 'Zum Heiligen Matthias' südlich von Bethlehem, heute Bethamar, erfolgte anscheinend an einem Sonntag. Die feierliche Liturgie (magna gloria dominica) dort,[34] der Willibald beiwohnte, verstärkt den bereits angesprochenen[35] negativen Befund in Willibalds Bericht. Dieser kennt im Heiligen Land keine organisierte Kirche. Die islamische Herrschaft duldet lediglich die Ausübung der Liturgie und die Verehrung der 'loca sancta'[36] durch die Pilger. Griechisch-orthodoxe Mönche versahen den Dienst an den Heiligen Stätten. Um sie geschart lebten grössere oder kleinere Gemeinschaften von Christen.

2.2 Volksfromme Bräuche im Umkreis frühmittelalterlicher Heligen- und Reliquienverehrung

Die Form der Pilgerfahrt ins Heilige Land war durch die islamische Herrschaft um 700 in Palästina geprägt. Die Toleranz des Islam ermöglichte das Bestehen christlicher Ortskirchen. Mönche unterhielten die Pilgerstätten vor Ort. Deren nie abreissende Anziehungskraft auf Pilger aus allen Jahrhunderten aber wuchs mit der Wundermacht und Hilfe an heiliger Stätte. Gerade das abendländische Frühmittelalter hatte auf der Grundlage der kirchlichen Lehre von der Heiligen- und Reliquienverehrung, die parallel zur Grabesverehrung Christi sich

[30] *Vita Willibaldi* (wie Anm. 1), S. 66–71, hier: S. 66 (99, 10).
[31] *Ebda* S. 57 (96, 16).
[32] *Ebda* S. 63 (99, 3–6).
[33] *Ebda* S. 62–64 (99, 6–8).
[34] *Ebda* S. 65 (99, 10).
[35] Weiter oben.
[36] Im Zusammenhang mit der Kirche von Nazareth spricht Willibald ein einziges Mal von Spannungen zwischen Mohammedanern und Christen. Die Kirche sei oftmals von Christen den heidnischen Sarazenen abgekauft worden, das diese sie zerstören wollten. Vgl. *Vita Willibaldi* (wie Anm. 1), S. 55 (95, 24).

entwickelt hatte, eine (für den heutigen Betracher übersteigerte) reale
Vorstellung der Hilfe am heiligen Ort entwickelt.[37] Das Umbetten heiliger
Leiber oder die Transferierung der Überreste von Heiligen aus Rom in
Kirchen des Langobardenreiches, nach Gallien und anderwohin,[38]
bestärkte die Sehnsucht abendländischer Pilger, den oder die Heilige an
ihrer ursprünglichen Grablege zu besuchen, noch mehr: es erregte den
Wunsch, an Erinnerungsstätten aus dem Leben Jesu aus verschiedenen
Motiven zu weilen.[39] Auch die Pilgerfahrt Willibalds ins Heilige Land
wäre ohne den altkirchlichen Brauch der Heiligenverehrung nur
bruchstückhaft analysiert. Hier kann nach einer Zusammenfassung der
'Heilige Orte' Palästinas nur noch auf Eigentümlichkeiten volksfrommen
Glaubens verwiesen werden.

Wie bereits im ersten Abschnitt der Pilgerfahrt, auf der Reise nach Rom
erwähnt, hatte Willibald zusammen mit seinem Gefährten viele heilige
Stätten aufgesucht. ' ... multa sanctorum illic oratoria, que illis in
commodu fuerunt, orando petiverunt ... '.[40] Dies bedeutet: Auf ihrer
Pilgerfahrt nach Rom besuchten sie alle erreichbaren abendländischen
'heiligen Orte' am Weg, ihre Reise ins Heilige Land aber wurde von ihnen
geradezu geführt! Haltepunkte nach Willibalds 'Itinerar' waren: Ephesus
mit der Siebenschläfer-Höhle und dem Grab des Apostels Johannes; auf
Cypern die Stadt Constantia mit dem Grab des hl. Epiphanias; in Syrien die
Stadt Emesa mit einer Schädelreliquie[41] des hl. Johannes; in Damaskus die
Grabstätte der hl. Annanias; in Jerusalem die Erinnerungsstätten aus dem
Leben des Herrn, vor allem an seine Passion, so an sein heiliges Kreuz und
sein Grab,[42] ebenso das Grab Mariens zu ihrem Gedächtnis;[43] die Kirche mit
dem Grab des Propheten Amos;[44] die Kirche mit dem Grab des hl. Sabas
bei Bethlehem; die Grabkirche des hl. Matthias;[45] das Grab des Propheten
Zacharias, der Patriarchen Abraham, Isaak und Jakob[46] in der Stadt
Aframia (= Hebron); die Stadt Diospole (= Lydda) in der Nähe von
Jerusalem mit dem Georgsgrab; die Festung Samaria/Sebaste mit dem

---

[37] H. Fichtenau, 'Zum Reliquienwesen im früheren Mittelalter.' In: MIÖG 60,
1952. S. 60–89. K. Guth, Guibert von Nogent und die hochmittelalterlich Kritik an der
Reliquienverehrung, (Ottobeuren 1970), bes. S. 15 ff.
[38] St. Beissel, Die Verehrung der Heiligen und ihrer Reliquien in Deutschland im
Mittelalter, (Nachdruck 1967 von 1892), bes. S. 63 ff.
[39] Vgl. weiter oben.
[40] Vita Willibaldi (wie Anm. 1), S. 40 (91, 13): '... multa sanctorum illic oratoria,
que illis in commodu fuerunt, orando petiverunt ...'
[41] Vita Willibaldi (wie Anm. 1), S. 49 (94, 12). Die Reliquie befand sich zu jener
Zeit nicht mehr dort.
[42] Ebda S. 58 ff.
[43] Ebda S. 61 (98, 9).
[44] A. Bauch (wie Anm. 1), S. 107, Anm. 140.
[45] Ebda S. 65 (99, 10).
[46] Ebda S. 64 (99, 13–15).

Grab des hl. Johannes des Täufers und der Propheten Abdias und Eliseus.[47] Diese Hinweise zu der Grab-Verehrung heiliger Männer und Frauen mögen in unserem Zusammenhang genügen.

Die Verehrung heiliger Stätten geschah im Gebet,[48] in der Liturgie und durch besondere Bräuche. Die selbstverständliche Einrichtung von 'Säulenheiligen' in der kleinasiatischen Stadt Milet[49] nahm der 'edle und ruhmreiche Kreuzesverehrer Christi'[50] ebenso zur Kenntnis wie zahlreiche Sonderbräuche an heiligen Stätten. In Kanaan trinkt man Wein aus einem der 6 Wasserkrüge in Erinnerung an das Weinwunder des Herrn, in Kapharnaum erinnert man sich an einen grossen Myrrhenbaum, unter dem sich die Zebedäus-Söhne (Johannes und Jakobus d. Ä.) ausgeruht haben sollen.[51] Neben der Stelle, an der Jesus nach der Tradition getauft wurde, hat sich nach Willibalds Bericht der Brauch eines heilenden Kultbades entwickelt: Kranke und Sieche tauchen am Fest der Epiphanie (6. Januar) im Jordanwasser unter, indem sie sich an ein von Ufer zu Ufer gespanntes Seil festhalten. Auch unfruchtbare Frauen erwarten dort nach einem Bad Heilung.[52] Fruchtbarkeit schenkt die ehemals bittere Quelle des Elisaus bei Jericho, dem heutigen Oasenort. Für Willibald liegt diese in der Segenskraft des Elisäus begründet.[53]

An dem noch unzerstörten Grab des Herrn – erst 1009 hatte Sultan Hakim den Grabesfelsen als Anti-Kultort zum Felsendom in Stücke schlagen lassen[54] – brennen nach des Pilgers Bericht 15 golden Gefässe mit Öl Tag und Nacht. Ähnlich wie das eherne Denkmal mitten in der Himmelfahrtskirche auf dem Ölberg, als Rundbau nach oben in der Mitte offen, erinnert die ewig brennende Lampe in diesem Erzmal an Jesu Weggang von der Erde. Ein magisch beeinflusster Durchkrieche-Brauch, zwischen den Säulen und der Wand der gleichen Kirche vollzogen, sollte die Pilger von ihren Sünden befreien.[55] In Bethelehem ermöglichte ein Tragaltar die Messfeier in der Grotte unter der Geburtskirche.[56] Die Ortsbeschreibung Willibalds erfasst in obengenannten Beispielen dazu jeweils exakt Umgebung wie Architektur. Sie bilden den sog. 'Sitz im Leben' für die christlichen oder halbchristlichen Bräuche. Heute erleichtert

---

[47] *Ebda* S. 69 (100, 15).
[48] *Ebda* S. 44 (92, 21): '... ut tutis itineris cursibus dilectabiles atque optabiles civitatis Hierusalem moenios peragrare speculareque per illorum pia precum praesidia ...' ('illorum', d.h. der Verwandten zuhause).
[49] *Ebda* S. 48 (93, 23–24).
[50] *Ebda* S. 44 (92, 18).
[51] *Vita Willibaldi*: ebda S. 54 (95, 21–29; 96, 2–3).
[52] *Vita Willibaldi*: ebda S. 56 (96, 19–23).
[53] *Ebda* S. 56 (97, 4–10).
[54] *Ebda* S. 102, Anm. 119.
[55] *Vita Willibaldi* (wie Anm. 1), S. 60 (97, 15–16).
[56] *Vita Willibaldi*: ebda S. 62 (98, 28–31).

Willibalds Bericht eine historische Topographie der heiligen Stätten. Das gilt besonders für Jerusalem.[57]

Nicht minder wertvoll erscheint Willibalds Erzählung als kulturhistorischer Bericht.[58] Farbig schildert dieser Merkwürdigkeiten über Land und Leute in einem ehemals christlichen Gebiet unter islamischer Herrschaft. Von des Islams Einstellung zum christlichen Pilgerwesen war bereits die Rede.[59] Willibalds Leben als Eremit an der Apostelkirche zu Konstantinopel (seit 727), sein Eindrücke im ostromischen Reich, stehen bereits ausserhalff bunserer Analyse. So soll nur noch an drei Begebenheiten erinnert werden, an die Bekanntschaft mit einem einheimischen Nomaden, an eine kleine Schmuggelaffäre, an das Erlebnis eines Vulkanausbruchs.

2.3 Kulturhistorische Beobachtungen des Pilgers

Auf der letzten Reise durchs Heilige Land (726) durchzogen die Pilger die Ebene Esdrelon zur Zeit der Olivenernte mit einem Äthiopier.[60] Es war eine weite Ebene, von Ölbäumen dicht bestanden. Die Bedrohung der kleinen Reisegesellschaft durch einen plötzlich auftauchenden Löwen wird von Hugeburc so lebendig geschildert, dass die Rettung aus dieser Gefahr einem Wunder gleicht. Der Äthiopier mit seinen beiden Kamelen, dessen Frau auf dem Maulesel sowie die Pilger wurden vom Löwen verschont. Dafür verschlang er Bauern bei der Olivenernte und zeigte dies durch Gebrüll an.

Mag diese gefährliche Szene den Zuhörern im kalten Germanien Schauer den Rücken hinuntergejagt haben, so erfüllte sie die Schmuggel-Episode, auf der gleichen Reise erlebt, mit Schmunzeln.[61] Sie verdeutlicht einerseits die strengen Zollbestimmungen in der Hafenstadt Tyrus bei der Ausfuhr wertvoller Fracht nach dem Westen, andererseits aber auch des Angelsachsen praktisches Geschick. Wie hätte er sonst einen ganzen Kürbis, mit kostbarem Balsam gefüllt, den Augen der Zöllner verbergen können! Mit einer List führte er diese hinters Licht. Indem er den Kürbis kunstvoll mit einem Rohr verschloss, das Rohr mit 'petre olea', wohl Olivenöl, aber anfüllte, gelang ihm die wertvolle Ausfuhr. Die Geruchsprobe bei der Gepäckdurchsuchung brachte keinen Hinweis. Willibald jedoch musste zusammen mit seinen Gefährten noch viele Tage auf ein Schiff in Tyrus warten, ebenso sein wertvoller Kürbis.

---

[57] Vita Willibaldi: ebda S. 58 f (Grabeskirche); 60 f (Marienüberlieferung).
[58] Die Schilderung des Aufenthaltes zwischen den beiden Jordanquellen zeigt Willibalds naturwissenschaftlich-beobachtendes Interesse: z.B. bei der Beschreibung der Lebensweise von Wasserbüffeln wie bei der Charakterisierung der Gastfreundlichkeit der Hirten. Vgl. Vita Willibaldi: ebda S. 56 (96, 9–14).
[59] Vgl. weiter oben.
[60] Vita Willibaldi: ebda S. 68 f (100, 22–29).
[61] Vita Willibaldi (wie Anm. 1), S. 68–70 (101, 1–17).

Gleichsam den erzählerischen Höhepunkt der Heilig-Land-Fahrt und deren dramatischen Abschluss bringt die Erlebnisschilderung über einen Vulkan-Ausbruch auf der Insel Vulcana, südöstlich von Sizilien.[62] Bevor er die Apeninnen-Halbinsel und damit bald Monte Cassino als vorläufigen Endpunkt seines Pilgerlebens erreichte (729), grub sich ein Naturschauspiel unvergesslich in des Erzählers Erinnerung ein. Bereits auf der Pilgerreise in den Nahen Osten hatte Willibald in der Bischofsstadt Catania auf Sizilien von dem Brauch gehört, dass die Lavaströme des Ätna nach Ausbruch durch den Segen mit der Reliquie der hl. Agatha zum Stehen gebracht wurden.[63] Doch eine Eruption hatte er 723 bei seinem Aufenthalt von drei Wochen in der genannten Stadt sicher nicht erlebt. Jetzt, auf der Rückreise, packte den angelsächsischen Pilger naturwissenschaftliches Interesse: Er wollte die 'Hölle des Theoderich' von innen sehen und den Gipfel des Vulkan-Berges besteigen. Die hohen Aschenmassen jedoch verhinderten den Anstieg. So mussten sich die Pilger mit dem wunderbar-schaurigen Schauspiel eines Vulkanausbruchs aus der Ferne begnügen. Die mit dem Feuer ausgeworfenen Bimssteinbrocken erinnern die Zuhörer an das Handwerk des Schreibens. Mit solchen Bimssteinstückchen war auch Hugeburcs Schreibfläche, ihre Pergamentblätter, geglättet worden.[64]

Im Leben des Mönchsbischofs von Eichstätt scheint die Pilgerfahrt ins Heilige Land verschiedene Funktionen erhalten zu haben: die der Busse, der Nachfolge an heiliger Stätte, die der persönlichen Bildung in der Kontaktzone dreier Kulturkreise. Sie war wie ein Vortasten 'auf der Suche nach Sinn', besser: nach den konkreten Teilsinnen seiner Lebensabschnitte. In der menschlichen Grundbefindlichkeit des 'Unterwegsseins' leuchtete ihm am Vorbild seines Herrn und Meisters der Totalsinn christlichen Lebens auf: Pilgerschaft als ständiger Versuch und Anruf, weiter auszugreifen. Für Willibald war dieser Zustand des Pilgerns stets von einer Lebensform gestützt, von der Regel der ältesten Mönchsgemeinschaft des Abendlandes. In der 'regula Sancti Benedicti', und später in der 'canonica recta constitutionis forma',[65] der Priesterweihe, fand seine Lebensreise ihre bleibende Gestalt, ob als Büsser,[66] Pilger oder Missionsbischof. Die 'institutio regularis vitae'[67] durchformte seine Lebensführung (disciplina

---

[62] Vgl. A. Bauch, *Biographien* (wie Anm. 1), S. 115, Anm. 210: Liparische Inseln. *Vita Willibaldi*: ebda S. 72 (101, 28–102, 10).

[63] *Vita Willibaldi* (wie Anm. 1), S. 46 f (93, 8–14).

[64] Vgl. dazu: W. Wattenbach, *Das Schriftwesen im Mittelalter*, 1. Aufl. (Leipzig 1871), S. 129–134 (3. Aufl. 1890) H. Foerster, *Abriss der lateinischen Paläeographie*, (Bern 1946), S. 47 f.

[65] *Vita Wynnebaldi*: ebda S. 144 (109, 24–25).

[66] Vgl. seine verschiedenen Malariaanfälle, Krankheiten: A. Bauch, *Biographien* (wie Anm. 1), S. 299 (Register!) oder seine vorübergehende Erblindung: *Vita Willibaldi* ebda S. 674 (99, 11–12).

[67] *Vita Willibaldi* (wie Anm. 1), S. 76 (102, 31).

vitae)[68] im Kloster wie unterwegs, zuerst aus eigenem Entschluss, dann im Auftrag der Kirche von Rom.[69] Bonifatius hatte ihn um seine Hilfe gebeten.[70] Mit Unterstützung seiner angelsächsischen Familienmitglieder[71] wird ihm, dem Heimatlosen aus Berufung, Deutschland, die fränkische Kirche, zu seiner endgültigen Heimat.

[68] *Vita Willibaldi:* ebda S. 84 (105, 21–26); ebda S. 74 (102,. 22–24): recte constitutionis formam et cenobalis vitae normam in semet ipso ostendendo prebebat (d.i. die Station in Monte Cassino 729). Ähnlich: ebda, S. 44; 92, 18–26, ebda S. 38: 90, 10–13; *Vita Wynnebaldi* S. 136: 107, 16–19; *Vita Wynnebaldi* S. 142: 108, 39–41; *Vita Wynnebaldi* S. 144: 109, 22–25.

[69] Auf Geheiss Papst Gregors III. (731-741) zieht Willibald nach Germanien, zuerst nach Thüringen, dann nach Bayern.

[70] Th. Schieffer, *Winfrid – Bonifatius.* (Freiburg/Br. 1954) (Neudruck Darmstadt 1972, mit einem Nachwort).

[71] Geschwister waren Abt Wynnibald und Walburga, Äbtissin von Heidenheim; Verwandte waren Lioba, Äbtissin von Tauberbischofsheim und Bonifatius. Zu Walburga vgl.: H. Holzbauer, *Mittelalterliche Heiligenverehrung. Heilige Walpurgis.* (Kevelaer 1972), passim. A. Bauch (wie Anm. 1), S. 250 F.

PROTESTANT IRENICISM IN THE SIXTEENTH AND SEVENTEENTH CENTURIES

G. H. M. Posthumus Meyjes

INTRODUCTION

In older dictionaries one will look in vain for the terms 'irenism' and 'irenicism'. One does find the corresponding adjectives like 'irenic' and 'irenical' – which have been in use since the seventeenth century[1] – but not the substantives 'irenism' and 'irenicism'. This holds for English as well as for French, German and Italian: 'irenisme', 'Irenismus' and 'Irenik', 'irenismo' are neologisms of a very recent date. It is possible to indicate the moment of their origin with some precision.[2]

They owe their existence to the encyclical *Humani Generis* of 1950. Here Pope Pius XII warns against all those who, in his words, 'out of grief over discord and division of the spirits, devote themselves with a misplaced zeal to remove the obstacles that keep people of good will apart.' He continues by stating that 'they accept some sort of "irenism" that seeks to arrest the advance of atheism with might and main and will not even stop short at a reconciliation of contradicting dogmatic positions.' And he concludes this paragraph: 'some, captured by such an unreflecting "irenism", even come to take for obstructions on the road to unity what in fact is based on the laws and precepts of Christ himself and on institutions founded by him'. In the encyclical the term *'irenismus'* is placed between quotation marks, just like, a little earlier, a whole series of 'new philosophies' like pragmatism,

---

[1] Cf. A. H. Murray, *New English Dictionary, on historical principles*, 1901, *i.v.* 'irenical'.

[2] Cf. *Dictionnaire de Théologie Catholique*, Tables générales (Paris 1967) *c.* 2323 *i.v.* 'Irénisme', and *Lexicon für Theologie und Kirche i.v.* 'Irenik, Irenismus', vol. 5, *c.* 749–50.

existentialism and historicism. One may conclude from this that the pope was aware of the fact that he was coining a new term.[3]

a. *Irenicism and Tolerance*
I shall not take over the negative and dogmatically coloured use of the term as coined by the pope. Instead, I propose tentatively to define irenicism as the endeavour to allay or to reconcile tensions or divisions between the confessions in a peaceful way. Considered in this light irenicism is close to religious tolerance. Both terms imply a search for conciliation between different religious persuasions. Still I would prefer to distinguish between the two, especially with regard to the period under consideration. Tolerance is a much broader concept. When one takes it to denote tolerance towards those who hold divergent views in religious matters, the concept has a very wide scope indeed, from freedom of conscience to total freedom, including the freedom to be of an atheistic persuasion (Coornhert).[4] The advocates of irenicism, however, never go that far.

Another mark of distinction is that the irenicists apparently belong to a tradition other than that of the defenders of religious tolerance. The latter certainly are indebted to humanism, but above all they draw from mystical and spiritualistic sources, like Sebastian Frank. With the former this is entirely lacking; their roots are to be found in humanism in a far more exclusive sense as well as – in the case of later irenicists – in the juridical thought of their day. Undoubtedly this must be seen in connection with the remarkable fact that none of the irenicists – irrespective of the confession in which they had been brought up – felt any affinity towards sectarian, heterodox or non-institutional groups or their advocates. Erasmus, Melanchthon, Bucer, Cassander, Junius, Casaubon, Hotman, or any others who share their views, differ very little on this point. For anabaptists, spiritualists, freethinkers or dissenters they had no sympathy at all, and it did not strike them as unjust that respective governments denied

[3] *Acta Apostolicae Sedis*, 42 (Roma 1950), pp. 561–77, *LThK*, *i.v.* 'Humani Generis', vol. 5, *c.* 524–26.
[4] Besides J. Lecler, *Histoire de la Tolérance*, 2 vols. (Paris, 1955) which is the most exhaustive study in the field, see E. Hassinger, *Religiöse Toleranz im 16. Jahrhundert*. Motive-Argumente-Formen der Verwirklichung. Vorträge der Aeneas Sylvius Stiftung an der Universität Basel, 6 (Basel/Stuttgart 1966); G. Güldner, *Das Toleranz-Problem in den Niederlanden im Ausgang des 16. Jahrhunderts*, Historische Studiën 403 (Lübeck/Hamburg 1968); H. R. Guggisberg, 'Wandel der Argumente für religiöse Toleranz und Glaubensfreiheit im 16. und 17. Jahrhundert', *Zur Geschichte der Toleranz und Religionsfreiheit*, herausgeg. v. H. Lutz (Darmstadt 1977), pp. 455–81. Most authors do not distinguish sufficiently between the different traditions and concepts of 'tolerance' and 'irenicism'. This is especially the case with H. A. Enno van Gelder, *The two Reformations in the 16th century. A Study of the Religious Aspects and Consequences of Renaissance and Humanism* (The Hague 1961).

those groups their existence. They did champion reconciliation, but not without limits. For them the limits were set by the idea of the catholic church and by this I mean that they developed their programmes of reconciliation within the context of the established or tolerated churches. For them state and government deserved at least as much respect as the church.

In this they differ considerably from the defenders of the idea of tolerance, and although the writings of these contained lots of irenical material, the irenicists never used them as a source of inspiration, at least not in the sixteenth century. Only in the seventeenth century, and more especially in its second half, did this situation change. It brought better opportunities for many of the 'stepchildren of Christianity', and all sorts of movements that had been driven underground in the sixteenth century could come out into the open. This was not without effect on the relations between the confessions, which naturally affected the nature of irenicism too.

All this implies that we can only speak of irenicism in a strict sense once the process of confessionalisation had begun; in other words when beside the traditional Roman Catholic Church other churches – Lutheran, Anglican, Calvinist – have appeared, are recognised or tolerated by the state, have gained independence and are living in coexistence side by side as more or less monolithic structures. Confessionalisation and irenicism are parallel phenomena and are subject to the same cycles of ebb and flow.

Here the term 'confessionalisation' should not cause misunderstanding. For us this term conjures up the vision of a multitude of confessions and, even if we feel shame or grief about it, we accept this situation as the effect of an inevitable historical development and take it for granted. For most people in the sixteenth and seventeenth centuries however this was entirely different. Even if we, with the advantage of hindsight, must come to the conclusion that many of them helped to create a confessionally divided Europe, they did not in the least intend to. On the contrary.

We must keep in mind that neither Lutherans, nor Anglicans or Calvinists could ever give up the pretence of belonging to the catholic church. From the Roman Catholic point of view they were heretics altogether, but not so the other way round. The protestant opinion was that the church of Rome had fallen into the clutches of heretics, who had adulterated and suppressed the Word of God, but they did not consider the church itself heretical. How could they, wishing to consider themselves members, and even the legitimate heirs and trustees of the church? They felt that the heritage which had been transmitted to them had been thrown out of gear by miserable mismanagement of the pope – or rather the Antichrist – in former ages.[5] They however had put things straight, at peril

---

[5] H. Bornkamm, 'Die religiöse und politische Problematik im Verhältnis der Konfessionen im Reich', *Zur Geschichte der Toleranz*, pp. 253–54.

of their lives and goods, and they were quite determined to see to it that this achievement, this cleansing of the Temple, would not be squandered.

It was because the representatives of all protestant denominations thought along these lines and, as is well known, the church of Rome was not backward in claiming such catholicity either, that confessional strife became so vehement. Far into the seventeenth century all established churches clung to the pretension of representing the catholic church as a whole. Moreover they considered themselves to be representatives of the sacred legal order as a whole – the common corps of Christendom – as developed in the Middle Ages and handed down to modern times.[6] The different denominations would each interpret this order in their own way – thus widening the gap between them – but nonetheless each pretended to be its most legitimate heir.

b. *Confessionalisation and irenicism*

In the pre-reformation period France, England and Spain had developed into autonomous nations and the Swiss cantons and German principalities were able to present themselves as independent states. A politically and nationally divided Europe formed the background to the reformation movement. Largely owing to this the process of confessionalisation showed considerable regional differences.[7]

In the second half of the sixteenth century the features of the different denominations became more and more clearly distinguished and many new confessions emerged. Everywhere constitutional arrangements came into being (Peace of Augsburg, Elisabethan settlement, Edict of Nantes etc.), each of them guaranteeing some freedom of confession to the followers of the new denominations. But this only partially set things at rest. Constantly they felt themselves threatened – ecclesiastically as well as politically – by the forces of the counter-reformation, particularly by the Jesuits. This entailed a certain solidarity between the new confessions but this was based more on negative than on positive grounds, as after all each considered his own confession to be the most pure.

The varying confessional developments in the different European countries made for very different situations in which the irenicists had to operate. Moreover the same parties were not everywhere in conflict. In Germany, where it all started, the adherents of Wittenberg and those of

---

[6] Cf. Franklin Le Van Baumer, 'The Conception of Christendom in Renaissance England', *Journal of the History of Ideas*, VI (1945), pp. 131–56 and 'The Church of England and the Common Corps of Christendom', *Journal of Modern History*, XVI (1944), pp. 1–21.

[7] Stephen Charles Neill and Ruth Rouse, *A History of the Ecumenical Movement* (London 1954); *Handbuch der Dogmen- und Theologiegeschichte*, herausgeg. v. Carl Andresen, 2, Die Lehrentwisklung im Rahmen der Konfessionalität (Göttingen 1980).

Rome had opposed each other since 1530 (Augsburg Confession). This situation was to continue for a long time because only under the terms of the Peace of Westphalia (1648) would the followers of Calvin come to share the liberties already conferred on the Lutherans a century earlier (Augsburg 1555).[8] In France the traditional church was not challenged from Wittenberg but from Geneva. Here the grim wars of religion followed, which were only temporarily ended by the proclamation of the Edict of Nantes (1598). In England the process developed quite differently again. Here a state-church emerged which, although it took over many elements from the church of Rome, could not tolerate believers who wished to remain loyal to that church. Besides, from the beginning the church in England was exposed to a strong influence from Geneva, which produced considerable tensions. Finally in the northern Netherlands Geneva gained the upper hand over Rome, but this did not mean an end to the strife, for here before long a serious dispute broke out among the adherents of the new confession.

In short, we find in Europe a considerable confessional diversity, and this had its consequences for irenicism. If we turn our attention to the developments in the Roman Catholic Church, the Council of Trent strikes us as an important watershed. As a direct result of this council the number of irenicists in this church sharply declined after the middle of the sixteenth century. Trent consciously broke off the irenical tradition within the church of Rome. One has to add immediately however that in some areas the introduction of the Tridentine decrees did not run smoothly. Where this was the case, one can observe a continuing irenical current. This holds particularly for France where, thanks to the favourable climate of Gallicanism, irenicism remained vigorous for quite some time to come.

In the world of protestantism we see a considerable diversification in this period and consequently irenicism branches out in accordance with the new confessional situations in the different countries. In the process the idea of reconciliation with the church of Rome recedes more and more into the background. Everyone polemicises with Bellarmin, including such irenicists as Junius and Casaubon, and the irenical arguments tend to concentrate on conciliation of controversies within protestantism itself. In England irenicists attempt a reconciliation between Anglicans and Puritans, in the Netherlands between Remonstrants and Contraremonstrants, while in Germany they try to overcome the controversy between Lutherans and Calvinists (Paraeus, Calixtus). Added to this there existed numerous confessional and consequently also irenical inter-relations and solidarities, across national borders and frequently strengthened by international political ties.

To avoid losing my way in this politically and ecclesiastically highly

---

[8] F. Dickmann, 'Das Problem der Gleichberechtigung der Konfessionen im Reich im 16. und 17 Jahrhundert', *Zur Geschichte der Toleranz*, pp. 203–51.

varied landscape, which I can only vaguely delineate, I shall have to restrict myself drastically. Leaving aside the greater part of the internal protestant controversies, I shall concentrate on the line that can be drawn from Erasmus to Grotius, or in other words the line of Christian humanism. I shall highlight a few stages along this line, beginning with Erasmus. I shall secondly look at some of his adherents in the midst of the sixteenth century, Bucer, Melanchthon and Cassander, and I shall conclude with some remarks on irenicism in the circle of the Republic of Letters.

I. ERASMUS AND IRENICISM

There can be no doubt that all irenicists from the early sixteenth century, whatever their confession, were inspired by Erasmus in their pursuit of unity, reconciliation and church reform. Why? What did they learn from him in this respect?[9]

Erasmus, a born philologist, was first of all interested in culture, and particularly in the culture of antiquity, which in his opinion was both crowned and completed by Christianity. At an early date he turned from the classical authors to the original text of the bible and the works of the early Fathers of the church. In their works he found the finest combination of antiquity and Christianity and the purest and fullest possible rendering of the values of *eruditio* and *pietas*. He dedicated himself to the inordinately heavy, but splendidly fulfilled lifework of revealing all these sources of early Christianity. He did this not for the love of it in itself, but in the expectation and with the express intention of contributing to the renewal of the Christianity of his day by confronting it with the documentary evidence of its own origins. A return to the sources, to wit scripture and the Fathers, would restore the simplicity and the vigour of the original faith. By means of the *philosophia Christi*, characterised by love and peace, the common corps of Christendom would be renewed and purified.

From this initial position his conciliation programme follows automatically. This is characterised in the first place by an aversion to all pressure and force in the matters of religion. 'Our religion', he says, 'is peace and unanimity'[10] and he condemns all those who obstruct an agreement by dogged intransigence. What is needed is mildness, meekness and love, and these not as abstract values, but as many fruits of a union with Christ, who is for him above all the example of meekness.

Referring to the parable of the wheat and the tares he says: 'Let the wheat and the tares grow together. The Owner of the field doesn't want the tares pulled out. He wants to wait until the time of harvest.' And he

[9] Robert Stupperich, *Der Humanismus und die Wiedervereinigung der Konfessionen* (Leipzig 1936); Lecler, *o.c.*, I, pp. 133–49; Enno van Gelder, *o.c.*, pp. 132–73.
[10] Erasmus, *Opus Epistolarum*, ed. Allen, V, p. 177.

continues 'Give the heretics time to mend their ways and if they don't, leave the punishment to the Owner of the field.'[11] Here his tolerance is manifest. But it was not boundless. He loathed extremism and radicalism, and in case public order was threatened by radicals, he deemed the government fully justified in reacting with force. The argument advanced here is that the Apostles prescribe obedience to the government.

A second argument, time and again recurring in his works, is that the warring parties should keep in touch, and above all that they should be aware of their common roots. For him these roots lie in *antiquitas*, that is the days of Christ, the Apostles and the early Fathers. This golden age of peace, unity and concord he glorifies immoderately as well as naively – considering as a result all that came after a degeneration. However, he was decidedly no spiritualist. He knew where to draw the line, in these matters as well as in others. By this I have in mind that he never totally gave up the idea of continuity, however thin the line had worn. One does get the impression that he would rather cut out the middle ages, for after all, what had they contributed to the unfolding of the *philosophia Christi*? Knowledge had been given precedence, at the expense of piety. All that logical subtlety and cobwebby scholasticism had only hidden the essentials from view. The confusion encountered on all sides was a direct result of this. Therefore one should not continue along these lines, but put first things first and reorientate in this respect back towards the Golden Age.

Wise and pious men should to his mind immerse themselves in the sources of the Word of God and the writings of the Apostles and, illuminated by the best interpreters of antiquity, condense from these the main points of the *philosophia Christi*. They should formulate the essence of faith in a few articles, with a minimum of dogmatic fixation. Remaining points should be left to individual free judgment. This, in outline, is what Erasmus proposed with respect to doctrine.[12]

Thirdly: all this culminated in his pursuit of a restoration of Christian life, of ethics. From the very beginning he gave the highest priority to this because for him faith was primarily a matter of life, not of dogma. This is eloquently expressed in one of his early sayings. 'What matters', he says, 'is that we rid our souls of envy, hate, pride and impurity'. And he continues, 'It will not be held against you if you don't know whether or not the Holy Spirit proceeds from the Father and the Son. But you'll not escape God's judgment if you won't exert yourself to bring forth the fruits of the Spirit, which are: love, joy and peace, patience and meekness'.[13]

With this message Erasmus has had an incalculable impact on the most disparate groups and individuals. I need not discuss this now. But, if one

[11] Cf. Lecler, *o.c.*, I, p. 140 with reference to R. Bainton, 'The Parable of the Tares', *Church History*, I (1932), pp. 82–5.

[12] Erasmus, *Opus Epistolarum*, ed. Allen, IV, p. 118 cited by Lecler, *o.c.*, I, p. 144.

[13] Erasmus, *Opus Epistolarum*, ed. Allen, V, p. 177, cited by Lecler, *o.c.*, I, p. 145.

deals with his importance for irenicism it would be an omission not to point to the fact that for him *philosophia Christi* and 'church' incontestably belonged together. He was convinced that the values of *eruditio* and *pietas* – and all that pertains to them – could only thrive and be secure in the context of the church catholic.[14] The course of his own life and the strife into which he was unwillingly drawn time and again only strengthened his conviction on this point.

II. ERASMIAN IRENICISM

Between 1530 and 1550 the best chances for a solution of religious controversy as proposed in the Erasmian reconciliation programme lay in Germany. The great humanist had many adherents among the theological champions of both sides, but also in governmental circles many kindred spirits were to be found – in the courts of the princes as well as in the emperor's court, and beyond Germany, even within the Curia itself. They all thought along the same lines, to wit, that in view of the repeated postponements of the general council the princes should take reform in hand, thus restoring religious unity within their territories.[15]

The stronger the Erasmian leanings of those theologians and civil servants the stronger became their conviction that the church stood in need of an organizational and ethical restoration. *Disciplina* and *pietas* were the catchwords here. They shared the persuasion that countless abuses had crept into the church, that many of her servants lived in glaring immorality, that even those highest in the ecclesiastical hierarchy had been corrupted by their craving for power; in a word, there was a crying need for reform. Erasmus had shown the way towards this goal: restructuring of religious life, both personal and ecclesiastical, on the model of the primitive church.

Restricting myself to the theologians and church authorities thinking in this spirit, on the Roman Catholic side Gropper, Pflug, Witzel and Contarini should be mentioned and – on the other side of the confessional border – their compeers, such as Bucer, the reformer of Strasbourg and later counsellor of Edward VI, Melanchton and Capito, fellow-worker of Bucer.

a. *Bucer*
Of these protestants Martin Bucer was closest to Erasmus, whom he equals

[14] Erasmus, *De sarcienda ecclesiae concordia*, ed. Clericus, V, *c.* 481.
[15] Cf. Pierre Fraenkel, *Einigungsbestrebungen in der Reformationszeit*, Institut für Europäische Geschichte, Vorträge Nr. 41 (Wiesbaden 1965); C. Augustijn, *De godsdienstgesprekken tussen Rooms-Katholicken en Protestanten van 1538 tot 1541*, Verhandelingen ... Teyler's godgeleerd genootschap, NS 30, (Haarlem 1967).

in his respect for the early church.[16] The days of the Fathers, and especially those of the Christian emperors who had so excellently served the church in their legislation, formed also for him the classical era in the fullest sense of the word. He exerted himself in explaining to opponents that in the Evangelical camp nothing but a restoration of this in their own days should be pursued. He did not deny the significance of Luther, but neither did he ascribe to him a decisive role. He did not see in him a pioneer but rather a follower, and more especially a follower of Erasmus, who for him was the reformer par excellence. 'What useful and necessary knowledge can there be for a Christian to gain apart from that which Erasmus of Rotterdam so abundantly taught, long before Luther?', he exclaimed.[17]

For none of the other reformers was the unity of the church so close to his heart as for Bucer. This is in accordance with his strongly socially oriented way of thought. All his life he was intent on removing tension and bringing about conciliation, irrespective of party, whether for anabaptists, Lutherans or Roman Catholics. This was founded on a markedly christocentric ecclesiology, with a strong emphasis on the Spirit, that keeps and binds all men within the unity of the Body of Christ.[18]

b. *Melanchthon*

Contrasting Bucer to the more famous Melanchthon, one will notice that the latter was at least as deeply involved with the cause of Erasmus and humanism as Bucer. But unlike Bucer he felt greatly indebted to Luther whom he designated as 'a herald of wisdom illuminated by God'. The twofold loyalty – both to humanism and reformation – following from this, and the concomitant tensions show throughout his works. He was more of a dogmatist than his humanist friends. He shared their veneration for the early church and their eagerness to restore its *disciplina* within the contemporary church. But he was more discriminating. For him everything was concentrated on the concept of *pura doctrina* – the essence of scripture – which he wanted reestablished in the church. This implied for example that if certain ecclesiastical customs or dogmatic views could not be justified by scripture (or the symbol), but were based on the *consensus* of the Fathers only, he disowned them, despite the Fathers. He was far more critical in his concept of tradition than the humanists, because – thanks to

[16] Cf. H. Bornkamm, *Martin Bucers Redeutung für die europäische Reformationsgeschichte, Bibliographia Bucerana* v. Robert Stupperich, Schriften des Vareins für Reformationsgeschichte, Nr. 169, Jg. 58. Heft 2 (Gütersloh 1952); Friedrich Wilhelm Kantzenbach, *Das Ringen um die Einheit der Kirche im Jahrhundert der Reformation*. Vertreter, Quellen und Motive des 'ökumenischen' Gedankens von Erasmus von Rotterdam bis George Calixt (Stuttgart, 1957).

[17] Cited by Kantzenbach, *o.c.*, p. 120.

[18] Cf. Bornkamm, *o.c.*, p. 28.

Luther – he felt so closely tied to scripture.[19] This critical attitude would also show in practice.

c. *Cassander*

Next I turn to George Cassander (1513–1566) from the southern Netherlands, a man who more than anyone else set his mark on the development of the irenical ideal. Perhaps one might venture to say that he moulded this ideal even more strongly than Erasmus, whom he admired greatly and acknowledged as his example. Cassander was not a protestant, but I think that in fact protestant irenicism in the age of confessionalism is more indebted to this Roman Catholic lay-theologian than to its own forerunners like Bucer and Melanchthon.

However this may be, it is quite remarkable that whilst his Roman Catholic brothers ignored or vilified him, Cassander's name and influence were long-lived in protestant irenicism. In France the protestant diplomat-scholar Jean Hotman belonged to his greatest admirers and wrote irenical treatises in his spirit. Besides he edited reprints of some of Cassander's works and was involved, behind the scenes, in the publication of his *Opera Omnia*, edited by Jean De Cordes in 1616.[20] In Germany the creator of the concept of the *consensus quinquesaecularis*, the Lutheran George Calixt, was profoundly influenced by him. But also a quite different type like the Scot John Dury – the untiring apostle of peace, whose despair about the dissension of the church would seek an outlet in apocalyptic and millenarian dreams – was charmed by Cassander for a while.[21] The most ardent propagator of Cassander's ideas however was the Arminian Hugo Grotius, who recognised so much of himself in Cassander that in 1641, instead of attempting something original, he reproduced the 80-year-old programme of Cassander, merely adding *Annotata* to it.[22]

Cassander launched his ideas in the aftermath of the Council of Trent, when – particularly in government-circles of Germany (emperor) and

---

[19] Cf. Kantzenbach, *o.c.*, pp. 93–118, Adolf Sperl, *Melanchthon zwischen Humanismus und Reformation*. Eine Untersuchung über den Wanden des Traditionsverständnisses bei Melanchthon und die damit zusammenhängend Grundfragen seiner Theologie, Forschungen zur Geschichte und Lehre des Protestantismus (München 1959).

[20] I intend to discuss the relationship between Hotman and Cassander elsewhere.

[21] Hans Leube, *Kalvinismus und Luthertum im Zeitalter der Orthodoxie*. Vol. I. Der Kampf um die Herrschaft im protestantsichen Deutschland (Leipzig 1928), pp. 230–31: 'In Elbing beschäftigte sich der Schotte (= Dury) mit dem Werke und den Anschauungen des katholischen Irenikers Georg Cassander. Es zeigt sich auch hierin die Richtigkeit der Behauptung Hermanns Conrings, dass Cassanders Werke zu denjenigen zählten, die am meisten gelesen und den tiefsten Einfluss auf die Theologie des 17 Jahrhunderts ausgeübt haben.'

[22] See H. C. Rogge, 'Hugo de Groot's denkbeelden over de hereeniging der kerken', *Teyler's Theol. Tijdschrift* II (1904), pp. 14 *et seq.*

France – the hope for a peaceful solution or the confessional problem was still very vivid. What were his ideas?[23]

1. Central in his thought is the church, taken in a very organic sense. Vital to the church are unity and concord. In his opinion the dissension that split her pertained primarily to the relation of scripture and tradition. His stand on this is that the only way to interpret scripture correctly is by accepting the Apostolic tradition as normative. In accordance with Vincent of Lerins he takes the latter to be characterised by 'antiquity', 'universality' and 'unanimity'. He considers tradition as the explication of scripture, and conversely, scripture as the implication of tradition.

2. After having stated thus the standard for treatment of the points at issue, he attempts a systematic arrangement of the many controversial points which keep the church divided. He distinguished (a) matters pertaining to the doctrine of the church and (b) matters on church order – ceremonies and liturgical questions included. Under both heads he subdivides fundamental and non-fundamental points, and so indicates what is and what is not open to discussion.

3. Elaborating on this in accordance with the traditional distinction between the 'Head' – Christ – and the 'Body' of the church, he states that division of the 'Head' is possible only on the strength of a doctrine which is contrary to scripture, and a division in the 'Body' only through lack of love. Because the protestants do not defend opinions contrary to scripture as regards the 'Head' – their christology is correct – division in this sense is out of the question. Consequently dissent can pertain only to the church and its quality of 'Body'. By this he means that the controversy is restricted to matters of church order and ceremony. Diversity in this field however does not imply destruction of unity on principal grounds. Moreover one can discuss diversity. Given a discussion in a spirit of love, then he would gladly accept the protestants as true brothers in the one body of the church catholic.

In other words, Cassander views the entire controversy under the aspect of schism, not of heresy. For him the protestants were a modern version of the Donatists, and so it is not merely accidental that in reading his expositions one is often reminded of St. Augustine's statements about the Donatists. An example: 'Everything pure, holy and in conformity with the Gospel and the Apostolic Tradition that I find, either in one or the other part of the Church I accept as belonging to the Church of Christ. Each Church that stands on the foundation of true doctrine and apostolic creed

[23] For Cassander see, M. E. Nolte, *Georgius Cassander en zijn oecumenisch streven* (Nijmegen 1951); Kantzenbach, *o.c.*, pp. 203–29; Richard Stauffer, 'Autour du Colloque de Poissy: Calvin et le "De officio pii ac publicae tranquillitatis vere amantis viri" ', *Actes du Colloque l'Amiral de Coligny et son temps* [Paris, 24–28 Oct. 1972] (Paris 1974), pp. 134–54; A. Stegmann, 'G. Cassander, victime des orthodoxies', *Aspects du Libertinisme au XVIe siècle* (Paris 1974), pp. 199–214.

... I consider a branch of the true Church, the Catholic Church of Christ.'[24]

Delighted as were all those who came from the school of Erasmus about this concept, it sounded treacherous to the champions of the contending parties. Calvin wrote a really caustic refutation, and Cassander's own church was hardly more friendly. From both sides he was reproached for leaving aside and glossing over the central issues in the controversy: the Mass, justification, the 'visible' church.

This takes me back to the beginning of this paragraph, where I referred to the fact that in Germany in the period 1530–1550 many thought in an Erasmian spirit, and conciliation by way of disputations was attempted. In the age to come elsewhere in Europe men resorted to these disputations. Here I can be brief about them. They all failed for manifold reasons. Restricting myself only to the religious factor, I think one may say that the line of fracture always showed up in the borderland between 'reform' and 'reformation', church-order and dogma, *disciplina* and *doctrina*. Those who stood in the Erasmian tradition pursued renewal and peace of the church through a restoration of *disciplina* and were more or less indifferent towards *doctrina* – or perhaps one should say, they were less interested in it. For the confessions involved this was quite different. Matters of discipline were by no means unimportant to them, but their central issue was doctrine.

In this respect it is not from the sometimes very abstract, rational and 'cold' form of the notion doctrine that should be taken into consideration, but the intention behind the formula. To the protagonists of the confessions nothing less was at issue than the true knowledge of God, and the right way of serving and honouring Him. Distinguish between dogma and life, dogma and ethics, they did not, and could not, since to them the one presupposed the other. A system of moral principles that was not founded upon the insight into God's nature in all its aspects, into what He gave to and exacted from man, they deemed irrelevant, however lofty and noble in themselves the values of such a system. This was the dividing-line between them and the Christian humanists, and all those who did not couple from the very beginning *disciplina* and *doctrina*. On this point all new confessions were equally unrelenting. This was the rock on which all disputations split.

III.   REPUBLIC OF LETTERS

To the question: where did irenical ideas flourish most luxuriantly within early seventeenth century western Christianity, there is but one answer: in the Republic of Letters. What is to be understood by this? The Republic of Letters was no organisation or institution, but a kind of international

---

[24] Cited by Kantzenbach, *o.c.*, p. 215.

fraternity of men of learning for whom a lifetime in the service of the *bonae litterae* represented the highest form of human existence. It is already implicit in this that the Republic of Letters was a child of humanism.[25]

The citizens of this Republic formed a body of like-minded, internationally orientated individuals who usually belong to the ruling diplomatic or scholarly circles. There were seldom any theologians among them. Many of them had had a literary education, but most of them were jurists. Theologically they were as a rule self-taught, but they differed in their confessions. If they were French these men tended to subscribe to the doctrine of Gallicanism – they were generally supporters of the 'politiques' – if English they were among the convinced members of the Church of England; if German they were Lutherans, and if Dutch they often showed Arminian leanings.

They used to keep closely in touch with each other, not by organising pleasant conferences, but by sending each other publications by themselves or by others, by regularly visiting each other or sending regards by the mouth of pupils or mutual friends. Above all however they kept up their relationships by exchanging letters, by means of which they informed each other on personal well-being and activities, presented scholarly problems and discoveries and kept each other up to date on political, literary and confessional issues. It is mainly from reading a number of these letters – of which, as is well known, hundreds lie in our libraries and archives, both printed and unprinted – that I came to the view that here, in the Republic of Letters, irenicism as it had developed in the sixteenth century lived on in the most unbroken form.

Before I go any further into the matter I want to introduce the *dramatis personae* whose letters I have consulted. They are Jacques Bongars and Jean Hotman, both protestant diplomat scholars in the service of Henry IV, Jacques De Thou, the famous historian (Roman Catholic), the classicist Isaac Casaubon, the later librarian of King James I; William Camden and Robert Cotton,[26] who will need no further introduction; Philip Camerarius (1537–1624), jurist and vice-chancellor of the university of Altdorf;[27] Bernegger, classical scholar and historian (Strasbourg) and Lingelsheim,[28] diplomat – all of them Germans and adherents of Luther. Finally from the Low Countries Gerard Vossius,[29] historian, and of course, the most famous of all, 'the miracle' Hugo Grotius, who like Vossius was an Arminian.

[25] P. Dibon, 'Communication in the respublica litteraria of the 17th century', *Res Publica Litterarum. Studies in the classical tradition*, I (1978), pp. 43–55.

[26] Kevin Sharpe, *Sir Robert Cotton 1586–1631. History and Politics in Early Modern England* (Oxford 1979).

[27] See Lecler, *o.c.*, I, pp. 287–89.

[28] See A. Reifferscheid, *Briefe G. M. Lingelsheims, N. Berneggers und Ihrer Freunde* (Heilbronn 1899).

[29] See C. S. M. Rademakers, *Gerardus Joannes Vossius (1577–1649)* (Zwolle 1967).

It goes without saying that with these few names the number of citizens of the Republic of Letters is by no means exhausted – moreover in a considerable number of local circles people thought and worked in the same spirit – but I consider these few men of stature representative of the whole. I add to this that their religious ideas were remarkably homogeneous which makes it easier for me to summarise them in a few points.

1. The citizens of the Republic of Letters all suffered strongly from the strife and enmity of the society of their day – in the churches, in the states and in the relationship between them, both nationally and internationally – and they were all passionate searchers after means to end these disputes. The most alluring picture which presented itself to them was antiquity. They were all obsessed by antiquity, both classical and early Christian, and they cherished the illusion that the products of this period – which they constantly made a tremendous effort to search out because they regarded them as exemplary – could show the way to overcome the confusion of their own times and to realise the lofty ambition of peace.

2. To this end they put their confidence in a strong government – of an aristocratic or aristo-monarchical structure – which would impose itself on the contending parties, particularly on the discord and divisions within Christendom in their own time. Irrespective of their confessional origins, they all dreamed of the restoration of Christianity on the model of the primitive church. They had strongly idealised notions of this church and believed that under the leadership of the Christian emperors in the *sanior aevus*[30] a state of peace and unity in state and church had been reached, so perfect that they could do no better than find in it a pattern and an inspiration for their own time.

3. But they did not delude themselves that the confessional discord which they experienced could be resolved from within by the efforts of preachers or other ecclesiastical leaders. Their opinion of such men was usually very negative.[31] This arose from the fact that in practice it always turned out to be the theologians of all people, who threw oil – instead of water – on the fires of religious strife, and incited the formation of factions and schism. Accordingly, the citizens of the Republic of Letters were only strengthened in their conviction that there was no hope of a policy of peace coming from the theologians, but that their hope had to be vested in a

---

[30] This expression, which appears to be related with the term *sanior pars* – well-known from the juridical discussions on the concept of *repraesentatio* – can be found, inter alia, in Grotius, *Pietas Ordinum Hollandiae ac Westfrisiae Vindicata* (Leiden 1613), p. 18.

[31] A few examples are given in my article 'Jean Hotman's Syllabus of eirenical literature', *Reform and Reformation: England and the Continent c. 1500–c. 1750* (Oxford 1979), pp. 179–80.

strong government. That, and that alone, could bring about a restoration of the common corps of Christendom.

4. As far as the relationship of church and state was concerned, it is remarkable that the members of this circle always looked at the church from the viewpoint of the state and its interests, and never the other way round. In the ideal picture of the common corps of Christendom which they cherished, an exalted function was undeniably attributed to the church, but it was a limited one. These limits were constituted by the principle that the church should never be in a position to come into conflict with public order. The task allotted to her was to allow the saving influx from above to flow into the common weal. In fact this meant that the church was to defend morality, and this concept was regarded as having more to do with unity than with truth.

For Hotman, for Grotius, and above all for their mutual friend Casaubon – who actually made the move and had gone over to the service of James I – England was the great example of a successful realisation of the common corps of Christendom. They held that the reformation on the continent should have taken place along the lines of the English reformation. In England it had been possible to avoid extremes, merely removing some excrescences and abuses, but otherwise keeping to the catholic groundwork. The early Christian tradition had been honoured and constantly taken as a guide in this reformation. But above all they were impressed with the way in which the relationship of church and state had been managed. The Church of England, strongly linked with the state as it was, embodied for them the ideal of a Christian commonwealth in its most successful form. Hooker, of course, was their great apostle. Hotman wanted nothing more eagerly than to copy the example of the Church of England in France and Grotius stated time and again that nowhere had the idea of the primitive church been so closely approached as in the *Ecclesia Anglicana*.[32]

My attempt to characterise irenicism as it flourished in the Republic of Letters should now be brought to an end. However attention should be paid to one more point, one that is of considerable importance for the history of the transmission of irenical thought.

Despair of what confessional strife had brought about in the common corps of Christendom and still – plainly visible – brought about daily, mobilised the scholarly talents of the Republic of Letters to develop their irenical programmes and to promote an irenical policy. Therefore they did not only search antiquity for shining examples, but they also looked for support for their dreams and efforts in the more recent past. In this as in all other matters they wanted to return to the *status quo ante* – the time of wholeness. Here the resemblance is striking: on the one hand they wanted

---

[32] See my article 'Jean Hotman and Hugo Grotius', *Grotiana*, N.S. II (1981), pp. 3–4.

to put scholasticism in parentheses and reach back directly to antiquity; on the other hand they would rather forget the nightmare of confessional strife and refer immediately to the untimely ruptured tradition of sixteenth century irenicism. After so much useless and unpromising struggle – so they thought – one is forced to admit that those apostles of peace had been perfectly right. Grotius expressed it thus: 'In short, it is my opinion that if Luther had had the spirit of Melanchthon and the patriarch of the West had had the sympathies of Cassander, it would have gone better with things in Europe, which is now in a miserable state and has been tormented with these pestilential wars for more than a century under the pretext of the Gospel of Peace.'[33]

I will not elaborate on this now, but I do want to state that among the citizens of the Republic of Letters interest in everything that the sixteenth century had yielded in the field of irenicism ran exceptionally high. Erasmus, Bucer, Melanchthon and Cassander were put upon the stage, reprints of their works were being prepared, so that their message of peace might be heard again. This happened not only to the great, but also to minor and less well-known figures from the same tradition, like the Hungarian Andrew Dudith (1533–1589), the Pole A. F. Modrzewski (Modrevius, 1503–1572) and many, many others who made their come-back. Attention was drawn also to the disputations in Regensburg (1541), Poissy (1561) and Sendomir (1570). With the assistance of the entire Republic of Letters and in the interest of the progress of irenicism Jean Hotman surveyed all this material.[34] This resulted in a long list of titles on which others would later elaborate.[35]

All this was carried by the idea that a division in the common corps of Christendom was an anomaly, a scandal, for which the separate confessions were to be held responsible. Each confession waged the battle in the name of Truth, but the guilt of all became apparent in the blood for which they called, the malice they bore and the weltering chaos they created. The irenicists were convinced that truth without love is impossible, that truth can only vindicate itself when showing a heartfelt desire for concord and peace. Only love rings true, and in its absence truth equals presumption and thus eliminates itself.

In conclusion I should like to give a quotation from a very personal letter, written by the diplomat–classicist Jacques Bongars to his friend

---

[33] Grotius to Hotman (26 August 1614), *Briefwisseling* (ed. Molhuysen) I [365], p. 347.

[34] See my art. mentioned above n. 31.

[35] Charles Read, *Daniel Chamier (1564–1621)* (Paris 1858), pp. 211–12, mentions the lists of Gaffarel, Colomiés and Graverol, which were published between 1645 and 1689. For bibliographical references see, Axel Hilmer Swinne, *Bibliographia Irenica 1500–1970. Internationale Bibliographie zur Friedenswissenschaft: kirkliche und politische Einigungs- und Friedensbestrebungen, Oekumene und Völkerverstandignug. Mit Faksimiles* (Hildesheim 1977).

Camarius, dated 1598. Musing over the confused times they lived in the Stoics came to his mind. The Stoics called the world their 'fatherland' and preached resignation towards the vicissitudes of Fate. He continues as follows:

'To us, I am speaking of the Stoics anyway – the "fatherland" is not identical with that immense, undulating movement in nature, the effect of which is that life is felt to be better now in one place and now in another. To us, our "fatherland" is the Church which as the Church Catholic has spread all over the earth and is never bound to one single spot. But my point is that in her I have found more to weigh me down than in all the rest of the body politic. For of her visibility which is being so much made of in books and sermons, I discern nothing. In fact, I think that this visibility has gone into exile – exile in Utopia.'[36]

A moving statement indeed, but is not one inclined to feel that what the irenicists actually pursued was at least as utopian?

[36] J. Bongars, *Lettres* (La Haye 1695), nr. 94 (3 December 1598), p. 431.

PAPAL POLICY AND SCHISMATIC MOVEMENTS IN THE SIXTEENTH AND SEVENTEENTH CENTURIES

Gerhard Müller

Translated from the German by Ian Hazlett

In the Roman Catholic view, a schism is the separation of a group from the church and from its governing authority, the pope. Anyone who conscientiously keeps the faith, but yet is disobedient to the bishop of Rome, lives as a schismatic, separated from the 'supernatural community founded by Christ'. However, accompanying this disobedience there is often criticism of Roman Catholic doctrine, with the result that it is necessary to make a charge of heresy, or the suspicion of heresy. Occasionally the boundary between heresy and schism is not too clear or overstepped.[1] Yet the fundamental difference between both is adhered to. This is true not just for contemporary canon law, but also indeed for the sixteenth and seventeenth century. At that time it was possible for schismatical movements to be heretical, but they did not have to be. This made a certain degree of flexibility possible, – the papacy and the Roman Curia were able to apply the rigour of canon law on schismatics whose heresy was acknowledged; but they were also able to show clemency if there was any hope of overcoming momentary disobedience. Finally, they could go further and 'dissimulate', that is, simply ignore what had taken place. Thereby it was simpler to deal with the problem as it stood. But the application of the law was kept in reserve for the future. All this did happen in the period to be dealt with here. Since our era is very broad, it is not possible to take everything into consideration. Besides, our intention is to confine ourselves to the most important schismatic and heretical

[1] Cf. J. Brosch and A. Scheuermann, Art. 'Schisma', in: *Lexikon für Theologie und Kirche*, 2nd ed., vol. 9 (1964), pp. 405 f.

94

movement which Rome had to deal with at that time, namely with England and Germany. As regards France, the Netherlands, Scandinavia, Bohemia or eastern Europe, important aspects in those situations could well be introduced; but the basic decisions are most clearly recognizable in the response to English and German developments.

But first of all it is appropriate to remind ourselves of the importance of both these lands in the Roman image. The Italians mainly understood themselves as a nation of ancient culture, and they did not know if this would be the same with the peoples living in the far north.[2] The old pattern of 'civilized nation' on the one hand, and barbarian peoples on the other no longer prevailed of course; but had it been completely overcome? The Italians, who not only formed the main body of curial officials but in particular occupied almost all the important posts as well, were more open and less reserved in their dealings with the French and Spanish. To the English and especially the Germans they felt much less close. In view of the ignorance of German Reformation history prevalent in seventeenth century Rome, and the false notions which were put across – hence it was for a while believed that a papal protest against the religio-political agreements of the German Imperial Estates had been articulated, a protest which in fact had not been registered[3] – it is almost a matter for surprise that there were not even more complications. One of the papal nuncios, Girolamo Aleandro, joked in 1531 that instead of the divine spirit – 'spirito divino' – there was in Germany the spirit of wine – 'spirito di vino', and because there was too much wine in Germany there were too many heresies.[4]

A century later, another nuncio, Gasparo Mattei, stated his intention to try and 'sound the Roman key-note'. Were he not to manage this, he would 'apologize – all the more so whenever someone, who himself was never in Germany, never mind at Imperial Diets, wants to play around with things from a distance which are not so easily managed in practice'.[5] Representatives of the pope who had crossed the Alps had to live with such difficulties – lack of understanding at the Roman Curia, and in most cases too no personal knowledge of the vernacular. It was certainly a remarkable exception when such an outstanding theologian as Reginald Pole was dispatched to his native land in order to help bring about the settlement of

---

[2] Cf. Barbara McClung Hallmann, 'Italian "National Superiority" and the Lutheran Question', in: *Archiv für Reformationsgeschichte*, vol. 71 (1980), pp. 134–147.

[3] Cf. Konrad Repgen, *Die Römische Jurie und der Westfälische Friede. Idee und Wirklichkeit des Papsttums im 16. und 17. Jahrhundert*, vol. I, 1st Teil: Papst, Kaiser und Reich 1521–1644 (Tübingen 1962), p. 11.

[4] Cf. Gerhard Müller, 'Zum Verständnis Aleanders', in: *Theologische Literaturzeitung*, 89, Jg. (1964) col. 531.

[5] Repgen, loc. cit., p. 497.

the English schism. To understand this, we have to go back somewhat. This we will do firstly by looking at England, and then turning in a second chapter to Roman religious policy in Germany.

1. THE BREAKDOWN OF UNION

1.1 *Henry VIII's Marriage-case*

Legal questions are for the most part not so easily answered as it might appear. This is particularly true whenever several states and thereby different legal traditions are concerned. The lawsuit over the marriage of the English king was of course conducted on the basis of canon law. Yet what made it so complicated was its immediate political consequences. If Henry's requirement was not met, there was then the danger that the *Defensor fidei* – he had as is well known received this title from Pope Leo X – would have recourse to deeds substantiating his disobedience to the pope, and so bringing about a schism. If however Henry's demands were acceded to, then Pope Clement VII, who was responsible for the handling of the case, would incur the enmity of the emperor, since his aunt would now be considered as having lived illegitimately with Henry all those years; she had also borne him a daughter. It is understandable that were Clement to give in to the emperor's wishes, he would in return expect the guarantee that the verdict be executed. There was nothing unusual about that; since the high middle ages the emperors had after all acted as the arm of the church when it was a question of putting judgements against heretics into effect. But it was at this level that the problem which was to be solved found itself. We do not have to trace the decision in all its various phases here. That is familiar enough. But it does demonstrate the close interaction of law and politics, religion and state which was characteristic of reformation times. Moreover, it indicates for us the discrepancy between the pretensions and the realities of papal power; it had never completely recovered from the losses sustained since Boniface VIII. At the Roman Curia there was plenty of talk, but little notice was taken in the different countries of Europe. It was also possible to negotiate, to engage in political manoeuvres. But then the pope had to shoulder responsibility for the risks – not only the French king, but Clement VII as well had experience of being suddenly handed over to enemy troops. Clement VII had hardly ever recovered from the *Sacco di Roma*. Accordingly his procrastination in the case of Henry VIII's marriage is understandable on various grounds; not only were the political difficulties well known, no matter what the outcome was going to be, but also there was the question of what was going to happen if the king's request were turned down, as was suggested by canon law. So long as he had no one to carry out the verdict, he was not able to risk provoking an English schism.

1.2   *The Schism*

Henry VIII however relieved him of this particular decision. In having himself acknowledged as Head of the English church by the English clergy in 1531, he set in motion the separation of the church of his country from the Roman obedience.[6] But even this failed to induce the pope to instigate decisive steps. Instead, the English king tried conversely to influence Clement VII through Francis I of France in his own favour. But that would have meant abandoning the legal position hitherto maintained by Rome, and from which she was no longer able to move. Accordingly Henry was urged to repudiate Anne Boleyn within a month and return to his legal spouse. Henry's response was the edict prohibiting the publication of anything coming from Rome directed against himself. In addition, the English parliament voted to abolish the annates, but it was left to the king to have it activated. Notwithstanding all this, the pope did confirm Henry VIII's candidate for the see of Canterbury. This enabled the new primate of the Church of England, Thomas Cranmer, to be consecrated in due form on 30 March 1533.

The latter did not take long to conclude Henry's marriage-suit in his favour.[7] In reply Clement threatened excommunication, – if the king did not dissolve his new union within a certain period and resume his marriage, the ban was to have legal force. On several occasions this deadline was extended. But the curia achieved nothing with it. Instead Henry called for a council, which was being demanded as well by the emperor and the Germans, without it being possible for Clement to consent to this wish, as is well known. Henceforth in England, new situations were being created independently of this, – payments to Rome were stopped, and the papal *potestas iurisdictionis* was transferred to the king. He is 'supreme head in earth of the Church of England'. Nor was the bishop of Rome to have any say in future nominations of bishops. Doctrine was to remain as it was however. It is true that the monasteries were abolished, yet the tendencies to associate with the reformation message were unable to make a breakthrough during the Henrician era.[8] Here we have then a clear instance of a 'schism'. It is only obedience to the bishop of Rome which is rescinded. His authority is considered as illegitimate. Yet no doctrinal change is linked with this. In consequence, a reunion would conceivably be much more likely than in the case of heresy, where any reunion negotiations would have to include the settlement of doctrinal questions. Yet this cannot blind

---

[6] Cf. Ludwig Freiherr von Pastor, *Geschichte der Päpste seit dem Ausgang des Mittelalters*, 4th vol., 2nd Abt.: Adrian VI und Klemens VII, 13th ed. (Freiburg 1956), p. 510.

[7] Cf. G. R. Elton, Art. 'Thomas Cranmer', in: *Theologische Realenzyklopädie* vol. 8 (Berlin 1981), p. 227.

[8] Cf. Erwin Iserloh, *Geschichte und Theologie der Reformation im Grundriss* (Paderborn 1980), pp. 161–163.

us to the fact that the outcome of this lawsuit caused considerable damage
to papal authority. The bull of excommunication against Luther in January
1521 had not by then had the desired effect;[9] on top of this there was now
the schism of an entire land. It is true that for quite some time the English
king had been in possession of special rights in regard to the church of his
land. At the time this helped to make the schism easy. All the same, until
this crisis England had remained a part of Roman Catholic Christendom.
The question was, what was the attitude of the other monarchs going to be?

Admittedly the English example did not set a precedent. But conversely,
no one was to be found who of his own accord or with Roman help
contemplated forcing England back to the Roman obedience. Pope Paul
III, who succeeded Clement VII in 1534, kept up the cautious policy of his
predecessor with Henry VIII. At the same time he tried with the aid of the
French to exert pressure on the schismatic. But his hopes turned out to be
just as unfounded as those of Clement. In July 1535 he therefore informed
the Christian monarchs that for more than two years now he had been
wanting to declare the excommunicated Henry devoid of all claims to his
kingdom as a 'heretic(!), an open adulterer, public murderer, robber of
God, and frequent perpetrator of high treason'.[10] After the other sovereigns
were urged to keep their distance from the schismastics and were even
granted the right 'to seize their persons and property',[11] was there any hope
that they would now proceed against Henry and his followers? The draft of
a bull to this effect was soon presented. Henry was given three months to
change his mind. But the key monarchs, Emperor Charles V and Francis of
France, gave no signs of being willing to go along with this. Accordingly,
Paul III deemed it better to make no promulgation for the time being. For
several months there was debate in Rome over the text, until the death of
Catherine of Aragon on 7 January 1536 dramatically altered the situation.
Charles's reputation, which had suffered from the fact that Henry had
repudiated his aunt, was re-established. In view of the inveterate enmity
between Charles V and Francis I, it was Henry who stood to gain. He was
not avoided or resisted as a schismatic. On the contrary he was wooed by
the opposing parties contesting for precedence in Christendom. This
meant however that Paul III did not publish his bull at all – why should he
make himself somewhat ridiculous when he knew full well that its contents
would not command obedience, more likely indeed derision?

The execution of Anne Boleyn provided an unexpected bonus. Rome
liked to think that unrest in the north of England was the beginning of the
end of Henry's rule. As a member of the house of York and with the task of

---

[9] Cf. the articles by Robert Stupperich and Martin Brecht in: *Der Reichstag zu
Worms 1521. Reichspolitik und Luthersache*, ed. Fritz Reuter (Worms 1971),
pp. 459–489.

[10] Cf. Pastor, vol. 5: Paul III, 13th ed. (Freiburg 1956), pp. 680 f.

[11] *Ibid.*, p. 681.

working for the termination of the schism, Reginald Pole was appointed legate. But again hopes were delusive. 'The total failure of the canonical sentences pronounced against Henry VIII' made it all too clear to the Roman Curia how restricted its spiritual influence had become. And the very sovereign that had been expected originally to bring the schism to an end was to form an alliance with Henry VIII in 1543;[12] Charles V himself, the *rex catholicus*, as he was entitled to call himself as king of Spain, and as emperor the most important secular arm of the church, ignored the requests, wishes and expectations of the pope. It was not just that the times were past when excommunicated sovereigns who had no desire to lose their territory had to make efforts to have the ban repealed; so too were the times when it was possible for other sovereigns to try and expand their own rule at the expense of excommunicated monarchs. Proprietary conditions were by now much too stabilized for an individual to remove someone who was excommunicate and take over his realm. The pope declared that Henry VIII was worse than the Turks, conferring on him a biblical title – Antichrist – when he characterized him as 'Son of Corruption' (II Thess. 2.3). On Henry's death he called upon the emperor and the French king to attend at last to the reunion of the English church.[13]

But the heir who succeeded to the throne was one who had been designated by the curia as illegitimate. Any return to the papal obedience was out of the question. On the contrary, the schism broadened out into heresy with the introduction of a new liturgy and the approximation to protestant doctrine.[14] For all that, the Roman Curia was to forgo spectacular measures. It was not only occupied with other problems – not least the ageing Paul III's concern for the safeguarding of his own family[15] – rather, it had no hope of any success with further warnings or declarations of opinion. Instead, England became a land of refuge for many on the continent who because of their faith had to abandon their spheres of activity. But new hopes were raised when Edward VI died in 1553, and was succeeded by his half sister, Mary.

1.3 *The Reunion*

Older than Edward, Mary had not abandoned Roman Catholicism; she based the legitimacy of her birth on a papal dispensation which had permitted Henry to marry Catherine of Aragon the widow of his elder brother. Not wanting to jeopardize her succession to Edward, it was not possible for Mary to take up contact with Rome publicly straight away. Instead, her priority was to establish her claims to the throne. And when

[12] *Ibid.*, pp. 474 and 488.
[13] *Ibid.*, pp. 497–689.
[14] Cf. T. M. Parker, *The English Reformation to 1558*, 2nd ed. (London 1966), pp. 97–125.
[15] Cf. Pastor, op. cit., pp. 574–676.

that met with success, political sense determined that no anti-papalist emotions were roused; particularly apprehensive about such feelings were those who were anxious about church property which had come into their possession. But in Rome the proclamation of Mary as queen was noted with great satisfaction. Pope Julius III renewed Reginald Pole's appointment as legate for England. Along with this, he entrusted Pole with the task of getting Charles V and Henry II of France to restore peace between them. This is not the place to go into this peace-mission, which made it difficult for Pole to have the English question resolved in line with Roman wishes.[16]

Yet basically what Pole was charged with was the solution commending itself. No other cardinal was so suited for it as Pole. His mother had made quite a contribution to Mary's upbringing,[17] and in fact already in September 1553 the latter asked him for a dispensation before her coronation, so that her conscience might be at ease;[18] and if on this occasion she had to make certain assurances which conflicted with her faith, Rome knew that this happened for political reasons, that better decisions could and should follow. Pole was insistent that he be permitted to travel to England; for if papal authority there was not going to be completely restored again and permanently established, then there was the danger that Mary's right to the throne might be endangered.[19]

Charles V's opinion was completely different. He wanted to strengthen Mary's position by a marriage with his son Philip. This made things awkward for the papal legate, as he knew that a marriage between Mary and a foreigner would come up against substantial resistance, and he was accordingly striving for an internal English solution – on behalf of a relation at that. Mary seems even to have contemplated the cardinal as a spouse – he was not yet ordained as a priest. This made his task so much more difficult. The emperor intended using all his power to prevent the collapse of his marriage-project. He had the curia toe the line, and it directed the legate strictly to acquiesce. This Pole did, expressing his hope that the union of Mary and Philip would contribute to the consolidation of the religious situation, that is to the return of England under the Roman obedience. Julius III let Pole know that he should not be impatient. The pope was also prepared to waive his legal rights on the question of church property and not demand immediate restitution,[20] as this would endanger

---

[16] Cf. *Nuntiaturberichte aus Deutschland nebst ergänzenden Arkenstücken*, 1st Abt., vol. 15: Friedenslegation des Reginald Pole zu Kaiser Karl V und König Heinrich II (1553–1556), compiled by Heinrich Lutz (Tübingen, 1981).

[17] Cf. Pastor, vol. 6: Julius III, Marcellus II und Paul IV, 13th ed. (Freiburg 1957), p. 181.

[18] Cf. *Nuntiaturberichte*, 1st Abt., vol. 15, p. 48.

[19] Cf. *ibid.*, p. 82.

[20] Cf. *ibid.*, pp. 102–224.

the reunion. However he was opposed by Charles V. He stated that in Germany he had seen that the question of church property was the most important one. There ought to be no yielding on this. Anyway, one ought to be under no illusions in the matter of doctrine: the English were not genuine followers of the reformation or of Rome![21] For all that, Julius III enlarged Pole's powers of negotiation and dispensation, since he did not overestimate the influence of Mary, not wanting to jeopardize the work of reintegration.

As is well-known, the English parliament began by repealing the Edwardine religious legislation and finally voted the 'return to the unity and obedience of the Church'.[22] On 30 November 1554, Legate Pole, Queen Mary, King Philip of Spain and parliament ratified the reunion. This solution has the appearance of being somewhat too facile; could it have been so easy to come to terms with the fact that a few years earlier a new liturgy had been introduced and that new articles of faith had been drawn up as well? But Rome made no demand that the heresy of the past be cleared up. No disputations were held. Instead, the act of 'returning to the unity of the church and to obedience vis-a-vis the Apostolic See' was simply registered with pleasure.[23] Thus the English church-question was treated as schism. This schism was terminated with an act of parliament, just as it had begun with one. By means of new bishops and through the influence of the legate everything which was now being waived could be made up for later. Parliament also re-enacted the old heresy laws, to enable the state to proceed against heretics. In the trial of the archbishop of Canterbury, Pope Paul IV was involved. On 4 December 1555, he excommunicated him, ordered his deposition and – in good medieval fashion – 'handed him over to the secular arm'.[24] So Cranmer then was also burned. But the new archbishop of Canterbury, Pole, encountered difficulties with Paul IV too. It is true that in Rome the policy hitherto in regard to church property was adhered to and its return not demanded, but Pole himself was summoned on the suspicion of heresy to Rome, where he was to explain himself. This did not come about. Pole died on 17 November 1558 – of greater moment however was that Mary as well passed away on the same day;[25] for with that, religio-political consequences followed swiftly.

1.4 *The definitive Separation*

In accordance with an order of Henry VIII, his daughter Elizabeth was considered as next in line to the throne. After Mary's death, she was

---

[21] Cf. *ibid.*, p. 216.
[22] *Ibid.*, p. 224.
[23] *Ibid.*, p. 231.
[24] Cf. Pastor, op. cit., pp. 582–591.
[25] Cf. *ibid.*, pp. 606–608.

proclaimed as queen and crowned without great difficulties. Previously, at Christmas in 1558 and also during the coronation service on 15 January 1559 in Westminster Abbey, Elizabeth demonstratively walked out of the Mass during the elevation.[26]

Next came 'the grant of the first fruits and tenths to the Crown' and the restoration of the royal supremacy. The queen though was not styled as 'supreme head', rather as 'supreme governor in all spiritual and ecclesiastical matters' – after Archbishop Heath of York had declared that a woman ought not teach in the church and accordingly ought not to be characterized as its head. In Rome naturally the question was immediately raised as to whether the papal response to this settlement would not have to be excommunication. But during the last months of Paul IV's pontificate it did not come to this, although many hoped that the new queen might not be able to stay in power if she was banned from the church.[27] Rome looked on idly as the Book of Common Prayer was again introduced in 1559.[28] Certainly almost the entire episcopate put up strong resistance, but almost the whole of the remaining clergy acquiesced. Since Paul IV died in August 1559,[29] it was left to his successor, Pius IV, to undertake measures aimed to avoid a consolidation of heresy or a definitive schism. But the limited prospects of success of an excommunication may have deterred him. Instead he tried to exert a favourable influence on English developments by dispatching a nuncio. It was certainly said that a papal excommunication would suspend Elizabeth's contacts with the catholic princes and occasion internal political unrest among the supporters of the old faith in her country.[30] But it was a question of whether these expectations or hopes were well-founded or not. It was felt that the nuncio had the power 'to excommunicate Elizabeth and pronounce her a rebel if she opposed his demands'.[31] But this was not the case; after the way in which hopes in Rome for action against the schismatic Henry had been too high, Pius pondered instead if more could be achieved by diplomatic than by canonical means. The pope did not even intervene initially for the liberation of imprisoned catholic bishops. Instead he started by trying to arrange for Elizabeth's representation at the Council of Trent. But the queen refused to receive the nuncio and did not enter into negotiations at all. The result was that in 1561 the question of excommunication was

---

[26] A. G. Dickens, *The English Reformation*, 4th ed. (London 1968), p. 297.

[27] Cf. Pastor, op. cit., pp. 614 f.

[28] Cf. G. J. Cuming/S. G. Hall, art. 'Book of Common Prayer', in: *Theologische Realenzyklopädie*, vol. 7 (Berlin 1981), p. 80. It is a question here of the 1552 edition; cf. on this C. H. Smyth, *Cranmer and the Reformation under Edward VI* (Westport 1970), pp. 228–268.

[29] Cf. Pastor, op. cit., pp. 616–620.

[30] Cf. Pastor, vol. 7: Pius IV, 13th ed. (Freiburg 1957), p. 443.

[31] *Ibid.*, p. 443, n.5.

renewed. Philip of Spain advised strongly against this, as did Emperor Ferdinand – therefore the execution of a papal sentence by the Hapsburgs was not to be expected. In consequence the idea was given up in Rome; it was felt indeed that the effect of a ban could be to put Elizabeth's catholic subjects in increased danger.[32] Thus things remained during Pius IV's pontificate.

But as is common knowledge, Pius V took the step of formally condemning Elizabeth – this was the last time a pope would excommunicate a ruling monarch and pronounce her claim to office void. From the beginning of his pontificate, Pius V did not regard the daughter of Henry and Anne Boleyn as legitimate queen. He also managed to find someone whom he believed to be capable of putting the execution of his sentence into effect, namely the duke of Alba. On the other hand this greatly annoyed the latter's king, Philip II, and understandably so, for the pope had got in touch with Alba directly. Pius was of the opinion that the time was ripe for declaring Elizabeth excommunicate, since in Mary Stuart a candidate was available for the English throne, and whose allegiance to Rome was beyond doubt. Above all however it was reckoned that most people in England were good catholics. Why they did not take up arms against their queen was because Elizabeth 'was not yet proclaimed as a heretic and deposed by a decree of the Apostolic See'. On the strength of this, a trial was conducted within a few days in which Pius pronounced the queen of England as having incurred excommunication and designated her right to the English throne as null and void. Her subjects were not bound to her by oath, indeed in relation to the punishment of the ban, they ought not to render her obedience.[33]

This was the recurrence of a piece of medieval thinking and behaviour. It is true that the bull was not published in Rome in the usual way – e.g. not at the 'Campo de' Fiori'[34], but it was issued to the duke of Alba, the kings of France and Spain and also in England itself. Anyone who retained a vestige of admiration for the medieval unity of church and state, law and politics can only register the inefficacy of the papal judgement with disenchantment. What smooth-talkers had intimated to the curia did not come about: there were often risings against Elizabeth, but not on account of this bull!

Philip of Spain wrote to the queen that 'no action by the Pope displeased him so much as the bull of excommunication'[35] – under these circumstances naturally an invasion of England by Alba was furthest from anyone's mind. And the straw of hope which was being clutched, that England must be brought to her knees by a trade embargo turned out to be

[32] Cf. ibid., p. 453 f.
[33] Cf. Pastor, vol. 8: Pius V, 13th ed. (Freiburg 1958), pp. 423–443.
[34] Cf. ibid., p. 438, n.5.
[35] Ibid., p. 440.

delusive. The shock of the impotence of this judgement then was also so deeply implanted that in the succeeding century the curia did not have recourse to this expedient again, when events in France seemed to call for its use.

The reunion which was supposed to be enforced by means of papal authority was therefore not achieved. The English national church remained schismatic, or heretical as well, according to how one looked at it. In Germany the situation was different, because here there was the territorial sovereignty alongside the national central authority; this broadened the room for manoeuvre in curial politics, but also made things difficult. In our second section we will go into the way in which matters were decided and acted upon in this field.

2. THE CONDEMNED HERESY

2.1 *The Emperor's responsibility*

With the Edict of Worms, Emperor Charles V identified himself with the condemnation of Luther and his supporters by Pope Leo X. Thereby he accepted the responsibility enjoined on him by medieval heresy law. Consequently Rome was able to hope that the power of the emperor was going to quell the commotion caused by Luther. Charles V also announced this in his Worms' Confession.[36] But as is well known, political difficulties did not allow the emperor for a long time to head a campaign for the suppression of the condemned heresy – to him there were other happenings more important than the religious movement in Germany.[37] Added to this was his conviction that a reform of the church was requisite; on this, platitudes certainly abounded in Rome, but no important decisions were taken. When in 1524 Charles disallowed the national council announced by the German estates, he complied with papal expectations. But he was unable to stir Pope Clement VII to convoke a general church council.[38] Only with the peace-treaties of 1529 with the pope and the king of France was it possible for him to tackle what his younger brother Ferdinand was

[36] Cf. Hans Wolter S. J., 'Das Bekenntnis des Kaisers', in: *Der Reichstag zu Worms*, pp. 222–236, and Wilhelm Borth, *Die Luthersache (Causa Lutheri) 1517–1524. Die Anfänge der Reformation als Frage von Politik und Recht* [Historische Studien 414] (Lübeck and Hamburg, 1970).

[37] Cf. the emphasis of Wolfgang Reinhard: 'Die kirchenpolitischen Vorstellungen Kaiser Karl V., ihre Grundlagen und ihr Wandel', in: Erwin Iserloh (ed.), *Confession Augustana und Confutatio. Der Augsburger Reichstag 1530 und die Einheit der Kirche* [Reformationsgeschichtliche Studien und Texte 118] (Münster/Westph. 1980), pp. 62–100.

[38] Cf. Gerhard Müller, 'Zur Vorgeschichte des Tridentums. Karl V. und das Konzil während des Pontifikates Clemens' VII', in *Concilium Tridentum*, ed. by Remigius Bäumer [Wege der Forschung 313] (Darmstadt 1979), pp. 74–112.

urgently bringing to his attention, i.e. defensive measures against the Turks and the restoration of church unity in Germany.[39]

It is conspicuous that from Bologna, where he had been meeting Clement VII, Charles invited the German estates to a diet, at which he intended to function as arbiter of the religious quarrels.[40] This was not in accordance with the law of heresy – it laid down that the secular power should and must only put the papal judgement into effect. But in regard to the contents of this announcement, nothing of course was determined yet. And Clement VII could be fairly certain that Charles V in his declared capacity was not going to make a pronouncement in favour of Lutheranism. There is a hint here however of independent magisterial action, which the protestant princes in Germany were already openly practising, and which pointed to a weakening of the Roman legal position. The emperor, though, opted for a middle way: He kept the papal legate fully informed and tried to gain his approval for religio-political compromises. But the legate, Cardinal Lorenzo Campeggio, remonstrated with the emperor that there was actually only *one* way to deal with heretics, namely force. Yet despite this, the emperor kept on trying to win the legate's consent to concessions, such as allowing the chalice to the laity or the marriage of priests. Campeggio the lawyer would have been the last person to have made a decision 'off his own bat'. He inquired in Rome if such concessions could be granted from there. When the reply was negative, his attitude was clear: If the emperor should promise anything to the evangelical estates then it would be without papal authority! Rome advised the legate 'to close his eyes' and correspondingly take no notice of agreements. There was no intention of legitimizing them, but also not to protest against them. Instead, the aim was to inflict the burden of the crisis on Charles V, as well as the responsibility for the future.[41]

The behaviour of the Roman Curia on the occasion of Ferdinand's election as Roman king demonstrates how easily law could be used and therefore manipulated to serve political ends. In order to be equipped for all contingencies, Charles made a request in 1530 for various bulls concerning the participation of the Saxon electoral duke in the election. Rome obliged and declared in one document that Electoral Duke John had no right to take part in the election. In another document however it was said that such an election was valid, even if he as excommunicate had taken part in it. In a

[39] Cf. Müller, 'Entstehung und geschichtliche Bedeutung des Augsburger Bekenntnisses', in *Luther. Zeitschrift der Luther-Gesellschaft*, 51 (1980) pp. 55–56.

[40] Cf. Müller, *Die römische Kurie und die Reformation 1523–1534. Kirche und Politik während des Pontifikates Clemens' VII.* [Quellen und Forschungen zur Reformationsgeschichte 38] (Gütersloh 1969), pp. 72–85.

[41] Cf. Müller, 'Kardinal Lorenzo Campeggio, die römische Kurie und der Augsburger Reichstag von 1530', in: *Nederlands Archief voor Kerkgeschiedenis*, 52 (1972), pp. 133–152.

third bull, his exclusion from the church was explicitly renewed and it was
stated that in consequence he should not participate in the election of the
Roman king. As justification, reference was made to Leo's verdict on
Luther, which does affect John as the Wittenberger's protector.[42] The
imperial court could now select for itself, as the occasion demanded,
whatever document seemed most suitable. In this, Rome only maintained
one line consistently: John of Saxony is to be regarded as debarred from the
church. But the legal inferences drawn from this were contradictory. The
question is whether with this, the medieval heresy law was being struck at
in its very heart. For it was not here a matter of an opportunist
promulgation, rather, of legal conclusions which no longer envisaged the
previous exclusion at all costs of a heretic from Christendom. But thereby
the settlement of a schism or the suppression of a heresy must have been
basically easier than was believed in the middle ages.

For the moment however it rested in the eyes of the Roman Curia with
the competence of the emperor. He should see to it how he might again
suppress heresy in Germany, or how he might come to an interim
agreement with it. In 1532 when the Turkish threat made plain to it the
desirability of gathering all German forces to resist, the curia encouraged
the emperor to come to such an arrangement. And so Charles V concluded
a cease-fire with the evangelical estates, which was to hold until a council or
the next diet. It was therefore a matter of an interim solution, but for all
that an act of understanding with people who as protectors of Luther were
certainly considered in Rome as notorious heretics. Yet in Rome, no
measures were taken against this, also not in 1539 when the emperor was
contemplating a new cease-fire, nor in 1540–41, when by means of
colloquies he attempted to bring about theological agreement. Instead,
efforts were made by the dispatch of Cardinal Gasparo Contarini to
promote these colloquies as much as possible.[43] But there was then no
willingness in fact to concede as much theologically to the protestants as the
legate had considered feasible. Thereby various options had not borne out
the expectations of success: neither had the emperor been able to effect the
return of the protestants to the Roman obedience through a policy of
moderation, nor had the attempt to reach theological agreement brought
success. Indeed the latter had to be more difficult after 1545, when the
Council of Trent defied reformation theology with Roman Catholic
doctrine.

Already in 1544 the curia had also indicated that, as always, it was
capable of speaking clearly whenever it considered it desirable. The
imperial recess of this year had met with firm resistance in Rome. The
surrender of church property to the evangelical estates which had been

---

[42] Cf. Müller, *Die römische Kurie*, pp. 128 f.
[43] Cf. Klaus Ganzer, Art. 'Gasparo Contarini', in *Theologische Realenzyklopädie*,
vol. 8 (Berlin 1981), p. 204.

ratified at Spires in 1544 and which really only gave subsequent legality to a *de facto* situation, was denounced by Paul III. In a letter of warning, standing in the tradition of similar communications, the emperor was emphatically and earnestly called upon to attend to his responsibility.[44] As always no one in Rome had any thought of capitulating to the facts. The legal position remained clear. Charles V ought to see to it how he was going to do justice to his responsibility.

Consequently the Schmalkaldic war 1546–47, that is the way of force, seemed to offer a solution. Officially it had not been begun because of the religious question, rather due to the action of the evangelical estates against Duke Henry of Braunschweig-Wolfenbuttel, but that does not tell us too much either. It was known – and the emperor himself also conceded the point – that the religious question was also involved.[45] A military victory over heresy was made no easier by the fact that precisely during Charles V's successful campaign a deep disagreement set him and Paul III at variance. At the Imperial Diet of 1548, the emperor was unable to bring the protestants back directly into the western church. Instead he decreed an Interim,[46] to remain in force until the council, which was going to deal definitively with the religious question. Thereby, in place of his personal responsibility that of a general church council was to take over. Although a council did meet in 1551–52, no solution emerged, as is known. Therefore Germany continued to be burdened with its religious question and in a certain way she was also left alone – was Rome not just getting somewhat used to it by now?

2.2 The Protest that Never Was

With the treaty of Passau in 1552, Charles V again had to pursue the path of negotiation. At that time, it was intended to look for a lasting solution. The emperor opted out of this by surrendering the imperial crown to his younger brother, who for decades now had been designated as his successor. Certainly in the 'religious peace' of 1555, the desire to restore the unity of the church in Germany had been determined.[47] But whether that was likely to succeed had to be doubted after the many fruitless efforts that had already been made. However, particularly with the granting of full

[44] In order to defend the emperor, Martin Luther replied to this with his caustic tract 'Against the Papacy at Rome, founded by the Devil', Weimar Edition, vol. 54, pp. 206–299.

[45] Cf. Karl Brandi, *Kaiser Karl V.* (München 1937), p. 471 and Gerhard Müller, 'Karl V. und Philipp der Grossmütige', in: *Jahrbuch der Hessischen Kirchengeschichtliche vereinigung*, vol. 12 (1961), p. 30).

[46] Cf. *Das Augsburger Interim von 1548*, ed. Joachim Mehlausen [Texte zur Geschichte der evangelischen Theologie 3] (Neukirchen, 1970).

[47] Cf. Gerhard Pfeiffer, art. 'Augsburger Religionsfriede', in: *Theologische Realenzyklopädie*, vol. 4 (Berlin 1979), pp. 639–645.

civil legitimacy for the adherents of the Augsburg Confession, the implementation of the heresy law had been broken off. Was Rome able to consent to this? Should the peace simply be acquiesced in without protest like the previous limited agreements? Or was it desirable to draw attention to their own legal positions in Rome? That it was possible to regard the latter as necessary is shown in the protest of the bishop of Augsburg, Cardinal Truchsess against the Religious Peace of Augsburg.[48] But there is no corresponding action by the papal nuncio.[49] This was also due to the deaths of Pope Julius III and Pope Marcellus II.[50] But that does not account for everything. For Pope Paul IV – otherwise reputed for his anti-Hapsburg policies – did not throughout his entire pontificate officially take cognizance of the Religious Peace; nor did he protest against it! Later in Rome it was considered inexplicable that no one spoke out in 1555, for the crucial legal positions had indeed been consolidated there.

Only eleven years later did the question become alive, when there was discussion about whether the still outstanding 'religious settlement' should be established. For, during the talks after 1555 one of the chief reasons why there were never any serious efforts to reach agreement was the dissensions among the followers of the *Confessio Augustana*.[51] There was the possibility of change in 1566, when Emperor Maximilian II placed all his influence at the disposal of the cause. But the papal legate, Cardinal Giovanni Francesco Commendone, worked to prevent a religious settlement, since in that an agreement with heretics and not their return to Roman doctrine was to be expected. The curia avoided 'any form of recognition of the Religious Peace of Augsburg'. At the same time however, it did not bear in mind what Maximilian II solemnly undertook at his election in accordance with the agreement of 1555, that 'the Religious Peace had become an established Imperial Statute'! And so for a long time now decisions on matters of principle had been taken, but which were circumvented when people like Commendone recommended that the religious question should by no means be dealt with at the diet. For the fundamental problems would indeed have to be faced ultimately. And it was the catholic estates who desired a confirmation of the 1555 Peace. This had worked out very much in favour of German catholicism, since by means of the 'religious proviso' the possibility of large areas going over to the reformation was prevented. Rome instructed the legate only to protest if the imperial recess was directed against 'the dogmatic decisions of the Council of Trent' – and so

[48] Cf. Repgen, op. cit., p. 10.
[49] Cf. *Nuntiaturberichte aus deutschland nebst ergänzenden Atkenstücken*, 1st Abt. vol. 17: Nuntiatur Delfinos, Legation Morones, Sendung Lippomanos (1554–1556); compiled by Helmut Goetz (Tübingen 1970).
[50] Julius III died on 23.3.1555, Marcellus II on 1.5.1555.
[51] Arthur Heidenhain, *Die Unionspolitik Landgraf Philipps von Hessen 1557–1562* (Halle/Saale, 1890).

the possibility of a formal protest was clearly kept in mind.[52] Certainly no one in the curia entertained illusions about the consequences of such a step. But thereby legal positions would have been maintained, which were otherwise in danger of falling into oblivion.

It is extremely informative to follow at this point the discussions between the legate's advisors on the issue of whether a protest was necessary or not. Whilst the Jesuit advisors argued against such a step, the canon lawyer Lancelotti recommended it. He also drafted a text, which later in Rome was explained as the Commendone-protest. Yet it was never ratified, remaining simply a proposal. The legate was not keen on such a step and did not go ahead with it. It was only later that he received the information that the curia too did not consider it necessary. Therefore Germany was left to her own devices. Although a few years later Pius V was to undertake serious measures against Elizabeth of England, as we have seen, no legal measures were instigated against the religio-political developments in central Europe. Thereby the possibility of an official schism was avoided, and it enabled an inward renewal of the catholic church in Germany to take place. In return, the unsatisfactory legal situation – from the canonical point of view – was put up with.[53] The intention was that it should remain at that. During the next century as well, Rome saw no reason to make a point of stating her opinion on the ecclesiastical situation in Germany. Only during the Thirty Years' War was there to be any change.

2.3 *Between Dissimulation and Protest*

The outbreak of war in 1618 led at first to considerable successes on the catholic side. In 1630–31, the first attempts were made to bring the fighting to an end.[54] Recent research has shown that in this respect, the Roman Curia was conspicuous in its hesitancy. This was due to the fact that the European policy of Urban VIII (1623–1644) was lacking 'the grand design'. This pope was primarily involved in Italy. He was prepared to make sacrifices for his own family, but hardly for religious interests in Germany. Konrad Repgen has demonstrated that for the Roman Curia a question of protocol was taken much more seriously than the religious situation in Germany. It had to do with a request from Urban to the emperor to let 'the newly-appointed prefect of Rome, the papal favourite, Taddeo Barberini have precedence over the imperial ambassador at certain

[52] Cf. Repgen, op. cit., pp. 100–140; also Walter Hollweg, *Der Augsburger Reichstag von 1566 und seine Bedeutung für die Entstehung der Reformierten Kirche und ihres Bekenntnisses* [Beiträge zur Geschichte und Lehre der Reformierten Kirche, 17] (Neukirche, 1964).
[53] Cf. Repgen, op. cit., pp. 116–142 and 388.
[54] Cf. Repgen, Art. 'Dreissjähriger Krieg', in: *Theologische Realenzyklopädie*, vol. 9, fasc. 2 (Berlin 1981), pp. 169–174.

ceremonial functions'. On this emotions ran high – not however on events in the distant north.[55] Granted that at those times questions of protocol were serious matters – they also led to serious tensions indeed between various German estates – it is nonetheless hard to conceive that the significance of negotiations in Germany with its consequences for the entire church could not have been more clearly perceived in the Roman Curia.

And so in 1630, the curia was concerned with the issue of whether the agreements come to should simply be accepted in a tacit manner. Although it was learned in Rome that in 1555 Cardinal Truchsess had made a protest, and although there was a demand that the abortive protest of 1566 be taken up again, Urban resolved in 1630 that the time was not ripe for a great protest. He wanted 'for political purposes in Germany . . . to avoid as far as possible every firm commitment, even if the consequences of such a commitment . . . would be of direct advantage to the Church'. Certainly from the beginning of 1631 Rome was speaking with a clear voice, but radical new courses were not being taken. She confined herself to directing the nuncio to represent 'the Roman legal position vis-a-vis a new religious peace', – to do this privately if necessary, but not officially. That was 'no really positive religious policy'.[56] It was only an attenuated form of dissimulating, which almost completely surrendered any claim to exercise influence.

A variation followed when Emperor Ferdinand II considered whether he should secure an ecclesiastical dispensation for his religio-political transactions – just as Mary had sought it before her coronation. This was new. At the time of the cease-fire of 1532, the Interim, the treaty of Passau or the Religious Peace of Augsburg, no one had 'asked' the apostolic see 'to give ecclesiastical approval to Imperial agreements by means of a Roman dispensation'. In contrast to Charles V and Ferdinand I, Ferdinand II considered this. In November 1631 the papal nuncio calculated 'that Rome would be officially petitioned for a dispensation by the Emperor'. In that way the curia would have had to come to a decision. Admittedly a dispensation would only have applied to the emperor personally, but undesirable consequences could arise from this too. The idea was therefore turned down. There was no willingness to seek a consensus, nor to grant a dispensation either. A protest was also considered – after the long silence it would also have been received in the imperial court only with surprise and incomprehension. There was therefore only one way out for the curia – the well-tried way of dissimulation. If this did not work, then the nuncio may express opposition. On no account was he to take on 'further commitments'. Also his opposition should remain on the private or semi-official level. An official commitment was to be avoided on the other hand.

[55] Cf. Repgen, *Die römische Kurie*, pp. 189–199.
[56] Cf. *ibid.*, pp. 239–259.

Thereby 'the Papacy . . . *consciously* let pass unused one of the rare chances of re-ordering the post-Tridentine relationship between Church and State'. The imperial estates had to find their own way and they would 'sometime or other' confront the curia 'with accomplished facts'. 'Then the question arose, how should one come to terms with this: Dissimulation? Protest? or a third possibility?'[57]

When the conclusion of peace appeared as a real possibility, Urban VIII exhorted the emperor in 1633 that he should 'give priority before every other human consideration to the preservation of the Catholic religion'. This sounds clear, but in the context of the negotiations of that time it simply testifies to the fact 'that the Pope cannot formally approve of the imminent peace'.[58] Once again then it was a matter of an internal German agreement, against which no protest was going to be raised; but equally, there was going to be no church approval from Rome. It is true that the nuncio was reproached for not defending strongly enough 'the Pope's measures against the German policy to the French', and not for having done too little in respect of the projected peace between the emperor and protestant Saxony! Without wielding any influence, the curia left the imperial theologians to their deliberations. Watching over the legal situation was felt to be enough – thereby everything was again committed to the future. And then Rome also reacted to the Peace of Prague of 1635 between Ferdinand II and Saxony without comment – politically, Urban VIII had capitulated.[59] But juridically, everything remained as it had been: Rome officially acknowledged nothing and was in a position to apply the old canonical norms again at a favourable opportunity.

For the first time a new nuncio, Gasparo Mattei made the proposal after 1640 to the curia to effect new legislation. This idea did not come from Rome, rather her representative in Germany. But in Italy German questions were not followed with much attention, despite this plan. Interest was limited simply to ensuring that no long-term solutions were agreed upon – as if the settlement of 1555 had not long since established itself as such!

The nuncio was so concerned with the idea of a protest that in April 1641 he pronounced a *protestatio*. Admittedly this was a protest against developments of which he was ignorant or was unclear about, so that it was 'easy for the Emperor' to ignore this action. What had been considered as a potent legal instrument shrivelled into a document; in Germany it was passed over in favour of the business of the day. On the other hand, Rome committed itself to the protest. This was because it stated the curia's intention now and in the future not to condescend to recognize religio-political agreements which 'did not correspond to the Roman view of

[57] Cf. *ibid.*, pp. 276–292.
[58] *Ibid.*, pp. 316–318.
[59] Cf. *ibid.*, pp. 349–387.

things'.[60] In May 1642 a further protest of the nuncio followed – he was unable to have a decisive influence on decision-making, but he also no longer wished to look on without comment. To those involved it was clear that the opposition was only able to serve the purpose of maintaining old legal positions, and that the nuncio was in no position to bring about religio-political amendments later. Also in Rome this variation was not pursued on principle. Fabio Chigi, who in winter 1643–44 was sent to Munster as extraordinary nuncio to the peace-talks,[61] 'had no instruction to protest at all events'.[62] Yet the developments of 1641–42 did remind people of the possibility of this legal instrument. At the same time, though, they also demonstrated their lack of political influence. For all that, Chigi protested in 1648 against the Peace of Westphalia as is known. He was unable to achieve anything with this other than enunciate the curial legal viewpoint. But it was certainly more honest to act in this way than to behave as if he knew nothing of the religio-political agreements. Accordingly it was a long route from dissimulation to protest. Both demeanours showed however that politically, Rome had changed from acting to reacting.

3. BETWEEN LAW AND POLITICS

In the period we have been looking at, the Roman Curia did keep to its rejection of schism and heresy. Initially it tried to convince the emperor how necessary it was that he should act: the execution of papal heresy-verdicts was incumbent upon him. But the political situation permitted no simplistic medieval solutions. Consequently the legal claims had to be put aside, indeed concealed. Yet they were not abandoned. Instead, they could again be brought to light when the opportunity or necessity arose. The latter occurred with the excommunication of Queen Elizabeth I and all who owed obedience to her; also with the protests against the Peace of Westphalia 1648. But in that case, excommunication proved just as ineffective as protest. Neither a schism nor a heresy could be overcome by those means in the sixteenth and seventeenth centuries. A reunion seemed however only conceivable when, as in England under Mary, the obedience under Rome was enacted. Theological compromises, such as were worked out in Regensburg in 1541, were on the other hand not accepted. After the outcome of the Council of Trent they were driven even further into the background. Consequently there was a concentration on the inner renewal of the catholic states, which were then able to follow pro-Rome policies.

---

[60] Ibid., pp. 506–508.
[61] Cf. Fritz Dickmann, Der Westfälische Frieden, 4th ed., ed. by Konrad Repgen (Munster/Westf., 1972).
[62] Repgen, Die römische Kurie, pp. 533 f.

Where that did not suffice, there continued for decades a retreat from the front line of religio-political affairs – by officially ignoring decisions that had been arrived at; or, there remained the possibility of protest to guard one's own legal position. Whether this indeed would later bring success politically, only the future could tell.

WAS O'CONNELL NECESSARY? SIR JOSEPH DILLON, SCOTLAND, AND THE MOVEMENT FOR CATHOLIC EMANCIPATION

B. Aspinwall

In 1835, Sir John Joseph Dillon wrote to Robert Peel: 'Having in 1812–1813 kept all Scotland quiet on the Catholic Question, although single handed, having contrived to get the General Assembly of the Church of Scotland to throw out a petition against Catholics and vote in their favour, Sir John Dillon has some insight in to the springs by which bodies of men are generally moved.'[1] Indeed he had, and therein lies a fascinating story of how catholic emancipation was almost accomplished in 1813.

In recent years historians have begun to reassess the traditional accounts of the period which immediately preceded catholic emancipation in 1829. The work of John Bossy, Eamon Duffy and R. W. Linker has reconsidered the mythology of the catholic revival in the late eighteenth and early nineteenth centuries.[2] This new look has been assisted by the revived catholic laity in the aftermath of Vatican II and in the 'ethnic revival' of the 1960s. British catholics want to emphasise the 'native' factors rather than the Irish or clerical elements: the new elite has discovered the old. But amid this exciting shift Scotland has been neglected. But, as Charles Butler observed over a hundred and sixty years ago, that is nothing new.[3]

---

[1] Sir John Joseph Dillon to Robert Peel, 7 January 1835: Peel Papers, British Library Add MSS 40409, f 188.

[2] John Bossy, *The English Catholic Community 1570–1830* (London 1975); Eamon A. Duffy, 'Ecclesiastical Democracy Detected 1779–1787' *Recusant History*, vol. 10, 1969–70, pp. 193–209, 309–331; vol. 13, 1975–76, pp. 123–48; R. W. Linker, 'English Roman Catholics and Emancipation: The Politics of Persuasion' *Journal of Ecclesiastical History*, vol. 27, 1976, pp. 151–80.

[3] Charles Butler, *Historical Memoirs respecting the English, Irish and Scottish Catholics*, 4 vols. (London 1819–21), vol. II, p. 436.

That neglect might be repaired by a consideration of the life and career of Sir John Joseph Dillon, a fellow barrister and member of the Catholic Board with Charles Butler and Edward Jerningham.[4] Although he claimed to have been the original convener of the meeting which established the board, Dillon always remained a staunchly independent character. His cosmopolitan background, wide experience and constant travels gave him an entree into many circles, but he was never fully integrated into any single one.

The son of William Mervyn Dillon of Proudston, Meath, Ireland, and Bedford Square, London, he was admitted to Lincoln's Inn in 1793, called to the bar in 1801 and died in Ipswich in 1837.[5] His family had seen service under the Austrian emperor and Dillon was a knight and baronet of the Holy Roman Empire. But the French Revolution, the Napoleonic Wars, the beginnings of significant shifts within the catholic community and the passage of the 1793 Catholic Relief Act, together with the integration of Ireland into the Union, were to reshape Dillon's life.[6]

He then entered upon a career within a rapidly changing world and within a revolutionised catholic community: the new polemical style of Bishop Milner was indicative of the erosion of the old catholic gentry.[7] With his aristocratic background, Dillon had little sympathy with French revolutionary sentiments. With his Irish family background and his connection with the aristocratic Fingall interest, he had little sympathy with the 1798 rebellion, the Threshers' movement or the popular catholic movement of O'Connell.[8] As a lawyer his instincts were essentially conservative: he naturally claimed to support 'restoration' rather than innovation.[9] As a legal adviser involved in the delicate matter of the duke of

[4] *Ibid.*, vol. II, pp. 498–505. J. J. Dillon to Grey, 17 May 1813; Grey Papers, Durham University, Department of Palaeography.

[5] See Sir J. J. Dillon, *Epitome of the Case for the claim of the Dillon family of Proudston to the Great Chamberlainship of All England* (London 1829), p. 2 for the family tree. Also see W. Betham, *The Baronetage of England* 4 vols. London 1803, vol. 3, p. 55; *Ipswich Journal* 11 February 1837. I am very grateful to Miss Yvonne McGowan of Lincoln's Inn Library and Mrs. P. Woodgate of Suffolk Record Office for information. *Gentleman's Magazine* September 1839, p. 317.

[6] See John Bossy, *The English Catholic Community*, pp. 295–323, and J. C. H. Aveling, *The Handle and the Axe: the Catholic Recusants of England: From Reformation to Emancipation* (London 1976), pp. 253–347.

[7] F. C. Husenbeth, *The Life of the Rt. Rev. John Milner D.D.* (Dublin 1862) especially pp. 170–284 and Bernard Ward, *The Eve of Catholic Emancipation*, 3 vols (London 1911), vol. I, pp. 99–140.

[8] *The Diary of Charles Abbot Lord Colchester* ed. by Charles, Lord Colchester, 3 vols. (London 1861), vol. II, pp. 121–22 and Michael Roberts *The Whig Party 1807–1812* (London 1939), pp. 7–102.

[9] See Paul Lucas 'A Collective Biography of Students and Barristers of Lincoln's Inn 1680–1804: a study in the "Aristocratic Resurgence of the Eighteenth Century" ' *Journal of Modern History*, vol. 46, 1974, pp. 227–261.

Sussex and his catholic wife, Lady Augusta Murray and her two children, he strenuously sought to avoid any public embarrassment of the royal family: such adverse publicity would merely fuel irresponsible radicalism in Britian. He continued in that role until 1809 and later acted unsuccessfully on behalf of the d'Este children.[10] That role drew him into close contact with the Prince Regent and the leading politicians of the day.[11]

Dillon considered his diplomatic skills would stand him in good stead when the imminent emancipation of catholics came to pass. A strict constructionist constitutional lawyer, he wished to avoid any popular demonstrations for or against catholic emancipation. A firm upholder of the union of Great Britain he stressed the need for national unity, for all property, all rank and all religion to rally round the throne. But though a unionist, he strongly believed that all three nations, England, Ireland and Scotland should have an equal share in that British national identity.[12] In his view, the acts of union with Scotland and with Ireland created a united kingdom but still left room for considerable diversity in practice. Unless English legislation were specifically recognised in the Act of Union, it did not apply to the whole of the kingdom. In this respect the *English* Test Acts operated against the legitimate ambitions of Scots and Irish. Some consideration had to be given to Scottish and Irish interests. The dominance of England to the detriment of Scottish and Irish aspirations was a serious danger to the union: English superiority in industry and enterprise, wealth and capacity, law and ecclesiastical institutions was assumed rather than proven.[13] England assumed an unwarrantable dominance over the rest of Great Britain: the irrelevant bigotry which

---

[10] See for example Sir J. J. Dillon to Earl Grey, 25 January, 2 February 1811; Grey Papers; Sir J. J. Dillon to Lord Sidmouth, 18 December 1812; Scottish Record Office Edinburgh, RH 2/I v. 99 ff 598–605.

[11] His views are usefully summarised in *De Immunitate Qua Gaudent Scoti, ex pacto Unionis Dissidentes Angliae Protestantes Et Catholici Jure Tolerantiae Omnis Jurisdictionis apud curias consistoriales Anglicanas et quad nuptas ab illis conficiendas apud templa Anglicanae Ecclesiae* (London 1834). His legal role is gathered in *The Case of the Children of His Royal Highness the Duke of Sussex* (London 1832).

[12] Sir John Dillon, *Legal Arguments occasioned by the project of a Union between Great Britain and Ireland on the Exclusion of the Roman Catholic Nobility and Gentry in Both Kingdoms from Parliament* (London 1799). Also see Lord Petre v. Lord Auckland and Lord Gower, 14 May 1800; *English Law Reports*, Vol. 126, Common Pleas, pp. 1202–1207.

[13] For example Sir John Joseph Dillon, *The Claims of the Irish Catholics Considered as they regard the Institutions of Scotland, Civil and Religious in a Letter Occasioned by a motion lately made in the Presbytery of Glasgow* (Glasgow, 1813), pp. 6–7; and his *Further Considerations on the Articles of Union between Great Britain and Ireland in respect of the Parliamentary Oaths in a Third Letter to Charles Butler Esq.* (London 1828), pp. 12–57.

Oxford divines exercised over government posed serious dangers to the integrity of the British Empire.[14] Dillon therefore wanted catholic emancipation as almost an agreed measure: justice, national self-interest and religion demanded no less.

A considerable landowner, Dillon with his social status and wealth had a stake in the country.[15] To reassure protestant opinion, he portrayed catholicism as essentially British, a characteristic which would be strengthened by curbing foreign influences and episcopal excesses within the catholic community. That programme provided personal fulfilment for Dillon as an aristocratic lawyer to exercise his diplomatic and legal skills, to air his knowledge of church history, and to publish numerous pamphlets to create an educated public opinion. But such an enterprise would have to outmanoeuvre and defeat the suspicious intransigance of Bishop Milner.

Milner, the London-born son of a Lancashire tailor, was a rather unattractive champion of catholic orthodoxy. Blunt of speech, harsh and even offensive in print, he was the vicar apostolic of the midland district of England as well as the agent of the Irish bishops.[16] An eager controversialist, he invariably saw doctrinal heresy and personal disloyalty to his church all around him. In particular he was anxious to crush any suspicion of democracy in the church, and in that he had already largely succeeded. Unfortunately, his methods were to sow dissension between the Scottish and English bishops as well as their Irish brethren. The catholic body was to be split into two warring camps for and against him. He was especially conscious of his pastoral office and status and sought to curb any lay initiatives. He was part of a larger socio-cultural clash within the catholic community. He proclaimed the plenipotential nature of papal power, which, contrary to catholic traditions, angered and embarrassed more informed, realistic, practical politicians, catholic and protestant.[17] For a quiet, judicious assessment of catholic faith and teaching would, it was believed, remove legitimate protestant fears, promote the understanding, if not the acceptance, of catholic doctrine, and so contribute to the early emancipation of catholics. In practical terms it meant reassuring protestant opinion by emphasising the patriotism of catholics, by challenging in print

[14] *The Claims of the Irish Catholics*, p. 11.

[15] Dillon owned lands in Worcester, Warwick, Wiltshire, East Anglia and, seemingly, Ireland. Betham, op. cit.

[16] Bernard Ward, *The Eve*, Vol. I, pp. 114–57 and vol. 2, pp. 23–154 gives a comprehensive account.

[17] See J. J. Dillon, *The Question as to the Admission of Catholics to Parliament Considered upon the principles of Existing Laws with supplemental observations on the Coronation Oath* (London, 1801), p. 32: also J. J. Dillon *Two Memoirs upon the Catholic Question with an essay upon the History and Effect of the Coronation Oath* (Bath, 1810) appendix pp. i–xxi. Also see C. Butler, *Historical Memoirs*, vol. 2, p. 116, vol. 3, p. 35.

the gross misrepresentations of catholic doctrines and their equally wild exaggerations by Bishop Milner.[18] It was, as Dillon stated, 'no article of catholic belief that the Pope is infallible: on the contrary, he is amenable to the general council of the church; and even in a general council of the church, catholics acknowledge no *infallibility* (except in matters strictly of religious *faith*) – not even in matters of church discipline.'[19] Like many other catholics of his time, Dillon, like Butler and Berington, limited papal authority to strictly religious matters, but even then he was prepared to see elements of positive doctrinal agreement with protestants.[20] He believed that traditionally, in patristic times, bishops had been elected by the faithful of the diocese, and held very limited views about the extent of episcopal power: 'I acknowledge NO POWER ON EARTH WHICH HAS A RIGHT TO CONTROL MY OPINIONS OR THE PUBLICATION OF THEM WITH RESPECT TO THE DISCIPLINE OF THE CATHOLIC CHURCH OR THE CONDUCT OF ITS MINISTERS IN MATTERS CONNECTED WITH THE MUNICIPAL LAW AND TEMPORAL POWER.'[21]

Similarly he argued on grounds of catholic tradition his own legal interest in the marriage of the duke of Sussex to Lady Augusta Murray, and the need to reassure protestants that the established church would not be threatened by catholic emancipation: catholics, like other dissenters, would still marry in the established church.[22] In marriage the sacrament was a mutual gift between the two partners, a process in which the clergy had little effective role. A catholic priest or a catholic church was not necessary, though desirable. Milner's demands for special catholic treatment in this regard were lacking a theological base, were part of a clerical resurgence and placed purely catholic marriages in jeopardy before the law of the land.[23] In these matters the aristocrat was sheltering behind the lay ideology of the church.

Widely read, particularly in Fleury, whose first English translator was to be John Henry Newman, Dillon's view coincided with those of the

---

[18] J. J. Dillon to Menzies of Pitfodels, 28 May 1813; Menzies of Pitfodels, GD 237; SRO.

[19] J. J. Dillon, *The Question as to the Admission of Catholics*, p. 32.

[20] Cf. Joseph Berington, *The History of the Decline and Fall of the Roman Catholic Religion in England* (London, 1813) especially pp. xviii–xxiii.

[21] *Two Memoirs*, appendix p. xxi.

[22] *Ibid.*, p. ii J. J. Dillon, *The Case of the Children . . . for a summary.* Dillon was deeply involved with the Prince of Wales. J. J. Dillon to Prince of Wales, 2 August 1808 (2498), 17 May 1809 (2565), 26 September 1809 (2609) in *The Correspondence of George Prince of Wales 1770–1812*, 8 vols. (London, 1963–69) vol. 6. Also see J. J. Dillon to Lord Liverpool, 20 September 1812, British Library, Add MS 38571, f. 192: J. J. Dillon to Lady Auckland, 19 September 1812; B.L. Add MS 38571, f. 196 and f. 211.

[23] J. J. Dillon, *Two Memoirs*, appendix, pp. ii–vi.

catholic universities consulted by Pitt's government.[24] They were part of that earlier English tradition, of that more recent cisalpinism which had flourished in the period 1787–1793, and personified in the Rev. Joseph Berington and Sir John Throckmorton.[25] In Ireland, they had much in common with Bishop Troy's view of limited papal temporal power. Protestants might be easily reassured. But that in itself almost proved to Milner the unsoundness of such views.

Adverse to partisanship in church and state, Dillon believed that cool reason and common sense would bring about catholic emancipation.[26] But he had failed to appreciate popular emotions. The 'No Popery' election of 1807 and the advent of Perceval drove him towards the Whigs, Grey and Grenville: Sir John Throckmorton and other catholic aristocrats were to give generous donations to Whig funds. Though later prepared to dally with Tory politicians, Lord Liverpool, Sidmouth, Wellington and Peel, Dillon clearly considered the Whigs more likely to grant concessions, to become a principled administration and to conciliate Ireland.[27] The 'moderates' were more likely to be in the ascendancy. Distrustful of the new clericalism which seemed to be growing in all denominations, Dillon sought to curb and to control its worst excesses by working with clerical 'moderates' of the old school; by using the traditional machinery of the catholic and presbyterian churches to ensure peaceful change; and by identifying the church with the laity, with all the people of God.[28] The recognition of deference to duly constituted authority and rank in their respective spheres would ensure orderly progress within a happy, harmonious community. With a sense of *noblesse oblige* and the acceptance of law, the poor could be given dignity and justice within the existing order.[29] Dillon's philosophy was consistent and comprehensive.

But Dillon was no mere intriguer. His social, political and family connections, allied to his legal and diplomatic knowledge, gave him entree

---

[24] Abbé Claude Fleury (1646–1725) author of the *Histoire Ecclésiastique* [originally published in 1691], 26 vols (Paris 1722–38). Significantly he was a lawyer before his ordination, and a Gallican sympathiser. J. H. Newman translated selections (Oxford, 1842–44). J. J. Dillon, *The Question*, p. 32.

[25] See Eamon A. Duffy, articles cited above and Gary Lee Nelson, *Charles Walmesley and English Episcopal Opposition to Cisalpinism 1782–87* (unpublished Ph.D., Tulane University, 1977).

[26] See J. J. Dillon to Grey, 21 February 1807; Grey Papers.

[27] Lord Liverpool to J. J. Dillon, n.d. 6, 9 May 1807, and 5 August 1809; B.L. Add MS 38320, ff. 6b, 7, 8; also J. J. Dillon to Liverpool, 20 September 1812; B.L. Add MS 38571, f. 192. J. J. Dillon to the Duke of Wellington, 18 April 1834; in *Wellington: Political Correspondence 1833–November 1834* eds. John Brooke and Julia Gandy (London 1975), pp. 506–7, and below.

[28] See for example J. J. Dillon, *The Claims*, pp. 11–17; and J. J. Dillon to Grey, 2 March 1813; Grey Papers.

[29] On this see below, p. 125.

into the highest councils in the land. His confidence in the power of reason and persuasion found expression in several pamphlets before he called the initial meeting of the Catholic Board. He constantly pressed for financial support of publications in support of catholic emancipation.[30] Other members of the board were less enthusiastic. Dillon therefore embarked on his own independent propaganda campaign. He offered himself independently to the Whig leadership as an intermediary, conciliator or negotiator with the Irish catholics. He acted independently in Scotland from 1810 to 1813. He was, in fact, an independent catholic Whig agent, though neither Whigs nor catholics gave any formal recognition to him.

The formation of the Catholic Board in the aftermath of the defeat of the Whig ministry of all the talents and the 'No Popery' election of 1807 was natural. Scottish interest in the board was apparent in the membership of the Vicars Apostolic, James Maxwell of Kirconnel and James Menzies of Pitfodels.[31] Dillon, whose father, William Mervyn, was also on the board, became a close friend of Menzies and an increasingly staunch admirer of Scotland. Known to the prince of Wales and the duke of Sussex, John Joseph Dillon was potentially a man of considerable clout. His association with royalty, his social position and his standing within the catholic community gave him entree into the inner circles of political power. He knew Charles James Fox, Grey, Grenville and later, Melbourne, on the Whig side, and Lord Liverpool, Windham, Sidmouth and later, Peel, on the Tory side.[32] In the aftermath of the 1813 failure, Dillon seems to have spent much time on the continent, in Paris and Rome, seeking to influence the papacy and publishing many pamphlets on the catholic question before his death in 1837. At the same time he was very active in pursuing the claims of the d'Estes, the duke of Sussex's children.[33] In both his religious and legal concerns, he found Scotland ever more attractive.

In some ways Dillon's campaign in Scotland was part of a larger campaign to outmanoeuvre, if not discredit, Bishop Milner. Nursing an intense dislike for Milner and the clerical-dominated church he represented, Dillon saw Scotland as a means of defeating that threat, securing his own social and political future and ensuring the continuance of

---

[30] For example, J. J. Dillon, *A Memoir Concerning the Political State of Malta* (London 1807); J. J. Dillon to Menzies, 3, 4, 5 February 1813; Menzies Papers.

[31] B. Ward, *The Eve*, vol. I, pp. 91–113, C. Butler, *Historical Memoirs*.

[32] Sir J. J. Dillon to Lord Melbourne, 21 December 1813; Melbourne Papers, Royal Archives Windsor.

[33] J. J. Dillon to Grey, 4 April 1821, 28 September 1832, 23 February 1834; J. J. Dillon to Menzies 27 July, 10 October 1814, reporting on two trips to Paris. Among the pamphlets are his *An Address to the Catholics of Ireland in Reply to that of Mr. O'Connell* (London 1822) and *Correspondence between E. Blount, Secretary of the British Catholic Association and Sir J. J. Dillon Knt. and Baron S.R.E. in Relation to a Work entitled Considerations on the Parliamentary Oaths* (Paris 1829).

the old British catholic tradition.[34] Politically, too, Scotland offered better potential for the Whigs if, as seemed likely, the Melville-Dundas dominance collapsed or was at least drastically recast.[35] With Scottish friends, happy personal experiences in the country and good relations with many presbyterian ministers, in a kirk still dominated by patrons resembling his ideal of British catholicism, Dillon found the prospect particularly attractive.

The reasons for Dillon's admiration for Scotland were personal, ideological and tactical. Within the catholic community, Dillon suspected that Bishop Milner was intriguing against Roman approval for his ideas. He therefore needed political success to contain that clerical threat. The three nations of Britain presented different problems to supporters of catholic emancipation. Ireland needed catholic emancipation as part of an attempt to pacify and stabilise the country. Unless that concession was granted to the movement's aristocratic leaders, more radical and more nationalist leadership would take over. The situation was already critical. Dillon's schemes could have only limited effect.

In Scotland the prospects were brighter. The repeal in England of the Test Acts would merely recognise the existing Scottish position: an established church able to accept the legal equality of dissenters without fear for her security.[36] There was also, Dillon believed, a political opportunity to be exploited.[37] The Melville-Dundas ascendancy seemed to be weakening. To Dillon, that interest would have to soften its views on catholic emancipation or give way to a revitalised Whig element in Scotland. In either case catholics could only gain. Similarly a demonstration of Scottish protestant liberality would dampen down the English extremism of the Protestant Union south of the border.

In England, aristocratic English catholicism presented little social or political threat. The protestant dissenting deputies, under the leadership of the unitarian, William Smith, M.P., could effectively check the intolerant wing of protestantism.[38] On the political front, the fluid nature of parliamentary alliances following the death of Perceval and the emerging liberal Toryism seemed to augur better times for catholics. If Scotland

---

[34] *Two Memoirs*, appendix.

[35] See Holden Furber, *Henry Dundas 1st Viscount Melville 1742–1814* (London, 1931), p. 286. Only 17 seats were certain in the government interest. Also see Cyril Mathieson, *The Life of Henry Dundas 1st Viscount Melville* (London 1933).

[36] [J. J. Dillon] *The Letters of Hiberno Anglicus* (London, 1811). Apparently largely written on a trip through the western isles in July.

[37] J. J. Dillon to Grey, 14 April 1812; stressing the tactical advantage to be derived from the absence of the Test Acts in Scotland, a theme fully developed in his *Letter to Canning* (London, 1812). Scotland and Ireland should enjoy equality with England within the kingdom.

[38] See my own M.A. dissertation on Smith (Manchester University, 1962) and Bernard Manning, *The Protestant Dissenting Deputies* (London, 1955).

remained at least neutral, politically and religiously, the catholic cause could only prosper. Scotland was therefore a vital factor in catholic calculations.

His admiration for Scotland reflected his social and political ideals. It was a case of like admiring like. Aristocratic control of patronage would naturally appeal to an Anglo-Irish catholic aristocrat with a tradition of patronising priests. With his low opinion of some catholic clergy, Dillon was impressed by the quality of Scottish clergy, and the loyalty of the faithful.[39] That offered a solution to the problem of an anglican establishment freed from its excessive legal supports and an antidote to the more militant clergy within the catholic community. For England seemed to be falling under the 'wrong' kind of Irish influences, as exemplified in the machinations of Milner, the Irish bishops' agent. The danger was that without or with his kind of catholic emancipation, the catholic body would fall under his ungentlemanly sway.[40] At the same time Dillon, with his close association with Grey and Grenville, seems to have been hoping for a revival of Whig fortunes in Scotland through support for the principle of catholic relief. Equally, the anglican divines of Oxford seemed to exercise too much influence far removed from everyday life: they, too, had to be curbed, in the national interest. Dillon, like his friends the Rev. Joseph Berington and Sir John Throckmorton, with their cisalpinism, were the catholic 'moderates'. Accommodation between such gentlemanly groups was relatively easy and painless. Dillon strove to avoid confrontation, to meet protestant fears and give some reassurances within the existing constitutional framework of church and state.[41] To his more belligerent co-religionists, like Milner, such compromise was equivalent to conformity.[42] Catholics and protestants of similar, less established, backgrounds, at the sharp end of competition and discrimination, were less able or willing to compromise. Newly inflamed with zeal they demanded total victory.

Religion, political considerations and personal interest combined to produce that admiration. Dillon, coached by Menzies of Pitfodels, found Scotland 'the most religious, moral, loyal and tolerant nation in Europe.'[43] The deep and simple faith of the Scottish presbyterian at communion

---

[39] 'Their religious respect for the last supper is equal to that of Catholics themselves and the meanest peasant of this country is so impressed with this that I have often found them introducing the subject when guiding me in the highlands on my way and reproach my country with a law which they consider "an impious abomination".' Also see *The Claims of the Irish Catholics*, pp. 12 and 28.

[40] *Two Memoirs*, appendix p. lx.

[41] *The Letters of Hiberno-Anglicus*, pp. 125–29 and *The Claims*, pp. 11–13.

[42] Dillon told Grey he should be in Ireland counteracting Milner's intrigues; Dillon to Grey, 25 January, 2 February 1811. Also *Two Memoirs*, pp. ii–ix.

[43] J. J. Dillon to Menzies, 27 October 1811; Menzies Papers, J. J. Dillon, *The Claims*, p. 4.

particularly impressed him. The ministers, with a few notable exceptions, were open, tolerant Christians: 'They are not the magistrates of the state but the ministers of the Almighty. Their support is in the sacredness of their office, in the morality of their habits, in the love and veneration of their flocks, in the sincere, honest, disinterested, free and conscientious attachment of their people, to the national religion of Scotland.'[44] The kirk, unlike the established churches of England and Ireland, did not fear the end of persecuting laws 'of which she both disdains the aid, and considers the absence, not merely as consistent with, but even as contributing to her security.'[45] The kirk and its members had to rely on their own example, labours and influence. Unlike England, Scotland was marked by calm, sober reflection. England was too easily disturbed by artificially created alarms and 'incendiary' machinations which were liable to destroy the very bonds of society.[46]

In Scotland, the principle of complete toleration, according to Dillon, was well established: episcopalians and catholics for over a hundred years had allegedly enjoyed freedom from government or parliamentary interference in the nomination of clergy, differing from the established church. Conviction and commitment were far more effective guarantees than any legal enactments for the security of the established church. Scotland could be a model for Great Britain.

In Ireland, Dillon saw the traditional aristocratic leadership of Lord Fingall being eroded.[47] It was being threatened by the more popular catholic movement of O'Connell and by the unconstitutional acts of government agents preventing respectable assemblies from airing grievances. In particular, Lord Fingall was arrested and a meeting dispersed, much to Dillon's dismay, in 1811.[48] Further, the more militant posture adopted by the Irish bishops from 1808 was a serious barrier to the peaceful passage of a measure of catholic relief. The agent of the Irish bishops in England, Bishop Milner, had antagonised the Whigs by his apparent deception of Ponsonby in 1808, as he was to in 1812–1813, and even later.[49] The room for moderates seemed to be diminishing at a rapid pace. Scotland seemed a more intellectual, tolerant and politically more manageable society. There, unlike the rest of Britain, the urbanity and tolerance of the Enlightenment still seemed to be in evidence.

[44] Ibid., pp. 6–7.

[45] Ibid., p. 5.

[46] Ibid., pp. 3–4.

[47] M. Roberts, The Whig Party, p. 101 and B. Ward, The Eve, Vol. I, pp. 127–57.

[48] J. J. Dillon, A Letter on the Apprehension of the Earl of Fingall with an account of the Dispersion of the Catholic Committee and of the proceeding at the aggregate meeting of the Catholics of Ireland on the 26th December 1811 (London, 1812); J. J. Dillon to Grey, 29 December 1811; Grey Papers.

[49] On this see M. Roberts, The Whig Party, pp. 58–102 and B. Ward, The Eve, vol. I, pp. 99–113.

Those fears seemed realised in popular religion and popular politics. Dillon feared the mob. He had vivid memories of the Gordon riots as a child, the example of the French Revolution, and his name had been placarded around London by radicals anxious to attack royal immorality.[50] He was appalled by Irish lawlessness. 'Three months ago an obsequious Catholic was shot by a *party of Catholics in the chapel* after Mass in the presence of 1,200 persons, *not one of whom* would interfere and give evidence against the offenders.[51] In West Meath, *the most complete organisation* is established of the most *desperate villainy*. All rogues now act in combination.'[52] Even the clergy connived at these outrages: 'the priest must wink at it or starve.' The Irish clergy were particularly baleful: 'There does not exist a body which requires more reform.'[53]

Dillon was appalled by the political activities of the Irish clergy:

> In fact most of the mischief has been by the Irish *clergy* who are exciting throughout Ireland a *religious* war. A body requiring more regulation and reform than the Catholic clergy of Ireland hardly exists. They have but one virtue and that they certainly possess, that of chastity. I wish they had that of temperance and still more, less *cupidity*. They are destroying the Catholic religion by their *rapacity*. In 1806, they put up the Threshers and now they have put up the country of West Meath which I left in a state little short of rebellion. The exactions of the priests are the principal grievance of which the people now complain.[54]

Dillon grew increasingly disenchanted with Ireland: 'No thing particular has occurred in the island of *madness* since I last wrote. Only the priest of Derry who created one of the scandalous riots which disgrace our cause whenever a Catholic meeting is held, has been convicted of exciting disorder. He was imprisoned only for a month. I should give him and many others like him at least six months.'[55] Enjoying a far higher standard of living than a presbyterian minister in Scotland, the priest pretends 'to exist solely on charity. These *dons gratuits* are the most unwarrantable exactions and the most flagrant usurpation of temporal authority.'[56] In

---

[50] S. Maccoby, *English Radicalism 1786–1832* (London 1955), pp. 215–71; Dillon was a relative of Fr. Dillon the pastor of Moorfields who died following the Gordon Riots.

[51] J. J. Dillon to Menzies, 14 October 1813; Menzies Papers.

[52] *Ibid.* The Irish, he claimed 'have not the steady courage of the Scotch nor the intrepidity of the English. I never saw a country in which amongst all classes there is so much general depravity.'

[53] Same to same, 10 February 1814; *ibid.*

[54] Same to same, 5 January 1814; also his letter to Menzies 17 October 1813; *ibid.*

[55] Same to same, 10 February 1814; *ibid.*

[56] Same to same, 5 January 1814; *ibid.*

short, the best thing for Ireland would be to commit all historical records to the flames, for history merely fans the flames of fanaticism.[57]

Whatever the validity of his complaints, Dillon was very concerned at the loss of aristocratic control over the priests and people. Dillon came from that secure and affluent class of men who, even in those days, did not reject the possibility of Christian reunion. He and Charles Butler could see many points of common ground between Christians. Partly on tactical grounds, partly from selfish career interest, and partly from eighteenth century views of enlightenment, they wished to tone down religious animosities: they had little sympathy with the catholicism of de Maistre or Bonald.[58] In a calmer atmosphere, a more rational consideration of catholic claims might be undertaken. Concessions would then be made willingly rather than under duress, such as the threat of rebellion in Ireland. English and, still more, Scottish catholics were fully aware of their minority position. Gentle persuasion and demonstrations of catholic patriotism would be more effective than the exuberant triumphalism of Bishop Milner and his kind, an attitude of mind, Dillon believed, 'confined to the periods of gothic barbarism.'[59] Scotland seemed a model for a British settlement. As Dillon said in 1812: 'Scotland exhibits the case of a church establishment preserved and cherished by the people and respected by those not of its communion, without any exclusive laws, without any other *guards* and *fences* than the piety and exemplary morals of its clergy – the free conscientious attachment of its members to its faith and doctrines.'[60] It was a model for a political solution and for a revived catholicism.

Dillon's admiration, then, was based on his personal ambition, his distaste for the changing character of Ireland, the clerical controversialism of Bishop Milner, his legal interest in the d'Este children, and political considerations, both Whig and catholic.[61] There was also a romantic tour of the western isles and a strong personal admiration: 'to take advantage of the stranger is something wholly inconsistent with Scottish character.'[62]

Dillon believed that he could play a useful role in British society as an intermediary in Ireland; though both Grey and Grenville formally refused,

---

[57] *Two Memoirs*, p. 54.

[58] For example see C. Butler, *Historical Memoirs*, Vol. 2, pp. 447–48; vol. 3, pp. 35–80; J. J. Dillon, *The Question*, p. 32.

[59] C. Butler, op. cit., vol. 2, p. 246; the 1810 petition speaks of catholics at Agincourt, Poitiers, Crecy and against the Spanish Armada. Also Arnold Pritchard, *Catholic Loyalism in Elizabethan England* (London 1979). J. J. Dillon, *A Letter to the Rt. Hon. George Canning M.P.* (London, 1812), p. 8.

[60] *Ibid.*, p. 14. Also see *The Claims*, pp. 3–16.

[61] J. J. Dillon to Grey, 10 May 1812; Grey Papers, 11 October 1809; *The Case of the Children of his R.H. the Duke of Sussex . . .*; J. J. Dillon to Menzies, 27 October 1811; Menzies Papers; M. Robers, *The Whig Party*, pp. 70–79.

[62] *Letters of Hiberno Anglicus*, pp. 125–7; J. J. Dillon to Menzies, 4 February 1813; Menzies Papers.

he still regularly corresponded with them.[63] He thought he might act in some capacity, perhaps abroad or even, given his interpretation of existing penal law, as a Scottish M.P. in the near future.[64] But these hopes invariably seemed to be thwarted, particularly by Bishop Milner.[65]

Dillon had been in close communication with Fox during the unsuccessful attempt to obtain some catholic relief.[66] He also had an interview with Grey and later corresponded with him regarding the application of the Test Act to catholics. In the process he evidently established good relations with Grey. Unfortunately, the Whigs had lost any credit with the Irish catholic democratic elements, whilst nationalist, anti-union sentiment was also running high. The Irish catholic aristocratic party was the Whigs' only hope. The Irish bishops, including Dillon's friends, Troy and Moylan, rejected any idea of a government veto on the appointment of bishops, particularly under Perceval's anti-catholic administration.[67] In 1808 Bishop Milner appeared to have given solemn encouragement to Ponsonby and the Whigs on the veto issue and then to have renegued. Ponsonby and the Whigs were outraged. Dillon and his kind, for whom the veto had certain attractions as an aristocratic ploy to control episcopal nominations, were furious with Milner. Sir John Throckmorton, a veteran of the Whig Friends of the People, a lavish financial supporter of the Whigs and author of a pamphlet which would have gone much further in accepting a royal veto, was hostile. Dillon berated Milner as completely untrustworthy.[68] The movement for catholic emancipation was emphasising the divergences between the 'clerical' and 'lay' catholics. It showed the internal battle within the catholic community.

The problem was to continue. Grenville, in his *Letter to Lord Fingall*, urged catholic acceptance of conditions which applied to virtually every country in Europe regarding the appointment of bishops (1810). Bishop Milner remained adamantly opposed to any such arrangement. The 1810 attempt to secure some catholic relief failed. Dillon again rushed into print. Showing scant regard for Milner, he was eager to reassure protestants (especially on the Royal Marriage Act). Since 1753 catholics had conformed by marrying in the anglican church. Milner now raised objections to this procedure. Dillon saw that as undermining protestant

[63] J. J. Dillon to Grey, 25 January 1811; and to Grey and Grenville, 2 February 1811; Grey Papers.

[64] Same to same, 26 February, 1 April, 2 September 1811; *ibid*; Dillon to Menzies, 5 February 1813; Menzies Papers.

[65] J. J. Dillon to Grey, 2 September 1811; 9 May, 4 June 1813; Grey Papers.

[66] J. J. Dillon to W. Windham, 3 February 1810; Windham Papers, B.L. Add MS 37889 f.1.

[67] J. J. Dillon to Grey, 2 September 1811, 4, 21 February, 3, 12, 16, 25 March 1812; Grey Papers: *An Essay on the Coronation Oath* (London 1807).

[68] J. J. Dillon, *Two Memoirs, passim*; and *The Letters of Hiberno-Anglicus*, pp. ix–xx.

trust in the security of the establishment, should concessions be made to catholics, and further alienating the religious groups: 'IN THE NAME OF RELIGION LET US OPEN THE DOORS OF RECONCILIATION AND NOT BE MOVED IN DEVISING PLANS FOR BUILDING NEW WALLS OF SEPARATION.'[69] Such an attitude was merely an attempt to impose clerical domination over the faithful:

> 'The Catholics of England would henceforward hold their honours and estates solely at the caprice of their clergy. I am unwilling to trust persons with powers which may be abused and upon the exercise of which it may not be easy to impose an effectual check. I am the last to impute improper motives to anyone; but I will say that if there existed an ambitious and intriguing churchman (and such have existed) grasping power in every form, burning with lust of control over every family, bigoted in an attachment to centuries of darkness which obscured during so long a period the brilliancy of Christianity and emulous of regaining the former aspirations of his order upon the civil right and liberties of Princes and of their subjects; if there existed such an individual, and he were a man versed in scholastic subtlety and in the arts of disputation, formed also by nature and superior ability to command an ascendancy over his co-operators in the ministry – he could not have devised an expedient better calculated to accomplish his views, than to suggest scruples in the minds of the laity and to order an alteration in the law of England in the article of marriage.'[70]

Theologically, as Dillon pointedly maintained, the sacrament was conferred by the two partners mutually; the priest did not confer the sacrament.[71]

Such ill-informed clergymen were a serious liability, according to Dillon. They suspended priests from all faculties without any form of trial, sometimes without even an accusation, and even to appeal against this action was considered an offence. Dillon was obviously referring to the case of Dr. O'Conor, author of *Columbanus ad Hibernos*, which had argued for an 'effectual veto' on the appointment of bishops. Milner had suspended him.[72]

Milner did not take opposition lightly. In his pamphlet *Instructions Addressed to the Catholics of the Midland Counties*, he vehemently denounced

---

[69] J. J. Dillon, *Two Memoirs*, appendix, p. ii, M. Roberts, *The Whig Party*, pp. 70–75.

[70] J. J. Dillon, *Two Memoirs*, appendix, p. ii.

[71] *Ibid.*, p. v.

[72] *Ibid.*, p. xiii et seq.: B. Ward, *The Eve*, vol. I, pp. 145–47.

Dillon as 'no Catholic, nor will any clergyman who knows him and knows his duty treat him as a Catholic.' Not only was Dillon described as 'ignorant' and 'degenerate', but called upon to prove himself a catholic.[73] Such attacks merely angered Dillon and confirmed his view that Milner was 'at the botton of the mischief which has ensued in Ireland.'[74] Dillon therefore sought to defend his position in a series of letters in the *Morning Chronicle* under the pen-names *Hiberno-Anglicus* and *Scotsman*.

Dillon felt himself free from such episcopal control and determined to act independently. Evidently aware that his 'party' were losing influence in Ireland as the Fingall group faded before the Catholic Association and Milner, and aware of the ascendancy of Milner in England, Dillon saw Scotland as a safe haven for himself and his schemes. Legally, he believed, the country offered more scope: in religion its catholic bishops were more likely to support his ideas, and politically the declining fortunes of the Dundas interest after 1807 gave the Whigs an opportunity. With the support of 'moderate' presbyterian ministers much could be done in Scotland: as he wrote to Grey, 'with a little management very important assistance might be obtained from this country in support of the Great Cause in which your lordship is so conspicuously engaged.'[75] Whether the Whigs really wanted office or not at the time is perhaps debatable, but at least Dillon's scheme might enable one of their principal measures to be pushed through against the administration. Either way the Whigs could only gain.

In January 1811, Dillon accompanied Lord Fingall to a Foxite dinner in Edinburgh.[76] General support for catholic claims was expressed. The *Edinburgh Review* and its contributors seemed very favourable to catholic relief. Impressed and detained by business, Dillon remained in Scotland. He cultivated the Whig interest in Scotland, particularly the marquis of Douglas. (Douglas, in contact with the European romantic revival, was well disposed to Italian art, and was related to William Beckford of Fonthill).[77] As Dillon became thoroughly acquainted with Scotland as a

---

[73] J. Milner (Wolverhampton 1811), p. 23 and appendix, pp. x–xiii. Also J. Milner, *Supplementary Memoirs of English Catholics* (London 1820), pp. 1–7, 137 n, 162–3, 168 and 196–99.

[74] J. J. Dillon to Grey, 20 June 1811, 2 September, 3 October 1811, 10 May 1812, 1 May 1813; J. J. Dillon, *Letter to Canning*, pp. 1–8.

[75] J. J. Dillon to Grey, 14 April 1812. Dillon seems to have been acting legally on behalf of the d'Este children and the Gordon family as well as indulging in political intrigue. See letters to Grey, 4 October 1807 and 11 October 1809.

[76] J. J. Dillon to Grey, 25 January 1811; Grey Papers. *The Edinburgh Review* (1810–12) had a series of favourable articles and book reviews on the catholic question.

[77] Lewis Melville, *The Life and Letters of William Beckford of Fonthill* (London 1910), pp. 285–8. The marquis of Douglas was his son-in-law.

tourist in the western isles, as a lawyer with Sir Ilay Campbell's great work and the Scottish church so he rhapsodised over all things Scottish:[78]

'In the first place there exists no *Test Act* in Scotland. All persons departing from the Established religion are allowed to hold civil offices and employments. Protestants, Episcopalians and Roman Catholics are upon the same footing, with the exception that to be enrolled in the list of freeholders it is necessary to subscribe to the *formula*. This grievance is however trifling when it is considered how few landed proprietors in Scotland have the right of voting for members of parliament. In Scotland the Catholics are magistrates, convers and hold a variety of offices. The absence of a Test Act in such an important part of the British islands, would in *itself* afford an argument in the course of this discussion. But another advantage might be obtained from this circumstance. With *little* difficulty it would be possible to bring forward a petition from the whole of Scotland against a continuance of the English Test Act. If *properly* supported I could *myself* have accomplished this object and it was with me a principal inducement to remain in Scotland.'[79]

The Scottish respect for communion was equal to that of catholics. Indeed he pointed out that the General Assembly in 1792 had petitioned parliament on the Test Act against the Dundas interest. Scottish opinion was liberal; Scottish members of both houses of parliament would neutralise hostile groups. 'Your lordship will observe that Mr. Dundas was compelled to declare himself *favourable* to Catholic emancipation at his election for this city.'[80]

At the same time Dillon began to move against Bishop Milner. He secured evidence from Rome, presumably from Abbé MacPherson, of Milner's intrigues in Rome. Dillon told Grey that he believed Milner had shifted to opposing catholic emancipation about 1804–5. Milner, he claimed, had written to Rome to arouse suspicions against the proposed catholic relief. Catholic claims would have to be considered without reference to that untrustworthy cleric, and even Charles Butler and the Catholic Board were not totally reliable under clerical pressure (Fortescue). Scotland seemed to offer a via media between the fanaticism of the Irish catholics and the English protestants. It was a point of view Dillon amply illustrated in his *Hiberno-Anglicus* letters.[81]

---

[78] J. J. Dillon to Grey, 14 April 1812; Grey Papers. Also letter 26 February 1813. For Ilay Campbell (1734–1832), see *D.N.B.*

[79] J. J. Dillon to Grey, 14 April 1812; Grey Papers.

[80] *Ibid.* Also see G. M. Ditchfield, 'The Scottish Campaign Against the Test Act 1790–91', *Historical Journal*, Vol. 23, 1980, pp. 37–61.

[81] J. J. Dillon to Grey, 14 April 1812; Grey Papers; J. J. Dillon, *De Immunitate*,

Scotland, Dillon claimed, with judicious prompting from Menzies of Pitfodels, was vastly superior to England. Toleration had economic benefits. Agriculture, industry and education were flourishing: 'England, however considerable, is only a part and not the most flourishing part, of the British Empire. The people of Scotland and of Ireland have therefore surely a right to protest against any system of general policy, adopted solely with reference to English prejudices and with a view to local establishments with which the Empire has no concern; but especially against a system which was guided principally by attention to the limited notions of clerical residents of an English university.'[82] Secondly, Scotland should not interfere in Irish attempts to secure equal rights, especially in matters involving the 'PROSTITUTION AND PROFANATION OF SACRED THINGS.'[83] Such interference would contradict Scottish opposition to the Test and Corporation Acts in 1791. Again, Scotland should allow other statutes to retain their identity within Great Britain: unlike the Irish, 'they have not been handed over, as persons incapable of conducting the administration of their affairs, to English subalterns.'[84] As Dillon wrote later in 1828: 'We are prone indeed to consider everything in England supreme and all that pertains to Scotland and Ireland subordinate and dependent.'[85] Dillon therefore began to build up influence and support for the catholic claims in Scotland. Alternatively, he had hopes of forming some kind of common front with the Scottish presbyterians for an attack on the Test and Corporation Acts, from which Scots suffered disproportionately.[86]

In 1812, therefore, Dillon sought to assist the passage of Canning's motion in support of catholic claims. He wrote *A Letter to Canning* and attempted to convince Grey that at worst the Scottish M.P.s would remain neutral, though he was very concerned about Milner's intrigues at Rome.[87] He sought to convince the Scottish kirk that they had no part in the issue; that their position was comparable to that of the Rev. Joseph Berington:

p. 98. *Historical Manuscripts Commission; The Papers of J. B. Fortescue preserved at Dropmore*, Vol. X (London, 1927) for the Dillon Grenville correspondence. J. J. Dillon, *The Letters of Hiberno-Anglicus*.

[82] J. J. Dillon, *The Claims of Irish Catholics*, II: J. J. Dillon to Menzies, 27 October 1811; Menzies Papers.

[83] *The Claims*, p. 14.

[84] *Ibid.*, pp. 20–21.

[85] *Further Considerations on the Articles of Union between Great Britain and Ireland in respect of the Parliamentary Oaths in a third letter to Charles Butler* (London, 1828), p. 42.

[86] J. J. Dillon, *The Claims*, pp. 25, 28; and his *Cursory Suggestions for the Consideration of the Approaching Meeting of British Catholics in a Letter to Edward Jerningham* (Glasgow, 1813), p. 7.

[87] Glasgow 1812: J. J. Dillon to Grey, 10 May 1812; Grey Papers; sending a copy of a letter from Rome regarding Milner's intrigues.

'The first pastor in my eyes will be more venerable when the Christian virtues, Faith and Charity, shall be the sole supporter of his chair.'[88]

All calculations were suddenly reassessed with the assassination of the prime minister, Perceval, on 11 May 1812. Grey and Grenville were nominated to the cabinet but refused to join, and before Lord Liverpool took over on 8 June 1812, Canning's motion in favour of catholic claims passed the Commons, 235–106: a similar motion in the Lords on 1 July by the marquis of Wellesley failed 125–126. But for catholics relief seemed at hand and for the Whigs, political power. The next session would probably see the attainment of both objectives.

The opposition was not idle. The Protestant Union had been formed and moves initiated against the catholic claims.[89] In the Glasgow presbytery, Rev. Dr. Lapslie, long an opponent of radicalism and a government pensioner, moved for the consideration of a petition against catholic claims. Dillon moved smartly to fend off this threat. He declined attendance at the Catholic Board meeting in London in February because 'I am putting down a "No Popery" cry attempted to be raised in Glasgow.'[90] He wrote a full statement which was in the press, ready for release if necessary: 'It has been the most difficult composition on which I ever exercised my pen.'[91] He opposed any petition on the part of the Scottish catholics and urged Menzies to send him 50 copies of his *Letter to Canning* for the presbytery committee meeting on 3 February 1813. In addition Dillon printed a *Letter to Edward Jerningham*.[92] He was particularly distressed that his agitation for an informed press campaign upon the British public had been consistently ignored. Even in the last year great effect might have followed. As always he was acting by himself: 'in no town or city of England could a pamphlet on our side be found, whilst shops were filled with calumnies against us.'[93] In Glasgow, 'I cannot describe to you in terms sufficiently strong the profligacy with which it is attempted to excite in that town a religious cry.'[94] But throughout the election year of 1812, Dillon had been actively priming Grey with his views on Scottish conditions, strengthening his connections with the Scottish Whigs, the marquis of Douglas, Jeffrey and Cathcart, which found echoes in the *Edinburgh*

---

[88] Joseph Berington, *The History of the Decline and Fall of the Roman Catholic Religion in England* (London, 1813), p. xix note.

[89] J. J. Dillon to Menzies, 28 February 1813; Menzies Papers: *Glasgow Chronicle*, 10 February 1813. E. P. Lascelles, *Granville Sharp and the Freedom of the Slaves in England* (London 1928), overlooks Sharp's activities in the Protestant Union.

[90] Glasgow Presbytery Records; preserved at the Scottish Record Office, Edinburgh; 6 January, 3, 17 February 1813; J. J. Dillon to Menzies, 25 January 1813 (?); Menzies Papers.

[91] *Ibid.*

[92] Glasgow, 1813.

[93] *Letter to Edward Jerningham.*

[94] J. J. Dillon to Menzies, 2 February 1813; Menzies Papers.

Review, and through his sympathy with the Glasgow weavers, establishing rapport with the solicitor-general for Scotland, Archibald Colquhoun and Lord Sidmouth in London.[95]

Dillon evidently was seeking out presbyterian support. With the blessing of Bishop Cameron, he published his pamphlet, *The Claims of the Irish Catholics*, and determined to prevent any Scottish catholic petition, he published his *Cursory Suggestions for the Consideration of an Approaching Meeting of British Catholics in a Letter to Edward Jerningham*.[96] However, on the day after the Glasgow presbytery debate, Dillon was more relaxed. He had attended the meeting with some 500 others. 'After the most learned, grave and eloquent debate which I ever heard on the Catholic Question', he was convinced that the majority within and without the gathering were favourably disposed in principle to catholic claims: 'the most eminent and distinguished members spoke successively against the motion of Mr. Lapslie.'[97] Reassured, he believed the Glasgow example was 'the most *important* in Scotland.'[98] Its influence would be considerable. To that end Dillon published full accounts of the proceedings in the *Glasgow Chronicle* under the name *Laicus*, and then as a pamphlet, which was widely distributed.[99] Some 400 went to the presbytery of Perth and Stirling. But he urgently needed more books and material with accurate statements of the catholic system, as his four hours discussion with Glasgow university divines showed that morning.

In public and private he was convinced of the liberality of the church of Scotland. The best speeches he had ever heard on behalf of catholics were those of the Glasgow presbytery divines: 'If any Catholic were present at the debate, I am convinced he must have been satisfied with the tone and temper of liberality which was displayed.'[100] Again, 'it is impossible for me to do justice to their personal kindness towards myself, and if I had favourable ideas of their body and of Scotch liberality before, they have been confirmed by what I have witnessed.'[101] Encouraged only by a letter

---

[95] J. J. Dillon to Grey, 28 January 1813; Grey Papers. *Edinburgh Review*, vol. 15, pp. 504–21; vol. 17, pp. 1–39; vol. 20, pp. 54–58; vol. 21, pp. 93–102. J. J. Dillon to Lord Sidmouth, 12 May, 10 November 18, 20, 31 December 1812; Scottish Record Office, RH 2/4 vol. 99, ff. 598–605, 608–9, 642–5. A. Colquhoun to Sidmouth, 22 November, 12, 17, 24 December 1812; Sidmouth to Dillon, 28 December 1812; *ibid*, ff. 525, 584–5, 595–6, 625, 636, 640–1.

[96] J. J. Dillon to Menzies, 2, 5, 12 February 1813; Menzies Papers.

[97] Same to same, 4 February 1813; *ibid*.

[98] *Ibid.*; *Glasgow Chronicle*, 20 February 1813; J. J. Dillon to Grey, 21 February 1813; Grey Papers; identifying himself as *Laicus*.

[99] J. J. Dillon to Menzies, 4, 20, 23 February 1813; Menzies Papers. *The Glasgow Courier*, 23 February 1813, carried complaints about reports of the Glasgow meeting.

[100] *Glasgow Courier*, 20 February 1813; report by *Laicus*.

[101] J. J. Dillon to Menzies, 4 February 1813; Menzies Papers.

from the duke of Sussex and one from Menzies, Dillon went to great pains to ensure that accurate reporting of the meeting paid handsome tribute to that liberality.

Even so, a petition hostile to catholic claims from Merse and Teviotdale presbytery passed and was presented to parliament.[102] Similarly one from Edinburgh was presented, though not before Dillon had exercised some influence over that presbytery.[103] To forestall the impact of these reverses, Dillon was keeping the Whig leadership fully informed.[104] He sent full details of the church of Scotland move against the Test Act, reported his discussion of the existing legal 'liberation' of catholics in Scotland with Jeffrey, Clark and Cathcart, and warned Lord Holland that legally only individuals rather than corporate bodies like churches could petition parliament. In some three weeks Dillon had travelled 800 miles in his diplomacy. The Edinburgh presbytery meeting gave Dillon further opportunities to stifle hostility to catholic claims. The proposal to introduce a petition against the catholic claims was first raised on 24 February, postponed and then debated on 1 March. The moderator communicated papers put into his hands 'in the name of certain Roman Catholics' but was refused a hearing.[105] Sir Henry Moncrieff, Mr. Andrew Thomson, Dr. Fleming, David Dickson and Dr. Campbell opposed Dr. Ritchie's motion. At a later meeting the dissentients, in an unprecedented step, demanded that the reasons for their dissent be fully recorded.[106] The *Glasgow Chronicle*, possibly through Dillon, gave a comprehensive account of the proceedings, in which Moncrieff deployed many arguments drawn from Dillon's works.[107] But the proposal to petition against catholic claims was carried 22–9.

Grey and the Whigs were warned in advance of these developments: scheming ecclesiastics were turning assemblies into political meetings. Never before, even in 1779, had the kirk dreamed of petitioning parliament. A presbytery, according to Dillon, could not petition parliament. A petition had to come through the General Assembly, otherwise 'Every fanatic, every visionary theorist may excite the kingdom of Scotland.'[108]

---

[102] *Glasgow Chronicle*, 6 March 1813: *Parliamentary Debates*.

[103] J. J. Dillon to Menzies, 23 February 1813: Records of the Presbytery of Edinburgh; Scottish Record Office CH2 121 20B, vol. 18, ff. 76, 77; 24 February, 1 March 1813.

[104] J. J. Dillon to Grey, 26 February–March 1813; and to Holland 26 February; Grey Papers.

[105] Edinburgh Presbytery Records, 24 February, 1 March 1813.

[106] *Ibid.*; 31 March 1813.

[107] *Ibid.*; *Glasgow Chronicle*, 6 March 1813.

[108] J. J. Dillon to Lord Holland, n.d. 1813; Grey Papers: also see G. M. Ditchfield, art. cit., and Eugene C. Black, *The Association: British Extra Parliamentary Political Organisation 1764–1793* (Cambridge Mass., 1963), pp. 131–73.

The synod of Merse and Teviotdale, which had already petitioned parliament against catholic claims, made an overture to the General Assembly to do the same.[109] Dillon therefore decided to remain in Scotland to keep lines of communication open with the Whigs in parliament. Late in April he reported that Glasgow and Ayr synods had voted against the catholic claims. But of 130 members, only 26 attended and the majority was only two against.[110] He was anxious about the forthcoming General Assembly, and republished his *Letter to Canning* with an appendix on the church of Scotland. While recommending Bishop Cameron to Grey, he claimed to have put Dr. Milner in 'a *straight waistcoat*'.[111] On the presbyterian side, Dillon was carefully watching the intrigues of the court party in the General Assembly, which he sought to counteract with the earl of Lauderdale.[112]

At the same time he was anxious to follow parliamentary developments. He expressed some support for Canning's amendment which would place some safeguards upon the appointment of catholic bishops in Britain, urging Grey that his letter should be placed before Ponsonby and Grattan before the second reading of the catholic bill (13 May).[113] His ideas, he claimed, were connected 'with the question of restoring to laymen their civil rights', which meant restraint upon episcopal authority.[114] He was equally anxious that the Fingall party in Ireland should forestall 'any injudicious proceedings' on the part of O'Connell and his supporters.[115] That was particularly important because the General Assembly would then avoid a 'No Popery' outcry. Such views might be supported by the Melrose interest in the General Assembly, but probably the Dundas group would oppose them.[116]

Dillon's concern for the General Assembly was timely. In the debate upon the catholic question, the solicitor-general, Archibald Colquhoun, speaking largely from Dillon's notes, made an excellent impression. Dillon himself was present in 'the assembly with his grace the commissioner, directing the proceedings of my friends.' When Dr. Ritchie, professor of Divinity in Edinburgh university, moved a hostile petition against catholics, the solicitor-general opposed in 'a brilliant, forceful and eloquent address.'[117] Supported by Principal Hill of St. Andrews, Dr. Lockhart, who

---

[109] Records of the Merse and Teviotdale Presbytery, SRO; 28 April 1813.

[110] J. J. Dillon to Grey, 7, 23 April 1813; Grey Papers.

[111] Same to same, 1 May 1813; *ibid.*

[112] *Ibid.*

[113] Same to same, 7 April, 1, 4 May 1813; *ibid.*

[114] Same to same, 1 May 1813; *ibid.*

[115] Same to same, 25 May 1813; *ibid.*

[116] Same to same, 28 May 1813; *ibid.*

[117] *Ibid.* Dillon was present in the assembly thoughout. See his letters to Grey, 25 May 1813 (two sent): Dillon to Menzies, 20 May 1813; Menzies Papers; where he claims to have defeated an anti-catholic petition and secured acceptance of the more

claimed 'The Catholic clergyman was a liberal enlightened Christian pastor and his flock were loyal and dutiful subjects', with messrs. Macdougal and Irvine, the solicitor-general forced the withdrawal of the petition.[118] A resolution favourably disposed to the catholic claims was substituted and submitted to parliament. It was something of a triumph for Dillon.

Unfortunately his rejoicing was shortlived. For at almost the same moment, Dillon's *bête noir*, Bishop Milner, had issued his *Brief Memorial* to members of parliament, strongly attacking the proposed legislation.[119] The first clause to be submitted to the Commons on allowing catholics to sit in parliament was defeated by a mere four votes. Ponsonby, to Canning's regret, lost patience and abandoned the bill. A glorious opportunity had been missed.

Shortly afterwards at a meeting of the Friends of Religious Liberty, chaired by the duke of Sussex, Lord Fingall warmly praised the liberality of the church of Scotland as embodied in its petition to parliament.[120] Dillon might continue to press his case with the Whigs and through Abbé Paul MacPherson in Rome, but in vain. He might help secure the Quarantotti rescript with which the vicars apostolic, apart from Milner, might agree. They might be prepared to concede similar conditions on the appointment of bishops, as in other European states. With the French captivity of the pope, that seemed eminently reasonable in Britain. But it was hopeless. Sir John Coxe Hippisley might hold a massive inquiry on the position of catholics and their bishops in other European countries in vain. Dillon might further intrigue with Cardinal Consalvi and seem to be involved in Plunkett's catholic bill of 1821, which was largely a re-run of the 1813 bill.[121] But again, thanks to Milner, it was defeated. The possibility of

favourable motion. See *Acts of the General Assembly of the Church of Scotland* (1813), pp. 933–34 and *Parliamentary Debates*, 1 June 1813, p. 486.

[118] Dillon seems to have written *A Report on the Discussion and Proceedings which recently took place in the General Assembly of the Church of Scotland Respecting the Catholic Claims* (Edinburgh 1813). J. J. Dillon to Menzies, 17 May; and his father Mervyn to Menzies, 1, 8 June 1813; Menzies Papers. The Appendix to the *Report* carries a synopsis of Dillon's *The Claims of the Irish Catholics*. A different version of the assembly emerges from George Cook, *Life of Principal Hill* (Edinburgh, 1820), pp. 276–7, 302–6.

[119] John Milner, *A Brief Memorial* (London 1813). J. J. Dillon to Grey, 28 May, 4 June 1813; Grey Papers. J. J. Dillon to Menzies, 1 June 1813; Menzies Papers. *Parliamentary Debates*, 25, pp. 1107–1115 (30 April): 26, pp. 1–49 (11 May), 110, 245–9, (19 May), 270–95 (20 May), 312–65 (24 May). B. Ward *The Eve*, pp. 42–74.

[120] *Glasgow Courier*, 17 June 1813. J. J. Dillon to Menzies, 8 June 1813; Menzies Papers. J. J. Dillon, *Cursory Suggestions*, pp. 16–19.

[121] B. Ward, *The Eve*, vol. 2, pp. 71–154 and vol. 3, pp. 57–93. J. J. Dillon to Grey, 4 April 1821; Grey Papers. Dillon claimed that had a certain cardinal lived catholic emancipation would have come then if not earlier. *De Immunitate Qua Gaudent*, pp. 117–118.

agreed change and the end of triumphalism was checked.

Dillon's ideal of Scotland as a model for the development of religious liberty and catholic emancipation was illusory. New political forces were forming; urban, democratic and severely nationalist. New intransigent religious attitudes were hardening, in which triumph and defeat were the only choices: true toleration, the possible exchange and understanding between Christian denominations, were halted. A new clerical-dominated church, more Roman than Rome, with a mass, quiescent flock, was replacing the older lay-dominated, underground form of catholicism. Dillon had fought the good fight for that cause, and narrowly but decidedly failed. O'Connell was the victor.

SECTION III: SPIRITUALITY

THE IRISH MISSION OF THE SEVENTH CENTURY; HISTORICAL FACT OR HISTORIOGRAPHICAL FICTION?

Knut Schäferdiek

In Ireland Christianity had been firmly established during the fifth century, even while at the same time in other parts of Europe it was losing ground which it had already held in late Roman times. Most of it could not be regained before the seventh century, but then its recovery also marked the beginning of a new period of expansion in the history of western Christianity. Meanwhile the Irish church, which in the sixth century as a result of Irish immigration also extended to Caledonia, had developed its particular features such as its fervent monastic spirituality, and it is to this spirituality of Irish monasticism that the seventh century revival of mission owed a very substantial part of its initial impulse. According to a view, however, apparently still quite common, to a large extent its agents too were Irish, recruited from the ranks of Irish monks on pilgrimage abroad.[1] Certainly it is generally admitted, that their ideal of *peregrinatio pro Christo* and ascetic *Heimatlosigkeit* neither emerged from missionary motives nor was aimed originally at mission. But it is taken for granted, that it was always disposed to develop vigorous missionary drive and thus the Irish pilgrims spontaneously devoted themselves to missionary work, as soon as they had become aware of the religious situation in a new pagan or semichristian environment. So they have often been looked upon as missionaries not of intention, but of vocation, gifted with particular charisma, intrepid and independent even in opposition to established secular or ecclesiastical authorities, giving the initial phase of medieval missionary history much of its distinctive character. Medieval hagiography

---

[1] Cf. e.g. W. H. Marnell (for full titles of literature referred to in abbreviated forms see the bibliography at the end of the article); as to the problem of estimating early medieval Irish influence on the continent in general, see Duft.

has certainly contributed a great deal to this view, arbitrarily using the statement of a saint's Irish origin as a hagiographical topos, and the concept also has certainly undergone corrections by modern historical criticism and is obviously far from being accepted without qualification by specialist historians. Nevertheless, it seems to enjoy lasting popularity, and that may well justify taking a closer look at it.

As early as 1912 Wilhelm Levison in his still important essay 'Die Ihren und die frankische Kirche' pointed out, that it is not possible exactly to define the part taken by the Irish in the conversion of the so-called German tribes.[2] He apparently regarded this as a problem arising from a lack of information and reliable sources. But possibly it is also or even in the first place a question of the subject itself. It may be interesting in this connection to take note of the linguistic discussion held on the matter. The idea of an outstanding part played by Irish missionaries amongst German speaking tribes caused philologists to speculate about eventual Irish influence on the ecclesiastical and spiritual terminology of Old High German. They did not succeed, however in furnishing a convincing proof of any Irish influence at all.[3] On the contrary, it appears that at least to a certain extent terminological traces of the bonifation Anglo-Saxon mission can probably be shown.[4] Negative results, of course, may well be indicative, too, and it seems quite possible that linguists were bound to fail in looking for clear traces of Irish Christian influence in Old German, because they based their work on an unfounded supposition, suggested to them by church historians.

In an uncritical but not at all uncommon manner problems of this kind are disguised by a simple identification of the presence of Irish monks on the one hand and Irish mission on the other. A more cautious way, however, is to cite recorded instances of actual Irish missionary activity as examples of Irish mission in general. But even this does not seem to be a satisfactory way either, though we have to keep in mind, that any picture to be derived from fragmentary sources will inevitably be fragmentary itself. The scarcity of instances, which can actually be cited, necessarily raises the question, what is their evidence really worth? Are they to be considered typical examples or rather untypical exceptions?

To form at least a rough idea not only of the direct part taken by Irish

[2] W. Levison, *Frühzeit*, p. 260 resp. *Mönchtum*, p. 107: 'Im einzelnen sind wir freilich nur ungenügend unterrichtet und wissen wenig mehr als ein paar Namen und die blosse Tatsache einer solchen Wirksamkeit von Iren, und der Anteil, der ihnen an der Bekehrung der deutschen Stämme zukommt, lässt sich doch nicht gerauer bestimmen.'

[3] I. Reiffenstein; cf. also J. Weisweiler/W. Betz, pp. 92–94; as to 'Glocke', which was supposed to be a certain trace of Irish influence cf. Harri Meier 'La cloche, die Glocke': *Neue Beiträge zur römanischen Etymologie*, hg. V. H. Meier, (Heidelberg, 1975), pp. 283–295.

[4] Cf. Weisweiler/Betz, pp. 90–92.

agents in seventh century Frankish mission, but also of the role missionary work generally did play within the sphere of contemporary Irish pilgrimage abroad, it is necessary to put those instances of Irish missionary activity really known to us into a broader context. They must be seen against the background of what we know of Irish presence and activity in the Frankish empire of the time. The period envisaged can be defined in terms of Irish pilgrimage as the time between the Burgundian monastic foundations of Columban in the late sixth century and the establishment of an Irish monastery at Honau, then an island in the Rhine near Strasburg, by the Alsatian ducal family of the Ettichons early in the eighth century. In terms of Frankish mission it is a period which brought to a close the formal Christianization of most of the remaining pagan parts of the empire except for some boundary regions of the north and north east.

The number of Irish monasteries founded in the Frankish empire during this period is relatively small. The first of them, Columban's monasteries in the Vosges, established successively in 591 and the following years, were to play a particular role, and require particular consideration. Honau on the contrary came into existence too late to be regarded here, for the time of its foundation no longer fell into the period of mission but into the subsequent one of ecclesiastical consolidation.[5]

About half a century after Columban's arrival in Burgundy, another famous Irish monk Fursey (Fursa), who previously had been engaged in missionary work in East Anglia, was granted opportunity by the Neustrian mayor of the palace Erchinoald (641–658) to settle with his companions at Lagny on the Marne about 18 miles east of Paris. Its importance, however, was soon thrown into the shade of Péronne on the Somme between St. Quentin and Amiens, established by Fursey's brother Foillan and a group of Irish monks at the place of Fursey's grave about 650. Its foundation too has been made possible by Erchinoald, but he is said to have expelled Foillan and some of the brethren from Péronne shortly after for reasons unknown to us. Nevertheless the further existence of the community does not seem to have been seriously affected by this event. Even Ultán, another brother of Fursey and apparently one of the expellees, could enter upon the office of the abbot at a later date. As *Peronna Scottorum* Péronne maintained its Irish character for a long time.[6] After their expulsion Foillan and his companions knew how to make use of political rivalries within the Frankish empire. They appealed to Itta, the widow of the Austrasian mayor of the palace Pippin the Older (623–640), and her daughter Gertrude, who had founded the monastery of Nivelles about 18 miles south of Brussels some time before. Now the Irish pilgrims, this time being homeless against their will, were given their support and granted the domain of Fosses some 22 miles south-east of Nivelles on a tributary of the

---

[5] For Honau see F. Prinz, p. 225.
[6] For Lagny and Péronne see Prinz, pp. 128 seq.

Sambre to establish another monastery. It could still be called a monastery of the Irish by Einhard as late as 830.[7]

Bishop Burgundofaro of Meaux, who held office during the second third of the seventh century and was deeply influenced by the Columbanian spirituality of Luxeuil, is said to have supported two Irish hermits. One of them was Fiachra, who established his cell within a short distance south-east of the episcopal town itself at the place of the present St. Fiacre. The other one was Killian, whom the bishop sent to the Artois, where he had his cell at Aubigny about 15 miles to the north-west of Arras.[8] A group of Irish pilgrims led by a bishop Romanus (Ronanus?) finally was given opportunity by Ansoald, bishop of Poitiers during the last quarter of the seventh century, to restore a decayed cell at Mazerolles, some 21 miles south-east of Poitiers.[9] Lure, a short distance south-east of Luxeuil, should not be included here. Being a filiation of Luxeuil it also shares its peculiar character, and thus was not an Irish monastery in a proper sense in spite of the fact that its founder Deicola, who by hagiographical imagination became a brother of Columban, may perhaps have been Irish (Dicuill).[10]

Three of the six Irish communities just mentioned had established themselves in the Christian hinterland of the Frankish empire. Fosses was situated at the edge of a vast forest region, which for the most part was yet to be opened up for settlement by colonization. Péronne had its place at the border of the proper mission area of northern Gaul, but it had been chosen because it was the place of Fursey's grave. So Aubigny is the only one on the mission field and also the only one which is mentioned by the sources within a missionary context. According to the Life of Burgundofaro, written in 869, but referring to an older life of Killian, Killian won the Artois for Christianity.[11] If this is true or partly true, the bishop of Meaux apparently had intended a missionary effort, when he sent Killian to the region. The double monastery of Nivelles was not an Irish establishment, but Gertrude, being the first abbess, intentionally had also enlisted monks from Ireland, because she wanted them to teach her community the scriptures. Thus they had been recruited for the spiritual benefit of the community itself and not for public preaching.[12]

There is no reason to ascribe particular missionary activity to the Irish man Fichori and his companion Chaidoc, generally considered a Briton,

[7] For Fosses see Prinz, p. 186.
[8] Cf. Prinz, p. 126.
[9] Cf. Prinz, p. 294.
[10] Cf. Prinz, p. 282.
[11] *Vita Faronis 100* (*MGH. Script. rer. Mer.* V., pp. 194, 9–12).
[12] For Nivelles see Prinz, p. 185s; cf. *Vita Gertrudis A2* (*MGH, Script. rer. Mer.* II, pp. 457, 2–9): '... de transmarinis regionibus gignaros homines ad docendum divini legis carmina, sibi et suis meditandum, Deo inspirante, meruisset habere'.

who are said to have converted to monastic life Richar, the founder of Centula/St. Riquier in the diocese of Amiens, at a date before 645.[13] The same is true of the wandering bishop Failbe, who is said to have been instrumental in the conversion of Sigiram, cupbearer of Clovis II and founder of the monasteries of Meobecque and Logoretum/St. Cyran in the region of Bourges, to monasticism at approximately the same time.[14] A particular reputation as Irish missionaries, however, has been attributed to Kilian of Würzeburg and his companions. They are regarded by hagiographical tradition as martyrs to the faith, because they met a violent death in a conflict with local secular power. This happened in the late seventh century, 688/9 being the date usually assumed, though not verifiable. That the Franconian region on the Main should still have been a quite pagan area and should even have had a heathen duke at this time, as the author of the *Passio Kiliani* of the late eighth of the ninth century wants to make us believe, seems to be very unlikely. Early in the eighth century the region was already serving as a base to the Thuringian mission. Kilian's reputation of being the 'Apostle of Franconia' is to be considered an effect of his veneration as a martyr, deliberately propagated by the church of Würzburg after the middle of the eighth century. We cannot even be sure, that he actually pursued any missionary work at all. In addition, his activity, whatever it may have looked like, can hardly have been of any considerable influence, for it was only the longing for spiritual self-assertion of the new Frankish bishopric on the Main, established by Boniface in 741, which kept Kilian's memory from being forgotten.[15]

At least we find ourselves on firm ground, when we turn to the missionary activity exercised by Columban in Alemannia on the eastern edge of the Lake Constance in 611/612, in a region of overlapping religious practices, Christian and pagan.[16] But he hardly stayed on the field for more than one and a half years, his achievement thus being just an episode, brought about only as a result of Columban's expulsion from Luxeuil. His disciple Gallus, it is true, remained in the country, when his master was forced to cross the Alps to the Lombard kingdom. He did not, however, continue the master's missionary work, but retired as a hermit into the seclusion of the Steinach valley to the place, which in the eighth century was to become the famous monastery of St. Gall. Columban himself has clearly described, what his pilgrimage was looking for on earth. Its destination was the *locus deserti*, a place in the wilderness which he had

---

[13] *Vita Richarii primigenia 2s.* (*MGH, Script. rer. Mer.* VII, pp. 445, 2–446, 1); cf. also Prinz, p. 128.

[14] *Vita Sigiramni 9* (*MGH, Script. rer. Mer.* IV, p. 611, 15–23); cf. also Prinz, p. 136.

[15] For Kilian see Dienemann.

[16] For Columban and his missionary activity see Knut Schäferdiek, 'Columbans Wirken im Frankenreich', in: *Die Iren und Europa*.

sought coming from overseas for the sake of the Lord.[17] It was a place of seclusion from the world, but it was also the place of a monastic settlement and therefore a necessity for a community of monks, who were to provide for their maintenance by cultivating the soil with their own hands. Thus the place of seclusion was not only a spiritual aim, but also an economic requirement, and it is important to be aware of the latter aspect. To take possession of the place, which they needed for their worldly as well as for their spiritual life, the pilgrims were dependent on the support of the mighty ones of this world, their freedom of movement and their independence thus being restricted. Columban had looked for such a place of seclusion as a condition of realising his ideal of spiritual life, and there is no evidence that he ever considered it a base for further evangelistic or missionary activity. Only after he had been forced to leave Luxeuil, his place of seclusion, did it occur to him to go to the heathen and have the gospel preached to them.[18] But when he wrote about this plan to the brethren left behind at Luxeuil, he had already given it up again, because he had been warned of the tepidity of the pagans.

Evidently, however, the question was not yet settled for him. After he had succeeded in escaping forced embarkation for Ireland, he is said by his hagiographer Jonas of Bobbio to have resolved to go to Italy;[19] but this may well be an idea of Jonas himself, derived from a particular Bobbian view. In fact Columban entered into negotiations at the Austrasian court, and as a result he agreed to pursue missionary work in the south eastern border district of Austrasia at least for a time.[20] To this end he settled with a group of monks at Bregenz, a semi-ruined former Roman camp, but one which was still inhabited, not indeed by Alemanni but by an indigenous subroman population. This evidently was not a place of seclusion, but had been deliberately chosen as a base for public activity.[21]

We are told even more. According to Jonas sometime during his stay at Bregenz Columban thought for a moment of shifting his field of action, intending to preach to Slavonic tribes.[22] If he had realised this intention, it would have taken him far beyond the sphere of Frankish power into the eastern parts of the Alpine region, well into a domain of unbroken paganism, while his field of work at Lake Constance had been for a long time politically subjected to Christian domination and was a borderland of Christian penetration. Even some of the Alemanni he met in the vicinity of

---

[17] *Columban*, Fp. II, 7; (ed. Walker, pp. 18, 25s): '. . . de loco deserto, quem pro domino meo Iesu Christo de trans mare expetivi . . .'

[18] *Columban*, Fp. IV, 5; (ed. Walker, p. 30, 10–12).

[19] *Ionas, Vita Columbani*, I, 25; (*MGH, Script. rer. Germ.* 37, p. 208, 5–8).

[20] *Ionas, Vita Columbani*, I, 27; (*MGH, Script. rer. Germ.* 37, p. 211, 8–21).

[21] *Ionas, Vita Columbani*, I, 27; (*MGH, Script. rer. Germ.* 37, p. 213, 8–21). *Walahfrid Strabo, Vita Galli*, I, 5; (*MGH, Script. rer. Mer.* IV, p. 288, 25–31) is mistaken in suggesting, that Bregenz, too, had been chosen as a place of solitude.

[22] *Ionas, Vita Columbani*, I, 27; (*MGH, Script. rer. Germ.* 37, pp. 216, 22–217, 10).

Bregenz, are said to have been already baptized without, however, abandoning heathen practices.[23] We do not know what were the considerations suggesting this plan, but there are at least two possible explanations. Columban may have developed a theory of mission of his own in opposition to the familiar political concept, which regarded care of mission as a duty of a Christian ruler and at the same time restricted missionary activity to the domain of his power and influence, thus making Christian religion also a symbol of political domination. Or he may already have been aware of the necessity to leave Austrasia, too, which actually arose from political reasons in 612, confronting him once again with the problem of defining his aims. In any case, however, it was only a momentary suggestion which was soon rejected. This time a vision is said to have decided the issue. If this narrative is based on reliable tradition, its story can be taken as a sign of an internal struggle called forth by the problem, whether to continue missionary work or not. It was solved by an overwheling experience, which allowed Columban's true desire to prevail, namely his longing for a contemplative way of life in the greatest possible seclusion from the world. As a result in preference to further missionary activity he resumed his pilgrimage for the sake of Christ, and once again it was to take him to a place of seclusion. Some 25 years later we will see his compatriot Fursey in a comparable manner retire from his East Anglian mission to live as a hermit.[24]

To a certain extent this kind of subliminal reluctance about missionary work may be explained by some words used by Jonas in a section of his life of Columban, which can be considered a sort of a programme.[25] When Columban had come to Gaul he had found *fides tantum*, only the faith, remaining of Christian religion, while it had appeared to him that there had been a nearly total lack of *paenitentiae medicamenta* and *amor mortificationis*, remedies of penitence and love of mortification. According to the formalistic concept of faith apparently underlying here, the words 'only the faith', at first sight somewhat surprising, must be taken to indicate the mere external conditions of Christianity. Remedies of penance and love of mortification, however, are the essentials of spiritual life, the essentials of Columban's proper message. On the other hand mere faith was exactly what medievel missionary practice was aiming at in the first instance, attempting to integrate its subjects into the institutional church as soon as possible by baptism subsequent to an external conversion, which usually could not be more than a declaration of formal consensus with the belief of

[23] *Ionas, Vita Columbani*, I, 27; (MGH, *Script. rer. Germ.* 37, pp. 213, 11–214/12).
[24] *Vita Fursei*, 8; (MGH, *Script. rer. Mer.* IV, pp. 437, 14–438, 7); cf. Beda, *Hist. eccl.* III, 19; (ed. Colgrave/Mynors, pp. 274–276).
[25] *Ionas, Vita Columbani*, I, 5; (MGH, *Script. rer. Germ.* 37, pp. 161, 3–162, 12 especially p. 161, 6–8): 'Fides tantum manebat christiana, nam penitentiae medicamenta et mortificationis amor vix vel paucis in ea repperiebatur locis'.

the church. Thus in a sense converting the heathen to Columban's view may well have meant preaching mere faith, something of preliminary value according to his own standards.

Columban certainly had not had the time for his preaching in Alemannia to achieve any lasting effects. To the west of his field of action, about 165 miles down the Rhine, lies Säckingen. Its monastery probably originated in a cell founded by Fridolin early in the seventh, or perhaps even in the sixth century.[26] His supposed Irish origin, however, is to be regarded as an arbitrary assertion by his tenth century hagiographer or his source.[27] What his part was in the Alemannian mission, if he took a part in it at all, is not known. There is a total lack of written sources on the Christianization of Alemannia. Nevertheless, it must have been accomplished during the seventh century. When Pirmin, the 'Apostle of the Alemanni', who certainly was not an Irishman, came to the Lake Constance and founded the famous monastery of Reichenau in 724, he did so as a reformer, but not for elementary mission. The sparse evidence we actually have, in any case does not give any reason to fill the gaps of our knowledge with supposed Celtic wandering saints. On the contrary, Lombard crosses of gold-foil from graves in central Alemannia between the Black Forest and the river Lech indicate influences of another origin.[28]

At the time of Columban's successor Eustasius (after 610–629) the Columbanian community of Luxeuil, probably cooperating with the Bavarian ducal dynasty of the Agilulfings, started the Bavarian mission and as a base established the monastery of Weltenburg on the Danube south-west of Ratisbon, which was then the ducal residence.[29] These activities, however, led by Eustasius himself, no longer fell into the range of what can be called Irish mission in a proper sense. As an Irish foundation Luxeuil, that is the whole group of the Columbanian monasteries of Annegray, Luxeuil and Fontaine, considered as a unity, is untypical, when compared with the Irish monasteries of Péronne, Fosses or Honau. While the latter were able to preserve their national Irish character for generations, Luxeuil underwent a rapid process of Frankization.[30] This is certainly one of the reasons for the great influence, which the Columbanian foundation and its

---

[26] For Säckingen see Prinz, p. 79.

[27] Irish origin: *Vita Fridolini*, 2; (*MGH, Script. rer. Mer.* III, pp. 355, 395); moreover, the *Vita* (*c.* 10, *ibid.*, p. 350, 35–38) makes Fridolin a contemporary of Clovis I. (482–511); for criticism see M. Koch, pp. 50–54; on the contrary, B. Widmer, pp. 113–117, considers the *Vita* to be reliable in both respects; but in any case it gives no reason to ascribe to Fridolin any missionary activity amongst Alemanni, cf. Widmer, pp. 129 seq.

[28] Cf. Wolfgang Müller, 'Die Christianisierung der Alemannen', in; *Zur Geschichte der Alemanne*, hg.v.W. Müller [Wege der Forschung C], (Darmstadt, 1975), pp. 401–429, especially pp. 412–416.

[29] For Weltenburg see Prinz, pp. 357 seq.

[30] Cf. Prinz, pp. 121–123.

monasticism were to exert during the seventh century. Frankization in this context is not to be understood in a strictly ethnical sense. It means an indigenization carried out by Galloroman and Burdundian agents as well as by Frankish ones. In 591 a small community of Irish pilgrims settled with the permission of the Burgundian king at Annegray. Only a few years later the capacity of the new monastery, depending on the agricultural acreage available, had reached its limits and Columban resolved to establish a second one at Luxeuil, also granted to him by the king. Even by then the majority of the members of the community probably were of non-Irish origin, and certainly this was the case when Columban himself was deported from Burgundy in 610 in consequence of a conflict with the queen grandmother Brunhild and the Burgundian king Theuderich II (596–613).

The Frankization of Luxeuil was caused by a rapid increase of the community which on its part was a result of the surprising resonance, which the Columbanian message met. Columban himself, however, was inclined at least during the later years of his Burgundian time to regard Luxeuil in spiritual respects as an isolated Irish island within an alien and even suspicious ecclesiastical environment.[31] This tendency is clearly to be seen from the position he held in the paschal controversy and from his uncompromising adherence to the traditional Irish way of calculating the date of Easter. Such a retreat into isolation would doubtless have reduced the possibilities of exerting continuous spiritual influence. Actually, however, it was not feasible. The paschal question did not remain a point of controversy between Columban and the Burgundian church, against which he had tried in vain to appeal for Roman support. On the contrary, it became controversial within the limits of his own community, too, and we may well assume that the Irish calculation was abandoned soon after Columban's expulsion from Burgundy. Altogether the process of Frankization, brought about by the growing influx of indigenous elements, eventually resulted in an effective adoption of the Irish spiritual impulse as impersonated by Columban and expressed by his rules, while at least one particular Irish factor, which by its isolating effects threatened to paralyse the obvious attraction of Columbanian spirituality, was rejected. In addition the Columbanian rule was complemented by the rule of Benedict, probably at the time of Columban's second successor Waldebert (629–680) at the latest.[32] What had originally started at Annegray as a small Irish community abroad, developed at Luxeuil into the centre of a spiritual

[31] Cf. Schäferdiek (see n.16). *Columban*, Fp. III, 2; (ed. Walker, p. 241, 19–22): 'Constat enim nos in nostraesse patria dum nullas istorum suscipimus regulas Callorum, sed in desertis sedentes, nulli molesti, cum nostrorum regulis manemus seniorum.'

[32] Cf. Prinz, pp. 268–289.

movement of its own within the Frankish empire, which has suitably been called Irofrankish.[33]

It was this Irofrankish centre Luxeuil, which sent Eustasius to organize missionary activity in Bavaria. Apart from this achievement, there is a series of names of saints, including above all the famous wandering and monastic bishops of the last third of the seventh and first third of the eighth century; Emmeran, Rupert, Corbinian and Erhard, traditionally connected with the Bavarian mission, though it is not clear in any case what part they really took in it. Most of them were also supposed to be of Irish origin, but these assumptions are altogether unsubstantiated. Some of the names, however, may well be associated with Irofrankish tradition.[34] Actual evidence of Irish presence in Bavaria takes us already to the period of ecclesiastical consolidation, the early eighth century being the phase of transition on the Bavarian scene also. Thus we do not need to discuss the 'wandering Britons' (venientes Brittones), the Bavarian bishops are warned of by Pope Gregory III in 738,[35] whoever these Britons may have been – Boniface, who certainly had been Gregory's source of information as to the Bavarian situation, speaks of Irish as Scottus, and Britannia is employed in Bonifation documents in a strict sense not including Hibernia. The first unquestionable witness of Irish presence in Bavaria is Virgil (Feirgil) of Salzburg. He came to the country in 745 together with his monastic bishop Dobdagrecus (Dub-dá-Crich) sent by Pippin the Younger. About two years later he entered upon the administration of the Salzburg bishopric in the position of an abbot of St. Peter's, not being consecrated bishop himself before 755.[36] The care of the mission to the Slavonic Carantanians was a task, which was incumbent on him as one of the duties of his office, and a consequence of an increasing Bavarian overlordship over the Carantanian princes.

Soon after the Bavarian mission had been started by monks from Luxeuil, effective missionary work began also in those northern parts of the Frankish empire, which in spite of some early attempts subsequent to the conversion of Clovis yet had remained rather inaccessible to Christian penetration.[37] Occasionally it extended even to England, where the bishops Agilbert from Neuster and Felix from Burgundy found their fields of action in Wessex and East Anglia respectively.[38] Its agents as far as they are

---

[33] Cf. Friedrich Prinz, 'Peregrinatio, Mönchtum und Mission,' in: Kirchengeschichte als Missionsgeschichte, pp. 445–465, especially pp. 425 seq.

[34] Cf. Prinz, pp. 345–351; 379–396.

[35] Bonifatius, Ep. 44; (ed. Rau, p. 128, 7-9).

[36] Cf. Herwig Wolfram, 'Der Zeitpunkt der Bischofsweihe Virgils von Salzburg': Mitteilungen des Instituts für österreichische Geschichtsforchung, 79 (1971), pp. 297–315.

[37] Cf. Knut Schäferdiek, 'Germananmission': Reallexikon für Antike und Christentum, 10, (Stuttgart 1978) col. 492–548, especially col. 538–540.

[38] Cf. Beda, Hist. eccl., III, 7; (ed. Colgrave/Mynors, p. 234); II, 16; (ibid., p. 190).

known to us are directly or indirectly inspired by the spiritual influence of Luxeuil and the Irofrankish movement. Even Killian of Aubigny, who as an Irishman was an exception within this circle, was made to preach in the Artois by Bishop Burgundofaro of Meaux, who on his part kept close connections with Luxeuil. It was in this circle of northgallic missionaries, that mission was understood to be an immediate challenge to spiritual life, which they were ready to respond to. In addition, one of these Irofrankish missionaries, the Aquitanian Amandus (d. after 675), 'Apostle of the Flemings', developed, as Wolfgang H. Fritze has pointed out, a universalistic concept of mission as opposed to the political one.[39] It demanded that the gospel be preached to all *gentes* in the sense not of individual pagans but of heathen nations. Amandus also tried to carry out this idea himself. Besides his achievement in northern Gaul and the Frankish-Frisian border region he went to the Carantanians, belonging to those Slavonic tribes Columban for a moment had thought of visiting some 25 years before, and to the Basques.[40] Thus zeal for mission was obviously transcending the traditional ideal of pilgrimage for the sake of Christ.

Certainly the picture we get from our sources, applying critical standards, excluding legendary material or hagiographic stereotypes and clearly distinguishing mission from spiritual influence in general, can be only a partial one. Nevertheless it seems to be sufficiently representative to allow an evaluation. The intense missionary activity in the peripheral regions of the seventh century Frankish empire is above all an achievement of the Irofrankish spiritual movement. Thus it is substantially indebted to the lasting effects of an original impulse of Irish monastic spirituality; but nevertheless it is not at all Irish itself, just as the Anglo-Saxon mission of the subsequent period is not Irish itself in spite of its Irish spiritual background. Direct Irish contribution may be found occasionally too, but it is far from being important as a whole, and must be considered rather exceptional than typical. Furthermore it did not spontaneously derive from the ascetic ideal of pilgrimage for the Lord's sake. If Irish monks on occasion showed themselves ready to take over missionary responsibilities, they did so rather because one of their aristocratic supporters and patrons succeeded in convincing them that they should do so, as King Theudebert of Austrasia with Columban or Bishop Burgundofaro of Meaux with Killian.

If we now devote our attention to the English scene, we shall see ourselves at once faced with quite another situation. Direct, substantial and far reaching Irish contribution to seventh century Anglo-Saxon Christianization is a firmly established fact, which simply cannot be questioned. It is therefore not necessary to outline the well-known

---

[39] W. H. Fritze, pp. 88–92.
[40] *Vita Amandi*, I, 16; (*MGH, Script. rer. Mer.* V, pp. 439, 22–440, 7): 20 (*ibid.*, pp. 443, 12–444, 5).

historical events in detail here.[41] We should rather confine ourselves to some particular aspects, which may perhaps be important for a proper understanding of the facts as well as of the phenomenon of the Irish mission in general.

Irish mission in England means first and foremost, of course, the mission of Lindisfarne, which up to the date of the synod of Whitby (664) was strictly speaking an achievement of Iona, Lindisfarne continuing to be a filiation of Columcille's famous foundation and receiving its abbots from there. The mission was initiated by king Oswald of Northumbria in 635/6, when he called for Irish monks from Iona to convert his subjects and caused them to establish their monastery at Lindisfarne, a place of seclusion as well as a place near to the royal residence at Bamburgh. The mission, however, did not start without difficulties. The first monastic missionary sent from Iona is said by tradition to have been too harsh, which may well mean that he was not content to preach merely the faith, that is to say that he had no sense of elementary mission in its common medieval understanding. Only after he was superseded by Aidan, did the work begin to progress. Its further extension beyond the borders of Northumbria into Middle Anglia, Essex and finally the heathen stronghold Mercia itself was exactly subsequent to the development of political power and influence of the Northumbrian kings in their struggle with Penda of Mercia for supremacy. Thus the Lindisfarne mission must be regarded as a very typical example of early medieval political mission. It originated from religious selfconsciousness of kingship, but not from a particular sense of mission supposed to be proper to Irish monasticism, notwithstanding the fact, that it was carried out by its Irish agents with high devotion once they had agreed to take over its responsibilities.

There were also Irish missionary activities in Anglo-Saxon England beside the achievement of Lindisfarne and its geographical sphere of influence, although they appear to have been rather subsidiary to other Christian activities on the field. Thus, having no information on the circumstances of the founding of Malmesbury and its early role, if there was any apart from being a centre of learning, we have at least to consider Fursey's mission in East Anglia and the missionary attempt of Dicuill at Bosham in the South Saxon kingdom. Fursey had taken up pilgrimage for the Lord's sake, and coming to England, he crossed the country to the uttermost east, where he was welcomed and granted a place to establish a monastery by the East Anglian king Sigibehrt.[42] He could indeed expect a friendly reception there, for Sigibehrt was a devout Christian, converted

---

[41] For details see H. Mayr-Harting, pp. 94–102; Knut Schäferdiek, 'Die Grundlegung der angelsächsischen Kirche', in Kirchengeschichte als Missionsgeschichte, pp. 149–191, especially pp. 173–178.

[42] Vita Fursei, 6s; (MGH, Script. rer. Mer. IV, pp. 436, 20–437, 11); cf. Beda, Hist. eccl., III, 19; (ed. Colgrave/Mynors, pp. 268–270).

during his exile in Gaul and obviously familiar with Irofrankish spirituality, and he had also got an apparently Irofrankish wandering bishop, Felix of Burgundy, already working in his realm.[43] Given these facts there is sufficient reason to wonder if it actually had been only by chance that Fursey chose just this way to East Anglia. Probably he was well aware of what he did heading for the East Anglian kingdom on his search for a proper place to establish his community. Moreover, judging from what can be seen elsewhere, we may well also assume, that the missionary activity ascribed to Fursey, but apparently soon left by him to others, belonged to the terms of this establishment agreed upon by the Irish pilgrim and his Anglian royal patron.

In Sussex an Irish monk Dicuill is said to have preached to the pagan inhabitants in vain.[44] Having as a base a little monastery at Bosham, he must have been granted the opportunity to settle there with his brethren by someone who was in a position and at the same time had reason to grant it, a description which is perfectly answered by the South Saxon King Aethelwalh (d. 685) himself. He had been converted and baptized at the suggestion of King Wulfhere of Mercia (657/8–674/5),[45] and consequently he was – if perhaps not eager himself – at least expected by his Mercian overlord to take measures for the conversion of his subjects, too. Most probably this is the proper historical context of Dicuill's unsuccessful South Saxon mission.

As a result of our attempt to obtain a general view of seventh century Irish mission it is evident, that the question asked at the beginning is not a question of its existence at all. The problem of fact or fiction as to the Irish mission is a problem of its evaluation regarding its extent, its effectiveness and its nature. Direct Irish mission, which of course is only a partial aspect of Irish cultural and spiritual influence as a whole, was fundamental to the establishment of Christianity in large parts of seventh century Anglo-Saxon England and rather subsidiary in some parts. On the continent, however, its part was apparently relatively unimportant both as to its extent and its effects, small also in relation to contemporary Irish presence in the Frankish empire in general. Thus the Lindisfarne mission was by far the most important Irish missionary achievement of the seventh century, while any other recorded Irish missionary activity can only be considered secondary in comparison with it and appears sometimes to have been overestimated.

At a critical point of his monastic life Columban thought of preaching to the heathen, and some time later he may even have formed a particular concept of mission comparable to the ideas, which later on were to move

---

[43] Beda, *Hist. eccl.*, III, 18; (ed. Colgrave/Mynors, pp. 266–268); II, 15; (*ibid.*, p. 190).
[44] Beda, *Hist. eccl.*, IV, 13; (ed. Colgrave/Mynors, p. 372).
[45] *Ibid.*

Amandus and above all the Anglo-Saxon missionaries. These considerations, however, were still only momentary, lacking an effective power of motivation. In the event his actual missionary activity was to him only an interruption of the pursuit of his proper spiritual aims, and a similar attitude seems to have been held by Fursey. Indeed, our evidence as to seventh century Irish mission does not confirm the assumption, that this mission generally was a spontaneous action deriving from a particular predisposition on the part of Irish monastic spirituality or even from an explicit concept of mission. One may suppose, however, a considerable latent, though perhaps never hesitating, readiness of many devoted Irish monks to get themselves engaged in missionary responsibilities and to take over missionary functions, if they were called for. Occasionally there may also have been difficulties arising from a conflict between different aims, monastic striving for individual spiritual perfection on the one hand and medieval missionary practice tending to external collective conversion on the other. These being the internal conditions of seventh century Irish mission, its activities did easily fit in with the contemporary pattern of political mission, and thus in the end kept a sense of what could be regarded as realistic, so avoiding becoming engaged in hopeless missionary adventures.

APPENDIX

Sources

Bede's *Ecclesiastical History of the English People*, ed. by Bertram Colgrave and R. A. B. Mynors, (Oxford, 1969); repr. 1972.
Bonifatii epistulae. Willibaldi vita Bonifatii/Briefe des Bonifatius, Willibalds Leben des Bonifatius, hg. u. übers. v. Reinhold Rau [Freiherr vom Stein-Gedächtnisausgabe IVb]. (Darmstadt, 1968).
Sancti Columbania opera, ed. by G. S. M. Walker [Scriptores Latini Hiberniae II], (Dublin, 1957); repr. 1970.
Fredegarii et aliorum chronica. Vitae sanctorum, ed. Bruno Krush [*Monumenta Germaniae Historica, Script. rer. Merov.* I, 2] (Hannover, 1888); repr. 1956.
Passiones vitaeque sanctorum aevi merovingici, ed. B. Krusch and W. Levison [*Monumenta Germaniae Historica, Script. rer. Merov.* II–VII], (Hannover/Leipzig 1896–1920) repr. 1977–1979.
Ionae vitae sanctorum Columbani, Vedastis, Iohannis, recognovit Bruno Krush [*Monumenta Germaniae Historica, Script. rer. Germ. in usum scholarum* 37], (Hannover/Leipzig, 1905).

Studies (see also for further bibliographical reference)
Wilhelm Levison, 'Die Iren und die fränkische Kirche': *Historische*

Zeitschrift, 109 (1912), pp. 1–22; repr. Id., *Aus rheinischer und fränkischer Frühzeit*, (Düsseldorf, 1948), pp. 247–263; *Mönchtum und Gesellschaft im Frühmittalalter*, hg. v. F. Prinz [Wege der Forschung, CCCXII], (Darmstadt, 1976), pp. 91–111.

James F. Kenney, *The Sources of the Early History of Ireland. I: Ecclesiastical*, (New York, 1929); repr. 1968.

Hans Freiherr von Campenhausen, *Die asketische Heimatlosigkeit im altkirchlichen und frühmittalalterlichen Mönchtum* [Sammlung gemeinvergständlicher Voträge 149], (Tübingen, 1930); repr.: Id., *Tradition und Leben*, (Tübingen, 1960), pp. 290–317.

Louis Gougaud, 'Les surnuméraires de l'émigration scottique (VIe–VIIIe siècles)': *Revue Bénédictine*, 43, (1931), pp. 296–302. Id., *Christianity in Celtic Lands*, (London, 1932).

J. Dienemann, *Der Kult des heiligen Kilian im 8. und 9 Jahrhundert* [Quellen und Forschungen zur Geschichte des Bistums und Hochstifts Würzburg X], (Würzburg, 1955).

Johannes Duft, 'Iromanie, Irophobie. Fragen um die frühmittelalterliche Irenmission exemplifiziert an St. Gallen und Alemannien': *Zeitschrift für schweizerische Kirchengeschichte*, 50 (1956), pp. 241–262.

Ingo Reiffenstein, *Das Althochdeutsche und die irische Mission im obereutschen Raum* [Innsbrucker Beitrage zur Kulturwissenschaft: Sonderheft 6], (Innsbruck, 1958).

Margit Koch, *Sankt Fridolin und sein Biograph Balther. Irische Heilige in der literarischen Darstellung des Mittelalters*. (Phil. Diss. Zürich 1959).

Friderich Prinz, *Frühes Mönchtum im Frankenreich*, (München/Wien, 1965).

Wolfgang H. Fritze, 'Universalis gentium confessio. Formeln, Träger und Wege universalmissionarischen Denkens im 7. Jahrhundert': *Frümittelalterliche Studien*, 3 (1969), pp. 78–130.

G. S. M. Walker, 'St. Columban: Monk or Missionary?': *The Mission of the Church and the Propagation of the Faith*, ed. by G. J. Cuming [Studies in Church History, 6], (Cambridge, 1970), pp. 39–44.

A. Angenendt, *Monachi peregrini. Studien zu Pirmin und den monastischen Vorstellungen des frühen Mittelalters* [Münstersche Mittelalterschriften, 6], (München, 1972).

Joseph Weisweiler/Werner Betz, 'Deutsche Frühzeit': *Deutsche Wortgeschichte*, hg. v. Friederich Maurer u. Heinz Rupp, I, (Berlin, 1974), pp. 55–133, in particular pp. 92–94.

Kurt-Ulrich Jäschke, 'Kolumban von Luxeuil und sein Wirken im alemannischen Raum': *Mönchtum, Episkopat und Adel zur Gründungszeit des Klosters Reichenau*, hg. v. Arno Borst [Vorträge und Forschungen, 20] (Sigmaringen, 1974), pp. 77–130.

John T. McNeill, *The Celtic Churches*, (Chicago/London, 1974).

Berthe Widmer, 'Die Vita des heiligen Fridolin': *Jahrbuch des Historischen Vereins des Kantons Glarus*, 65 (1974), pp. 100–191.

Walter Berschin, 'Gallus abbas vindicatus': *Historisches Jahrbuch der Görres-*

Gesellschaft, 95 (1975), pp. 257–277.

Henry Mayr-Harting, *The Coming of Christianity to England*, (New York, 1977).

Kirchengeschichte als Missionsgeschichte II, 1. Die Kirche des früheren Mittelalters, hg. v. Knut Schäferdiek (München, 1978).

William H. Marnell, *Light from the West. The Irish Mission and the Emergence of Modern Europe*, (New York, 1978).

Die Iren und Europa im früheren Mittelalter, hg. v. Heinz Löwe, (Stuttgart, 1982).

ORDRE ET LIBERTÉ DANS L'EGLISE: L'INFLUENCE DE CLUNY AUX XIe ET XIIe SIÈCLES

Marcel Pacaut

L'histoire de Cluny a, depuis très longtemps, tellement attiré les historiens qu'il semble difficile de prétendre la renouveler. Après avoir été éclairée, dans son contenu interne – la fondation du monastère, le développement de l'ordre, ses coutûmes, son organisation, etc. – elle a, depuis quelques années, retenu l'attention des spécialistes qui ont cherché avant tout à estimer le rôle des moines clunisiens dans l'Eglise et dans la société. Il suffit de citer, pour le constater, et en s'en tenant aux publications les plus importantes, les travaux de J. F. Lemarignier et G. Duby en France, de H. E. J. Cowdrey en Angleterre, de C. Violante en Italie, etc.[1] Ces études, qui n'aboutissent pas à des conclusions uniformes, montrent d'une façon générale d'une part combien l'interprétation de certains documents fort connus demeure parfois délicate, d'autre part combien il est des arguments dont on n'avait pas jusqu'ici assez souligné la relative importance. C'est à partir de cette double préoccupation que j'ai conduit mon enquête sur l'influence que les clunisiens ont exercée pour conforter l'ordre et l'autorité dans l'Eglise, ou au contraire pour les contester et exalter l'autonomie et la liberté, en la limitant chronologiquement à l'époque de la grandeur de l'ordre – depuis ses débuts jusqu'à l'abbatiat de Pierre le Vénérable, qui marque à la fois l'essai de renouvellement et le debut de l'atonie – et en considerant l'Eglise

---

[1] J. F. Lemarignier, 'Structures monastiques et structures politiques dans la France de la fin du Xème siècle et du début du XIème siècle', dans *Il monachesimo nell'alto Medio evo* (Spolète, 1957), pp. 357–400. G. Duby, *Les trois ordres ou l'imaginaire du féodalisme* (Paris, 1978). H. E. J. Cowdrey, *The Cluniacs and the Gregorian Reform* (Oxford, 1970). C. Violante, 'Il monachesimo cluniacense di fronte al Mondo politico-ecclesiastico', dans *Spiritualita cluniacense* (Todi, 1960), pp. 153–242. On pourrait relever aussi G. Tellenbach, J. Wollasch, etc.

dans sa signification la plus large incluant les clercs et les laiques. Sans reprendre nécessairement des analyses maintes fois accomplies, j'examinerai successivement le problème de l'intégration de Cluny à l'ordere de l'Eglise (donc de la contribution qu'elle y apporte ou des restrictions qu'elle y oppose au nom de la liberté), la question de l'autorité a l'intérieur de la congrégation et des oppositions qu'elle suscite, la mesure enfin de la place tenue par les clunisiens en faveur de l'ordre politique et social ou au détriment de celui-ci.

Dès sa naissance, Cluny est placée sous le signe de la liberté et sous la garantie romaine. Ce sont là les deux arguments majeurs qui déterminent et doivent régler son comportement à l'intérieur de l'Eglise. Le nouveau monastère est libre: il n'est soumis à aucune puissance séculière et ecclésiastique – 'Il nous a plu d'insérer, écrit Guillaume le Pieux dans la Charte de fondation, une clause en vertu de laquelle les moines ici réunis ne seront soumis au joug d'aucune puissance terrestre, pas même à la nôtre, ni à celle de nos parents, ni à celle de la grandeur royale. Aucun prince séculier, aucun évêque, pas davantage le pontife du siège romain, ne pourront s'emparer des biens des dits serviteurs de Dieu . . .' Mais, payant un cens au Saint-Siège, dont il reconnait ainsi la propriété éminente, il est sous sa protection – 'Ô saints apôtres Pierre et Paul, . . . soyez les tuteurs et les défenseurs de ce lieu de Cluny et des serviteurs que Dieu s'y donne'. Le document, c'est évident, ne concerne dans ces termes que le temporel du monastère, dont il entend que les moines jouissent librement sans aucune contrainte ou menace extérieure et qu'il considère comme la condition nécessaire au maintien du respect de la règle bénédictine (libre élection de l'abbé) et à l'exercise des activités spirituelles des moines (qui ne doivent pas être troublés par les tracas du monde et qui doivent posséder des biens pour travailler et vivre). Mais, en faisant du pape le protecteur *unique* de ses biens, il lui accorde un rôle auquel aucun autre pouvoir ne peut prétendre, encore que, aussitôt, il le limite: d'une part, le pontife est seulement 'le tuteur et le défenseur', fonction qui ne donne aucune autorité directe sur l'établissement; d'autre part, il n'a pas le droit d'intervenir dans la gestion temporelle, ce qui fait fi en quelque sort de la donation de l'abbaye aux saints Pierre et Paul et de la propriété éminente de ceux-ci reconnue par le paiement d'uns cens. Il y a là, dès le départ, une certaine ambiguité, que l'on retrouve tout au long de l'histoire de l'exemption clunisienne, c'est à dire de la réalisation de l'indépendance à l'égard de la hiérarchie de l'Eglise séculière.

Il est utile, sans entrer dans les détails, de relever les phases successives de la mise en place de ce privilège qui résulte de l'esprit de la Charte de fondation (celle-ci ne contenant absolument pas la liberté 'spirituelle'), des démélés en quelque sorte naturels avec l'évêque de Mâcon, du développement de la pratique de l'exemption par l'Eglise romaine (qui vise sans doute à étendre son influence et son autorité), poussée en cela par diverses personnalités du monde monastique, parmi lesquelles avant tout

Abbon de Fleury. Il faut noter toutefois que, d'une façon générale, l'ambiguité à été maintenue, plus ou moins fortement, entre la liberté clunisienne et l'autorité pontificale. A première vue, cependant, l'évolution parait simple et logique. Elle s'accomplit en trois phases successives.

1. Jusqu'en 998, les bulles pontificales adressées à Cluny ou la concernant tendent uniquement à confirmer et garantir la Charte de fondation et à accorder la protection des biens de l'abbaye et de ses dépendances. C'est donc l'Eglise romaine qui exerce son autorité, qui conforte son ordre en maintenant et en renforçant ses liens avec des établissements qui relèvent de sa propriété et sont ainsi 'de son droit'. Il n'y a pas de liberté clunisienne et le jeune monastère ne proteste nullement contre ce statut.

C'est en 928 que l'on voit le pape, en l'occurence Jean X, intervenir pour la première fois à propos de l'exécution du testament de Bernon relatif à l'abbaye de Gigny. Il s'adresse alors au roi de France et à l'archevêque de Lyon, ainsi qu'à deux comtes (Hugues et Gilbert) pour leur demander d'aider Cluny à obtenir ce qui lui est dû en précisant que l'abbaye est sous la protection du Saint-Siège (*sub nostra ditione*).[2] Il agit d'ailleurs semblablement à l'égard d'autres monastères aux biens desquels il accorde sa garantie (St. Gall, Fulda, etc. . . .). En 931, Jean XI confirme les possessions temporelles de Cluny, y compris des chapelles et des dîmes, et il interdit que quiconque y porte atteinte; en même temps, il renouvelle l'obligation de la libre élection de l'abbé et précise que la monastère peut accueillir des moines venus d'ailleurs et cherchant une ascèse plus rude, ce qui revient à approuver et aider la diffusion de la réforme clunisienne.[3] La même année, il confirme à nouveau le temporel ainsi que la possession par Cluny du monastère de Charlieu, dont il rappelle qu'il est *juris Ecclesiae romanae*.[4] Ce faisant, il approuve la mise en application de la réforme que Charlieu a acceptée, en faisant très clairement mention de son autorité comme si c'était lui qui, ayant pouvoir à Charlieu, transférait cette maison à Cluny. En 936, 937 et 938, Léon VII, à son tour, confirme les possessions clunisiennes et les garantit.[5] En 938, la formule qu'il emploie lie la sujétion de Cluny à l'Eglise romaine et la libre disposition de son temporel: c'est pour autant que l'abbaye est sujette que personne ne peut lui porter atteinte ('Romanae tantum sedi ita subjectum est nunquam aut canonico aut laico aut etiam abbati . . .') si bien qu'il y a presque une assimilation entre les propriétés directes et la propriété éminente de la Papauté et qu'au plan juridique, concernant le temporel, la personnalité de Cluny semble disparaitre. Après Léon VII – qui adresse des diplômes analogues à d'autres monastères: Subiaco, Fulda, Fleury, Saint-Martin de Tours, Agapet II, en 949, énumère dans un chartre plus solennelle tous les biens et possessions de

---

[2] *Patrologia Latina*, t. CXXXII, col. 812.
[3] Id., col. 1055–1058.
[4] Id., col. 1058–1059.
[5] Id., col. 1068–1069, 1070–1071, 1074–1075.

Cluny et les garantit en même temps que la libre élection de l'abbé.[6] Quoi qu'on en ait dit parfois, le 'privilège' ne concerne que le temporel et le respect de la règle bénédictine.[7] Entre 965 et 972, Jean XIII prie les métropolitains et évêques d'Arles, Lyons, Vienne, Clermont, Valence, Besançon, Châlon, Avignon, Genève, Lausanne, Viviers, Bâle et plus particulièrement celui de Mâcon, de protéger les établissements clunisiens et d'excommunier ceux qui s'en prennent à leurs biens: il n'y a aucun argument nouveau, si ce n'est que cette bulle témoigne de l'extension de la réforme clunisienne au duché et comté de Bourgogne ainsi qu'en Auvergne et dans la vallée du Rhône.[8] Il en est de même de l'acte adressé par Benoît VII à Mayeul en 978 sur un point particulier.[9]

2. A partir de Grégoire V et jusqu'à Grégoire VII, une seconde période s'ouvre, qui est celle de l'exemption, c'est-à-dire de la liberté de Cluny, en matière ecclésiastique et spirituelle, vis à vis de l'évêque de Mâcon, donc de sa non-sujétion à celui-ci. C'est la période où se lient la liberté monastique et l'autorité romaine, puisque la première ne peut être créée et garantie que par la seconde et que l'une et l'autre n'ont de sens que dans la mesure où elles se confortent mutuellement. Il faut noter, toutefois, que cette pratique pontificale, pour laquelle milite Abbon de Fleury et qui va conduire la Papauté à accorder quasiment une pleine liberté à Cluny, de façon sans doute plus solennelle et plus vigoureuse qu'aux autres instituts monastiques, n'es pas véritablement innovée en sa faveur. Benoît VII déjà, pour Vézelay, le Mont-Cassin, Besalu, et Jean XV pour Aniane avaient accordé des privilèges qui ouvraient la voie.[10] Par ailleurs, on doit souligner qu'en certains diplômes pontificaux il peut y avoir une ambiguïté à propos de l'extension des droits aux autres établissements de la congrégation, du fait que, jusque dans les années 1050, celle-ci comporte sous l'autorité de l'abbaye-mère, uniquement des prieurés dont l'abbé de Cluny est, au plan théorique et juridique, le seul véritable abbé.

Le mouvement débute en 998 avec la bulle de Grégoire V qui renouvelle la protection du Saint-Siège, énumère les possessions de l'établissement dans divers diocèses, les répartit chaque fois en deux catégories – les monastères ou cellae, les églises ou chapelles, mais accorde en outre qu'aucun évêque ou prêtre ou diacre ne puissent procéder à des ordinations, consécrations ou célébrations de messes à Cluny sans y être autorisé par l'abbé, et que désormais les abbés nouvellement élus seront consacrés par

[6] *P.L.*, t. CXXXIII, col. 900–902.
[7] L'interdiction à tout évêque ou comte, en l'occurence à l'évêque et au comte de Mâcon d' 'ordinare' sur les monastères de St. Jean et de St. Martin, proches de Mâcon, ne pouvant pas concerner la juridiction spirituelle de l'évêque, sinon elle ne serait pas liée, comme le texte le formule sans ambiguïté, au droit du comte qui, lui, ne peut être que temporel.
[8] *P.L.*, t. CXXXV, col. 990–991.
[9] *P.L.*, t. CXXXVII, col. 332.
[10] Id., col. 323, 326, 334, 835.

l'évêque de leur choix.[11] C'est donc l'exclusion de l'évêque de Mâcon et la mise en marche de l'autonomie. En 1016, Benoît VIII, qui a accordé deux ans auparavant des privilèges de même ordre au Mont-Cassin,[12] enjoint aux évêques de Bourgogne et d'Aquitaine de condamner les laïques (nommément désignés) qui portent atteinte aux biens des clunisiens (Odilon s'en est plaint à Rome). Cela revient donc à rappeler la garantie donnée au temporel sans faire d'allusion directe à l'exemption. Cependant, il est aussi déclaré que Cluny, aidée et protégée par l'Eglise romaine ainsi que par les rois de France et de Bourgogne, s'est développée de telle façon qu'elle a été libre de la sujetion à toute autorité à l'exception du pouvoir romain, et que c'est là, est-il precisé, ce qui constitue sa 'libertas', la formule étant assez imprécise pour que l'on estime soit qu'elle ne concerne que les possessions soit qu'elle englobe aussi l'autonomie a l'encontre de l'ordinaire.[13]

En fait, l'évêque de Mâcon et d'autre prélats résistent alors à l'application de l'exemption partielle accordée par Grégoire V, ce qui explique sans doute la prudence de Benoît VIII. Dans les années 1024–1032, le conflit éclate avec violence entre l'abbé Odilon et les évêques. Le pape Jean XIX soutient à fond les clunisiens: en 1027, en renouvelant la garantie temporelle, il réaffirme la liberté des ordinations et consécrations et y ajoute l'interdiction pour tout évêque de mettre en interdit Cluny ou d'excommunier un de ses moines, ce dernier privilège ne semblant pas s'applique à tous les religieux de l'ordere et donc à tous les établissements.[14] En 1049, Léon IX reprend l'ensemble en précisant que l'ordinaire n'a pas autorité pour consacrer le saint Chrème et les saintes Huiles. En 1055, Victor II agit de même et énumère les monastères et églises de la congrégation. En 1058, c'est au tour d'Etienne IX d'intervenir, puis d'Alexandre II en 1063 et de Grégoire VII en 1076.[15] Ainsi, Cluny a obtenu la pleine liberté. A s'en tenir aux textes, la juridiction ordinaire de l'évêque ne s'exerce en aucune façon, en aucun cas, sur elle (ni consécration, ni ordination, ni bénédiction, ni exercice du pouvoir de correction et condamnation); elle est propriétaire de nombreuses églises où ses moines célèbrent le culte pour les fidèles (laïques). Elle est uniquement dans la dépendance de l'Eglise romaine, qui juge de toutes les causes dans lesquelles elle est partie, et qui, depuis 1046 commence à envoyer des légats qui règlent ces différends, mais qui cherchent aussi à faire de l'abbaye un centre de l'action pontificale. Tout parait aller pour le mieux à la fois pour la liberté clunisienne, qui renforce la puissance et l'ascendant des clunisiens, et

---

[11] Id., col. 932, 935.
[12] P.L., t. CXXXIX, col. 1592.
[13] Id., col. 1601–1603.
[14] P.L., t. CXLI, col. 1135–1137.
[15] P.L., t. CXLIII, col. 607–609, 803–808 et 879–884; t. CXLVI, col. 1293–1295; t. CXLVIII, col. 401–466.

pour l'autorité du pape qui la garantit et en tire profit. N'écrit-on pas d'ailleurs alors que la protection temporelle et l'exemption constituent pour Cluny la *libertas romana*?

3. En s'en tenant encore à une analyse élémentaire des documents, on constate que, à partir de Grégoire VII, cette articulation se renforce du fait que le Saint Siège indique que ses privilèges s'appliquent à l'ensemble des établissements clunisiens, ce qui exalte cette fois l'autorité de l'abbé de Cluny et sur son ordre et dans l'Eglise, puisque la juridiction épiscopale est partout exclue et qu'il devient le chef tout à fait indépendant, sauf à l'égard du pape, d'une immense communauté répartie dans les diverses régions de la Chrétienté. C'est dès Etienne IX, il faut le noter, que l'élargissement – qui était peut-être déjà contenu de façon ambigüe dans les diplômes antérieurs – commence à prendre forme au plan logique, lorsque ce pape approuve et ordonne l'intégration de Vézelay, monastère déjà exempt, à l'ordre en tant qu'abbaye d'obédience. Dès lors, en effet, à moins d'accepter un désordre inextricable, il ne peut y avoir à la fois des établissements exempts et d'autres non exempts (ce qui était à la rigueur concevable si Cluny seule l'était). Il faut donc que tous jouissent de la liberté romaine. La citation dans la privilège de Grégoire VII de 1076 de neuf abbayes d'obédience marque l'affirmation de cette obligation de clarification.

Urbain II n'a donc ensuite qu'à préciser davantage, d'autant plus qu'à cette époque et pendant les premières années du XIIème siècle de nouvelles abbayes d'obédience s'agrègent a la congrégation. De neuf en 1076, elles passent à treize en 1088, puis à dix-huit en 1118: St. Martial de Limoges, St. Eparche d'Angoulême, St. Jean d'Angeley, St. Cyprien de Poitiers, Lézat, Moissac, Figeac, St. Gilles, Mozac, Thiers, Menat, Vézelay, St. Germain d'Auxerre, Unicourt en Cambraisis, Pontoise, St. Bertin, St. Vulmair, St. Benoît sur le Po.[16] Il faut remarquer d'ailleurs que cette liste va être sujette à des variations du fait que certaines abbayes reprendront leur liberté ou seront au contraire réduites à l'état de prieuré. Quoi qu'il en soit, elles bénéficient de l'exemption comme toutes les maisons de l'ordre. Dès 1088, Urbain II indique que les évêques dans les diocèses desquels sont situées les établissements clunisiens (cellae) n'ont aucune autorité sur les moines.[17] En 1095 et en 1097, il renouvelle solennellement la protection de l'Eglise romaine, la garantie des biens et la liberté.[18] La même année 1097, il redit que l'exemption s'étend à toutes les 'cellae'.[19] En 1100 Pascal II reprend tout cela et énumère les abbayes d'obédience, en même temps qu'il demand aux évêques de France de protéger les clunisiens.[20] En Février 1106, il rappelle à l'évêque de Mâcon qu'il n'a aucun droit sur Cluny et fixe les limites

---

[16] Bulle de Gelase II, *P.L.*, t. CLXIII, col. 509–510.
[17] *P.L.*, t. CLI, col. 291.
[18] Id., col. 410–412 et 485–488.
[19] Id., col. 493.
[20] *P.L.*, t. CLXIII, col. 51–53, 53–54 et encore 56–58.

territoriales du ban clunisien.[21] D'autres bulles confirment la protection et l'exemption en 1106, 1109 (au novel abbé Pons) et 1114.[22] Gelase II agit de même en 1118[23] et, après lui, Calixte II, Honorius II, Innocent II.[24]

Cependant, en même temps que cette liberté s'épanoussait, on voyait s'exprimer une restriction en faveur de l'évêque sur un point particulier, à savoir le droit sur les paroisses, plus particulièrement la prérogative canoniquement reconnue à l'ordinaire d'y instituer les curés. La chronologie, en ce domaine, n'est pas toujours facile à suivre, car les formules qui mentionnent cette réserve apparaissent dans certaines bulles sans être répétées dans d'autres qui leur sont postérieures et reviennent ensuite. A ma conaissance, c'est en 1088, dans une lettre adressée à l'abbé Huges et qui traite d'abord de l'attribution du titre de primat à l'archevêque de Tolède (acceptée sans gaité de coeur par Cluny), qu'Urbain II renouvelle protection et exemption, en précisant d'une part qu'aucun légat n'aura autorité sur la congrégation, sauf celui qui aura reçu spécialement mission du pape ('nisi cui a nobis idipsum specialiter injunctum fuerit'), d'autre part que les évêques ne pourront rien 'juger' des affaires clunisiennes, sauf le droit qu'ils sont connus avoir tenu jusque là ('salvo tamen jure episcoporum quod in eis hactenus habuisse noscuntur').[25] Cette formule très imprécise n'est pas reprise dans le grand privilège de 1095 qui accorde à l'abbé l'usage de la dalmatique et de la mitre – mais la mention du légat est maintenue: 'nulli apostolicae sedis legato, sine certo Romani pontificis precepto'.[26] En revanche, en 1097, les termes concernent clairement les paroisses: pour les églises qui sont en sa possession, Cluny a le droit de choisir le desservant, que l'évêque institue et qu'en conséquence il soumet à sa jurisdiction dans l'exercice de son office ('liceat vobis seu fratribus in ecclesiis vestris presbyteros eligere, ita tamen ut ab episcopis vel ab episcoporum vicariis animarum curam absque venalitate suscipiant').[27] En 1100, Pascal II emploie une formule analogue en déclarant que les églises, chapelles et cimetières appartenant aux clunisiens doivent être libres et à l'abri de toute exaction, sauf le droit reconnu a l'évêque sur les prêtres ('praeter consuetam episcopi paratam justitiam in presbyteris').[28] Mais il ne la répète pas dans la bulle solennelle expédiée à l'abbé Pons en 1109. Gélase II, de son côté, n'inscrit aucune clause de réserve. A l'inverse, Calixte II et ses successeurs le font. Désormais, et pour un certain temps la chancellerie pontificale va veiller dans toute la mesure du possible à introduire cette mention dans

[21] Id., col. 201.
[22] Id., col. 204–205, 261, 262, 281, 356, 359.
[23] Id., col. 492, 509–510.
[24] Id., col. 1256; P.L., t. CLXVI, col. 1226.
[25] P.L., t. CLI, col. 291.
[26] Id., col. 412.
[27] Id., col. 487.
[28] P.L., t. CLXIII, col. 51.

toutes les bulles d'exemption, sans y parvenir d'ailleurs toujours. Elle tendre aussi à réserver le droit du Sante-Siège lui-même ('Salva sedis apostolicae auctoritate et episcopi canonica reverentia').

Il est possible, à partir de ces diplômes de dresser un premier bilan qui fait apparaitre d'abord l'importance de cette liberté romaine. Car l'exemption a non seulement contribué a mettre les clunisiens à l'abri d'entreprises, épiscopales ou autres, qui auraient pu géner leur épanouissement spirituel – à une époque où de nombreaux évêques étaient avides de puissance – elle a aussi grandement favorisé le développment de l'ordre, puisque, à partir d'une certaine époque, il suffisait de s'intégrer à Cluny pour devenir exempt. Par ailleurs, en luttant pour son exemption, celle-ci invitait d'autres instituts monastiques à faire de même – et c'est bien ainsi que vont agir Saint Benigne de Dijon, Fruttuaria, etc. Cette liberté, enfin, renforçait l'autorité de l'abbé de Cluny, qui dirigeait ainsi une immense congrégation autonome, en même temps qu'elle exaltait la puissance pontificale, seule apte à l'accorder et s'attachait par là en dépendance direct de très nombreux monastères. Toute cette histoire montre, en effet, que la papauté n'a jamais cessé d'oeuvrer pour la grandeur et l'indépendance des Clunisiens, d'abord en accordant avec solennité et minutie sa guarantie aux possessions temporelles qui étaient de leur droit éminent de par la chartre de fondation, puis en distribuant les 'libertés' spirituelles de façon à soustraire les couvents à la juridiction épiscopale. En contre-partie, l'Eglise romaine savait pouvoir attendre sans difficulté la fidélité, le soutien et la collaboration des clunisiens dans ses diverses entreprises, cette coopération, fondée sur la liberté monastique, confortant son autorité. La réserve du droit de l'ordinaire sur les paroisses, qui apparait très tard et se généralise lentement, ne serait, dans ces condition, qu'un rappel pour une saine gestion du culte à une époque ou le statut paroissial se précise.

Il est permis, toutefois, tout en reconnaissant qu'une telle vision est en partie exact, de se demander si elle n'est pas incomplète et même parfois déformée. Car, de toutes façons, il y a dans l'analyse même du contenu une ambiguïté à propos de laquelle il est impossible de dire qu'elle ne pouvait pas conduire logiquement à des malentendus, à savoir que la liberté clunisienne doit conforter à la fois la puissance de l'ordre et l'autorité de l'Eglise romaine. Qu'elle puisse participer à cette double entreprise, c'est possible. Mais il n'est pas du tout déraisonnable de considérer que Cluny a d'abord estimé devoir renforcer sa propre grandeur, l'exaltation de l'autorité romaine devenant secondaire pour elle et l'autonomie étant conçue comme une pleine et totale liberté sans référence au service à rendre au Saint-Siège, dont l'unique fonction en cette maitière, était de la garantir –, tandis que les papes, à l'inverse, jugeaient qu'un ordre exempt devait les servir et travailler pour leur exaltation.

Une lecture plus attentive de cette histoire, ou une autre lecture, permettent de le constater. Force est de relever, en effet, que, si l'accord semble profond entre la papauté et Cluny jusqu'a l'époque de Grégoire VII, il y a, pendant toute cette période, un conflit permanent d'une exceptionelle gravité entre les clunisiens et l'épiscopat. Non pas seulement entre le monastère de Cluny et l'évêque de Mâcon, ou entre tel prieuré et tel évêque, à propos de l'exercice de la juridiction épiscopale à l'intérieur de l'établissement et sur les religieux qui y résident, mais, porté par les grands abbés, entre le monachisme et la hiérarchie épiscopale au sujet des structure mêmes de l'Eglise. Dès Mayeul sans doute, mais certainement avec Odilon, un projet s'élabore selon lequel il reviendrait aux moines de prendre en charge l'encardrement des fidèles et la poursuite de la christianisation de la société, la crise morale du clergé séculier facilitant d'ailleurs et expliquant peut-être cette démarche. Certes, il ne s'agit pas selon eux de supprimer l'épiscopat, mais seulement de la réduire à des fonctions sacramentelles ou encore à le faire émaner des milieux monastiques (évêques – moines) en confiant aux moines la tâche fondamentale de 'diriger' spirituellement la société, et d'abord l'aristocratie – G. Duby ecrit 'monachiser',[29] Il suffit de lire à ce suject les invectives d'Adalberon de Laon contre Odilon et contre les clunisiens pour mesurer la violence du débat, qui conduit l'évêque à rappeler que les moines sont, en théorie au moins, des laïques. Odilon est traité de 'maître de l'ordre belliqueux', de 'bellator' 'alors que son office serait d'oraison, trainant dans un palais somptueux alors qu'il devrait vivre comme un pauvre, qui court à Rome prier le pape alors qu'il devrait prier Dieu.'[30] Il est le 'roi Odilon', un 'usurpateur'. La critique est excessive sans doute et même injuste, mais il n'en demeure pas moins qu' Adalberon a bien senti ce qu'étaient les intentions et les ambitions clunisienes, c'est-à-dire pour le moins une entière liberté développée aux dépens de l'épiscopat, d'autant plus que, contrairement à ce qu'il écrit, les moines ne sont plus des laïques. Ils sont même tous en pratique des prêtres; ils célèbrent la messe 'sans interruption, mettant à cet office tant de dignité, de piété, de vénération, qu'ils semblent plutôt des anges que des hommes'.[31] Et ils vont être poussés davantage encore à se substituer aux prêtres séculiers par la crise morale du clergé, évêques et clercs se conduisant, dès cette époque et dans les années suivantes (Adalberon écrit vers 1030), de façon telle que s'élève contre eux une contestation en quelque sorte légitime – et dont les mouvements hérétiques de cette même décennie témoignent, ainsi que, un peu plus tard, la Pataria. Les intrigues, les trafics, la corruption se développent autour des sièges épiscopaux, et d'abord pour l'acquisition de ces sièges, au point que Raoul Glaber y voit l'un des signes d'un dérèglement général au même titre que les épidémies et les famines.

Ainsi conçu le project clunisien rejoindrait à première vue le programme de la réforme grégorienne, puisque l'une et l'autre ont pour objectif une plus profonde christianisation de la société accomplie d'abord par une

---

[29] *Les trois ordres ou l'imaginaire du féodalisme*, p. 74.
[30] *Carmen ad Robertum regem*, V, 156.
[31] R. Glaber, *Hist.*, IV, 13.

épuration et une restauration du clergé (contre la simonie et le concubinage), et il est bien vrai que Grégoriens et Clunisiens ont oeuvré côte à côte en ce sens et qu'ils ont même pu s'entre-encourager. De la même façon, la papauté grégorienne a favorisé la poursuite de la réforme monastique entreprise et dirigée par les Clunisiens, parce que c'était là un autre moyen d'approfondir la christianisation (pour les âmes d'élite attirées par l'idéal monacal) et qu'elle allait tout naturellement trouver dans ces monastères des religieux capable et désireux de diffuser les mêmes thèmes spirituels et moraux. C'est la raison pour laquelle apparaissent à cette époque, et non auparavant, les abbayes d'obédience, c'est-à-dire des établissement confiés par le Saint-Siège à Cluny pour y rétablir ordre et discipline ou pour les mieux surveiller – et ce sont souvent des cadeaux empoissonnés dont se plaindra à l'époque suivante Pierre le Vénérable. Mais, à côté de cet accord sur deux points très importants, que de divergences! Sans vouloir reprendre les débats qui, depuis très longtemps, ont opposé les spécialistes et au cours desquels encore récemment se sont illustrés K. Hallinger, G. Tellenbach, E. H. J. Cowdrey et d'autres,[32] il est nécessaire de souligner combien, sur deux arguments fondamentaux, les positions étaient différentes; d'une part, quant à la prétentation de Grégoire VII et de ses partisans de ne concevoir et accepter aucun autre programme réformateur que le leur, étant noté que leur propos reposait sur une rupture délibérée avec les pouvoirs laïcs qui le refusaient et sur l'affirmation selon laquelle la réforme devait être mise en place autoritairement par une Eglise romaine toute puissante; d'autre part, quant à leur attachement indubitable aux structures épiscopales, sous réserve de faire soumettre les évêques au contrôle effectif du pape, la réforme ayant justement pour but de restaurer la dignité des prélats afin qu'ils soient en droit d'exercer leur office pour le meilleur bien des âmes et la plus grande gloire de l'Eglise. Sur ces deux propositions, Cluny, c'est évident, était fortement réticente. Elle était attachée à la reforme en général et a la réforme monastique en particulier, mais elle entendait en établir les dispositions et les méthodes selon sa propre analyse, et d'abord sans rompre avec les pouvoirs laïcs, sans que ses moines soient considérés comme de simples exécutants d'un programme conçu ailleurs et imposé de l'extérieur. Elle ne croyait pas à la possibilité d'une véritable restauration épiscopale; elle ne la souhaitait pas; peut-être même ne la voulait-elles pas. De ce fait, il y avait automatiquement un grave malentendu sur la signification de la 'liberté clunisienne – liberté romaine', et donc de l'exemption, celle-ci étant considérée par les clunisiens comme une réelle liberté, mais tenue par la papauté comme le moyen de diriger directement la congrégation pour la mettre au service de sa cause. Il y avait

---

[32] K. Hallinger, *Gorze-Kluny* (Rome 1950); O. Brackmann, *Zur politischen Bedeutung der Kluniacensichen Bewegung* (Darmstaddt, 1955); G. Tellenbach, *Neue Forschungen über Cluny und die Cluniacenser* (Fribourg en Br., 1951); E. H. J. Cowdrey, ouv. cit.

aussi des réserves de la part des moines quant aux prétensions théocratiques de Grégoire VII, illustrées avant tout par la déposition du roi de Germanie.

Une lecture attentive des bulles adressées par le pape à Cluny témoigne de ce malaise, de ces malentendus, de ces divergences. En Mars 1074, Grégoire VII s'adresse à l'abbé Hugues pour s'étonner de ce que celui-ci ne l'ait point encore visité. Il lui demande de faire prier ses moines pour le succès de son pontificat, 'parce que, si nous ne méritons pas d'obtenir l'aide divine par leur intervention et celle des autres fidèles, nous ne pourrons pas éviter le péril pour l'Eglise'.[33] Cette lettre constitue donc un appel pour que les clunisiens assistent le pape dans la lutte qu'il va engager. En Janvier 1075, il écrit à nouveau sur le même ton.[34] Puis, en Décembre 1076, alors que le conflit des investitures a pris un tour extrêmement violent, il confirme, on l'a dit, toutes les possessions clunisiennes ainsi que l'exemption.[35] C'est pour lui, peut-on croire, l'occasion de solliciter un engagement plus net des clunisiens et d'obtenir leur soutien le plus ferme ainsi que d'apporter, dans un accord délibéré, l'appui du Saint-Siège en faveur de la réforme et de l'hégémonie clunisiennes dans les milieux monastiques. C'est d'ailleurs l'époque où il agit de la même façon à l'égard de la Chaise-Dieu, dont il recherche l'assistance. Mais il ne semble pas atteindre aux résultats escomptés. En 1078, il fait à nouveau état a l'abbé Hugues de sa situation difficile;[36] en Janvier 1079, il lui écrit: 'Pourquoi, frère très cher, ne mesures-tu pas, ne prends-tu pas en considération quel péril, quel malheur menacent la Sainte Eglise' ('Cur, frater charissime, non perpendis, non consideras in quanto periculo, in quanta miseria Sancta versatur Ecclesia').[37] Et c'est sans doute cette indifférence qui explique son intervention en Avril 1079 pour prier Cluny de rendre certains biens à l'éveque de Mâcon[38] et ses réserves pour certaines entreprises clunisiennes en Espagne.[39]

Dès lors, on peut se demander quelle est la signification exacte du fameux discourse qu'ils prononce au synode de Latran en Mai 1080 et par lequel il exalte dans la forme les mérites des clunisiens.[40] L'allocution, une lecture attentive le montre, s'articule en trois parties.

Dans la première, le pape déclare que 'bien qu'outre-mont beaucoup de monastères aient été fondés pour l'honneur de Dieu tout-puissant et des Bienheureux apôtres Pierre et Paul', Cluny, parmi tous, du fait qu'il 'adhère par un droit spécial comme un bien particulier et propre aux

[33] *P.L.*, t. CLXVIII, col. 338.
[34] Id., col. 339–341.
[35] Id., col. 461–466.
[36] Id., col. 506–507.
[37] Id., col. 526.
[38] Id., col. 537.
[39] Id., col. 575–576 (Juin 1080).
[40] Texte cité par Urbain II, *P. L.*, t. CLI, col. 291–293; édité par E. H. J. Cowdrey ouv. cité, pp. 272–273.

Bienheureux Pierre et Paul, a été principalement assigné depuis ses origines à l'honneur et à la protection de ce siège saint et apostolique'.[41] Peut-être ce propos ne constitue-t-il qu'un rappel historique purement formel, mais peut-être aussi est-ce un moyen de souligner que les clunisiens ont des devoirs spéciaux à l'égard de la papauté et ne peuvent s'y dérober.

Dans la seconde partie, le pontife note que grâce à ce privilège originel (l'apôtre Pierre) et grâce a la clémence divine, Cluny a dépassé tous les autres 'pour le service de Dieu et la ferveur spirituelle'. Mais cela a été du aussi à la sainteté de ses abbés, qui se sont succédé par libre élection, en imitant là 'la dignité et la liberté de la Sainte Eglise romaine', et qui, de ce fait, ne sont tombés dans aucune dépendance, mais sont demeurés en revanche dans la sujétion du Saint-Siège pour sa défense. Autrement dit, Cluny l'a jusqu'alors emporté en sainteté et en ferveur et est restée libre parce qu'elle à été protégée par la papauté, qu'elle doit donc aider.

La troisième partie, dès lors, est simple. Grégoire VII renouvelle la protection et l'exemption afin que Cluny soit 'sous les *seules ailes* apostoliques', à l'abri de tout trouble et vive en paix 'dans le sein de l'Eglise romaine, pour l'honneur de Dieu tout-puissant et des bienheureux apôtres Pierre et Paul'. C'est à nouveau le rappel des obligations dues au pape.

Par la suite, aux moments les plus difficiles du combat grégorien, on ne décèle aucune initiative nouvelle. En 1088, au début de son pontificat, Urbain II, confirmant les privilèges clunisiens, précise, on l'a dit, qu'aucun légat pontifical, 'sauf injonction de (sa) part' ne peut avoir autorité à Cluny.[42] C'est laisser entendre que celle-ci n'a pas accepté aisément les légations autoritaires du temps de Grégoire VII, c'est-à-dire l'invitation à mettre en application la réforme et à poursuivre la lutte sur l'investiture selon les seules directives romaines. Urbain II, en outre, ancien clunisien, très sensible à la spiritualité clunisienne et attaché au monachisme, tire les conséquences de tout cette évolution.[43] Il entend restaurer la dignité et l'autorité des évêques en même temps qu'ils tient à aider la poursuite de la réforme proprement monastique. Il reprend donc et amplifie les privilèges accordés aux clunisiens, mais il leur demande de rester à leur place, dans leur secteur, l'exemption étant la garantie du soutien pontifical pour leurs entreprises monastiques (d'où l'accroissement du nombre des abbayes d'obédience), cette politique étant compensée par l'acces de nombreaux religieux à l'épiscopat. Après Pascal II et Gelase II, qui ont peut-être des

---

[41] '. . . Cum ultra montes multa sint monasteria ad honorem Dei omnipotentis et beatorum apostolorum Petri et Pauli nobiliter et religiose fundata, inter omnia quoddam in illis partibus habetur, quod quasi peculiare et proprium beato Petro et huic ecclesiae speciali iure adheret, Cluniacum videlicet, ad honorem et tutelem huius sanctae et apostolicae sedis ab ipsis primordiis principaliter adsignatum' (*ibid.*, p. 272).

[42] *P.L.*, t. CLI, col. 295; et encore en 1095, col. 410.

[43] A. Becker, *Papst Urban II* (Stuttgart, 1964).

idées moines fermes là-dessus, Calixte II renforce plus délibérément encore les structures épiscopales. Dès lors, Cluny perd son ascendant. Après la crise de l'abbatiat de Pons, dû peut-être entre autres causes à cette mutation. Pierre le Vénérable en prend son parti et oeuvre tout à fait admirablement au sein de la communauté monastique pour l'amélioration spirituelle du monachisme.

Tout cela, finalement, montre que Cluny n'a pas seulement contribué à diffuser les désirs d'autonomie dans le clergé régulier tout en tendent à accroître son autorité, mais que, dans la recherche d'une plus grande liberté et d'une plus réelle indépendance, elle a introduit un certain désordre dans l'Eglise, contre lequel les papes réagissent dès la fin de XIème siècle. Dès lors, la clause de réserve des droits de l'ordinaire dans les privilèges d'exemption manifeste davantage qu'un simple désir de bonne gestion. Elle est l'indice d'une volonté de rappel de la règle: liberté a l'intérieur du monastère et de la congrégation, soumission à la loi à l'extérieur. C'est la raison pour laquelle, semble-t-il, à la période suivante, la chancellerie romaine après Gratien ira jusqu'à renoncer à formuler cette clause, tellement il apparaitra alors évident qu'il est impossible (impensable) d'entamer la juridiction de l'évêque sur ses fidèles – seuls les moines et religieux pouvant y échapper. Alexandre III, qui s'appliquera à remettre en ordre les institutions et qui soulignera que les monastères censiers du Saint-Siège ne sont pas obligatoirement exempts, précisera, en un certain nombre de cas, que la liberté monastique doit respecter non seulement l'autorité des évêques sur les paroisses (droit de présentation du patron, concession de la cura animarum par eux seuls) mais aussi leurs pouvoirs en matière de bénédiction (chrèmes, huiles), de consécration et d'ordination. D'autres établissements, certes, continueront à jouir de la pleine exemption (sauf l'institution des curés), mais le simple fait que quelques-uns ne bénéficient que d'une semi-exemption, illustre la volonté soutenue de restreindre et de circonscrire l'indépendance monastique. De plus, le même pontife tiendra à faire mentionner dans tous les privilèges la réserve des droits du Saint-Siège ('Salva sedis apostolicae auctoritate') pour mieux marquer que la liberté monastique ne peut pas etre cette totale indépendance, considérée peut-être dans certains milieux réguliers et sous l'influence de Cluny comme la conséquence logique et normale du mouvement de libération du monachisme.[44] En 1178, l'archevêque de Canterbury Richard exprime clairement cette attitude lorsqu'il écrit au pape pour dénoncer l'abbé de Malmesbury qui refuse de se soumettre à son ordinaire, l'évêque de Salisbury:

> Si, en effet, dit-il, on n'apporte pas à ce mal un remède plus sérieux, il est à craindre que, de même que les abbés échappent aux évêques, de

---

[44] Voir M. Pacaut, *Alexandre III. Étude sur la conception du pouvoir pontifical dans sa pensée et dans son oeuvre* (Paris, 1956), pp. 295–300.

même les évêques échapperont aux archêveques et les doyens à leurs archidiacres et a leurs prélats. Et qu'est-ce que cette forme de l'ordre juste (justitia) ou plutôt cette déformation du droit, qui consiste à empêcher les disciples d'être d'accord avec leurs maitres, les fils d'obéir à leurs pères, les soldats de suivre leurs princes, les serviteurs de se soumettre à leurs seigneurs? Que signifie de soustraire les abbés à la juridiction des évêques et d'armer les enfants contre leurs parents?[45]

Saint Bernard, rappelons-le, avait précédemment protesté en des termes encore plus vifs.

L'exemption, la recherche de l'autonomie et de la liberté tendent à accroître la puissance de Cluny, à faciliter le développement de l'ordre et à renforcer l'autorité de l'abbé de la maison-mère sur les établissements et les moines. L'histoire des institutions clunisiennes est, à première vue, bien connue et illustre clairement ce fait.

Peut-être cependant n'a-t-on pas toujours assez souligné que cette autorité, qui se dévelope de façon telle que l'abbé de Cluny apparait comme un monarque tout puissant et quasiment autocrate, est fondée d'abord sur la charte de fondation, c'est à dire, concernant ce point particulier, sur la règle de saint Benoît qui exalte le pouvoir et la responsabilité du chef du monastère: ce dernier scelle l'union des moines du fait qu'il est élu par eux; ceux-ci lui doivent pleine et total obéissance d'autant plus que l'objectif principal du monachisme est de 'renoncer à sa volonté propre'; en outre, il règne et gouverne toute sa vie sans que, sauf circonstance exceptionnelle, aucune juridiction ne puisse le destituer (encore que, la règle ne suggérant en aucune façon l'exemption, l'évêque pourrait intervenir en cas de manquement grave à ses devoirs; mais un fois l'exemption obtenue, il ne reste que le pape, que l'on voit d'ailleurs intervenir dans les conflits qui s'élèvent sous l'abbatiat de Pons). Il résulte de là que le moine n'a pas à obéir à d'autre personne qu'à l'abbé. De plus, la règle insiste, pour l'élection abbatiale, sur la notion de *sanior pars*, c'est-à-dire sur l'argument selon lequel, en cas de contestation, ont raison ceux qui sont les plus sains les plus vertueux – et aussi les plus anciens, ce qui sous-entend aussi qu'il faut choisir le plus vertueux car, du fait qu'il est le plus vertueux, il est le meilleur, donc le plus légitime. Une telle reflexion conduit à considérer que le pouvoir est légitime s'il est exercé par des hommes vertueux et dignes, donc qu'un moine peut être contraint à ne pas obéir aux autorités considérées comme illégitimes par rapport à eux ou indignes (les laïques, les évêques). On voit là combien la règle, qui exalte la puissance abbatiale, est susceptible d'éliminer toutes les autres autorités, et on retrouve là une argumentation qui a sans doute été avancée en faveur de l'exemption, ne serait-ce qu'à partir de critiques adressées à juste titre à des évêques.

C'est donc en se fondant sur la constitution bénédictine que les abbés de

---

[45] *P.L.*, t. CC, col. 1457–1458.

Cluny ont maintenu et renforcé leur autorité sur leurs religieux. Dès Odon, qui laisse des 'lieutenants' dans les établissements où il introduit la réforme, le mouvement prend forme en faveur d'un système centralisé et dirigé par le chef de l'abbaye-mère. Il se développe avec une vigueur accrue sous Mayeul, et surtout sous Odilon qui paraît bien en avoir le mieux saisi le sens profond et avoir conçu que les réalisations devaient dépasser le cadre étroit du monachisme clunisien et même du monachisme en général. Hugues le perpétue, mais il en est avant tout l'héritier qui garde et fait fructifier de façon extraordinaire l'héritage reçu. Chez tous, les principes sont les mêmes: nécessité de l'autorité, justification de celle-ci par le service rendu et par l'obligation de maintenir l'union. Bernon écrivait déjà que 'Dieu veut que l'homme commande à l'homme'[46] Odon insistait sur le service que l'Eglise, et plus particulièrement les moines comparés a Marie-Madelaine, rendent à la société.[47] Odilon exprimait sans détour que c'était en gouvernant ses religieux qu'il était le plus utile à tous.[48] Quant à Hugues, faisant de l'abbé le berger du troupeau, il déclare que 'tous les clunisiens lui ont été confiés' et qu'il doit les 'tenir' avec fermeté.[49]

Autrement dit, il y a un seul pasteur, un seul chef, un seul roi, un seul souverain. Cela se traduit, on le sait, dans l'organisation par le fait que presque tous les établissements sont des prieurés et non des abbayes, la congrégation se développant soit par réformation de couvents réduits à l'état de prieuré, soit par fondation de maisons qui reçoivent ce statut. L'abbé de Cluny est l'abbé de chaque prieuré; ou encore, il est l'abbé d'une unique très vaste communauté répartie en un grand nombre de couvents, mais constituant en quelque sorte une seule abbaye. C'est lui qui nomme les prieurs: il peut les relever de leur charge ou les muter; il reçoit d'eux un serment de fidélité qui renforce le voeu bénédictin d'obéissance. Par ailleurs, il controle leur gestion directement ou par l'intermédiaire d'officiers délégués par lui; il surveille particulièrement les novices qui, si l'on en croit certains auteurs, devraient théoriquement faire profession à Cluny même.[50]

Il existe cependant des couvents qui gardent le statut d'abbaye. Ce sont les abbayes d'obédience, dont il a précédemment été dit d'une part qu'elles sont très peu nombreuses, d'autre part qu'elles apparaissent assez tardivement soit en conséquence d'une politique hégémonique des abbés de Cluny (qui veulent s'imposer et tiennent à contrôler certains grands établissements afin de limiter une possible concurrence), soit, le plus souvent, à la demande ou sous l'injonction du pape qui espère ainsi voir la réforme s'introduire dans ces maisons qui sont en difficulté. En 1076, par

[46] *Testament, Bibl. Cluniac*, éd. Marillier, (1614), col. 9.
[47] Id., col. 137.
[48] Raoul Glaber, *Hist.*, V, 4.
[49] *Bibl. Cluniac.*, col. 502.
[50] Aini U. Berlière, *L'ordere monastique des origines au XIIème siècle* (Paris, 1924).

exemple, Grégoire VII soumet à Cluny la vieille abbaye de Gigny, fondation première de Bernon, qui va d'ailleurs devenir un simple prieuré.

> Les moines de Gigny, écrit-il, dont le monastère appartient en propre à saint-Pierre, prince des Apôtres, nous ont adressé une requête afin d'obtenir notre compassion et notre aide. Leur monastère, qui autrefois brillait par sa piété, a maintenant perdu toute sa vigueur, à cause de la sollicitude décroissante des abbés et des prévots et souffre même d'une pénurie de biens temporels. Pour mettre fin à cette situation lamentable, les moines eux-mêmes nous ont suggéré un remède et nous ont supplié de l'officialiser: nous devrions confier ce monastère à ta vigilance pour que, là où elle déclinait par somnolence, la piété renaisse sous ta direction zélée et qu'avec l'aide de Dieu elle attire les bienfaits temporels. Aussi te confion-nous à toi, Hugues, le monastère de Gigny.[51]

Les abbés de maisons d'obédience continuent à être élus librement par les moines, mais ils jurent fidélité à l'abbé de Cluny qui inspecte leur gestion. Tout cela illustre le souci d'autorité et de centralisation qui constitue l'apport principal des clunisiens dans l'histoire monastique, encore qu'ils ne soient pas les seuls à agir ainsi et que l'on retrouve la même tendance dans d'autres congrégations ou chez d'autres réformateurs (Richard de St. Vanne, Guillaume de Volpiano).

Si l'on pousse plus avant l'analyse à ce propos, force est de remarquer d'abord que l'autorité 'monarchique' de l'abbé est très particulièrement exaltée, et la centralisation accomplie d'une manière qui peut à l'extrême paraitre aberrante. D'une part, en effet, contrairement à la règle de saint Benoît, l'abbé n'est pas élu par les moines en toute liberté. Bernon, on le sait, a cédé par testament l'abbaye à Odon, qu'il a donc lui-même désigné comme abbé (927). En 942, avant de partir pour son troisième voyage à Rome, Odon nomme à son tour Aymard pour lui succéder. Ce dernier, gravement malade, remet sa charge à Mayeul en 948 en obtenant l'assentiment des autres moines. ('Avec tous mes frères, fils et comme moi-même serviteurs du bienheureux Pierre, nous élisons notre frère et fils déjà cher Mayeul et nous proclamons aux moines qu'il est abbé').[52] En Janvier 994, Mayeul procède exactement de la même facon en faveur d'Odilon, choisi comme coadjuteur dès Mai 993. En revanche, Odilon agit différemment, mais il a pris soin d'exprimer avec force le souhait que soit élu Hugues de Semur, qu'il avait fait grand prieur.[53] D'autre part, seuls les

---

[51] B. Gasper, *Histoire de Gigny* (Lons-le-Saunier, 1843, texte latin). La donation par le pape à Cluny est le plus souvent précédée de la cession par une autorité locale, généralement laïque – le fondateur de l'établiseement.

[52] *Recueil des chartres de l'abbaye de Cluny*, éd. Bernard et Bruel, no. 883.

[53] J. Gaudemet, *Les élections dans l'Eglise latine des origines au XVIème siècle* (Paris, 1979), pp. 221–225.

moines de Cluny participent à cette désignation, les profès des prieurés en étant exclus, ce qui contredit la notion d'une vaste 'familia' monastique distribuée en plusiers établissements et apporte aux religieux de la maison-mère un privilège qui les associe particulièrement à l'autorité de l'abbé.[54]

Il faut se garder par ailleurs, de considérer cette autorité, dans ses fondements et son agencement, comme la transposition du système vassalique à l'intérieur d'un institut monastique, ainsi que l'ont fait certains historiens. Certes, il y a des liens de dépendance entre l'abbay-mère et ses prieurés et entre certains prieurés chefs de filiation et des maisons rattachées à eux (rôle particulier de Souvigny, de St. Martin des Champs, de Lewes, etc.), de même qu'il y a entre les hommes qui les dirigent échanges de serments de fidélité. Mais, d'une part, le fondement de l'autorité abbatiale ne cesse d'être celui que définit la règle bénédictine, à savoir que l'abbé tient la place du Christ dans le monastère et qu'il est le maitre (magister) de la spritualité, de plus un chef dont le pouvoir est-en quelque sorte absolu dans la mesure où ses décisions ne contredisent pas les coutûmes de l'ordre: autant d'éléments qui sont étrangers à la féodalité. D'autre part, il n'est nul besoin de se référer au système vassalique du simple fait que l'on constate des subordinations – car toute organisation des pouvoirs et des administrations serait alors censée reproduire ce système. Quant aux engagements de fidélité, ils expriment sous un forme particulière et dans des circonstances spéciales (pluralité des couvents) le voeu bénédictin d'obéissance. Tout au plus, l'usage qu'on en fait et la manière dont on les accomplit traduisent des moeurs qui sont celles de la société féodale, mais cela est tout à fait normal et représente seulement l'expression formelle, l'enveloppe extérieure d'engagements et de relations qui ressortissent à d'autres valeurs. Les abbés d'obédience et les prieurs ne sont d'ailleurs pas engagés par un contrat obligeant à des services en certains cas, mais astreints à une obéissance permanente.[55]

On doit cependant relever, plus particulièrement à propos des abbayes d'obédience, mais aussi à propos de prieurés qui ne sont pas des fondations clunisiennes et ont été données à Cluny, que l'exaltation de l'autorité pour maintenir l'ordre dans le secteur monastique à été facilitée par la défense de la liberté des etablissements face à la puissance séculière. Fort souvent, il a fallu intervenir pour sauver l'indépendance de monastères isolés, menacés de tomber sous la coupe de laïques (et d'être ruinés par eux) ou sous le controle abusif de la hiérarchie ecclésiastique, ou simplement accablés de difficultés économiques ou détériorés intérieurement par le relâchement. Dans tous ces cas, l'objectif étant de libérer de l'emprise d'autres pouvoirs ou de l'emprise du mal, il s'agissait donc d'un combat libératoire qui ne pouvait s'accomplir qu'à la condition d'être dirigé par un pouvoir fort et

---

[54] M. Pacaut, 'De l'aberration à la logique. Essai sur les mutations de quelques structures ecclésiastiques', dans *Revue Historique*, 1972, pp. 313–324.

[55] J.-F. Lemarignier, *Structures . . .*, art. cité.

contraignant, ce qui oblige à nuancer les appréciations que l'on pourrait porter sur les ambiguités clunisiennes et sur le rôle spécial dévolu aux moines de l'abbay-mère dans l'élection abbatiale. Ces derniers, en effet, sont sans doute plus aptes à garder entre eux les principes fondamentaux et l'idéal de la réforme: ils y sont plus naturellement attachés et surtout ils y ont intérêt, puisque c'est là la seule justification acceptable de leur privilège.

Il n'en demeure pas moins que, tout au cours de son histoire, l'autorité de l'abbé et celle de l'abbaye de Cluny ont été considérées par certains comme particulièrement pesantes et contraignantes, au point que l'on peut avancer sans exagération qu'il y a eu en permanence contestation à leur encontre et recherche vigoureuse de la liberté. Ce mouvement apparaît clairement dans la seconde moitié du XIème siècle et prend une ampleur considérable au XIIème siècle. Il se concrétise donc à partir du moment où les religieux et les établissements concernés cessent de percevoir les avantages de la réforme et de l'intégration, soit qu'ils ne tiennent pas tellement à se réformer, soit que la régénération clunisienne leur semble plutôt fade et qu'ils commencent, au contraire, à ressentir les inconvénients de la centralisation, avec les excès d'Odilon et de Hugues. Il est aisé de la constater en suivant les relations avec les abbayes d'obédience, ces remarques permettant de mieux comprendre certaines hésitations de la papauté qui cherche à aider la réforme monastique (donc à soumettre à Cluny), mais qui est sensible aux abus de la puissance clunisienne, et aux désirs d'autonomie des monastères. Sans doute peut-on le vérifier aussi pour bon nombre de prieurés. G. de Valous a étudié les combats de Vézelay, de St. Gilles, St. Bertin, St. Jean d'Angely, Baume, St. Germain d'Auxerre, St. Martial de Limoges, et E. H. J. Cowdrey lui-même en relève quelques'uns.[56]

Sans vouloir entrer dans les détails et reprendre des évènements bien rapportés dans ces ouvrages et dans d'autres, notons que St. Gilles, monastère ancien relevant directement de l'Eglise romaine et exempt depuis 985, est confié à Cluny en 1066 par la Comtesse de Toulouse et son fils. L'abbé Bérald, élu en 1067, réagit contre cette décision et, dans un premier temps, Alexandre II, puis Grégoire VII le soutiennent. Mais, en 1076, Grégoire VII l'excommunie (cela serait il lié à la réforme grégorienne?) et force les récalcitrants à se soumettre à Hugues de Cluny, qu'il charge de nommer un nouvel abbé. La lutte, apaisée par cette contrainte, reprend sous Urbain II et se poursuit jusque dans les années 1160, Cluny receivant d'une façon générale l'appui des pontifes romains. En 1162, en revanche, Alexandre III, qui est fort réticent à l'encontre de Cluny dont l'attitude dans le schisme pontifical est ambigüe, soustrait St-Gilles a l'obédience de l'ordre.[57] Vézelay, de son côté, résiste dès son intégration a la congrégation clunisienne en 1026 (par le Comte de Nevers)

---

[56] *Le monachisme clunisien des origines au XVème siècle* (Ligué, Paris, 1935), t. II, pp. 57–59, E. H. J. Cowdrey, ouv. cité, pp. 85 sq.

[57] G. de Valous, ouv. cité, p. 58; E. H. J. Cowdrey, ouv. cité, p. 95.

contre la mainmise d'Odilon et n'accepte jamais cette sujétion malgré les injonctions de la papauté (Pascal II, Calixte II surtout); en 1162, elle retrouve, elle aussi, sa liberté.[58] Baume-les-Messieurs, enfin, qui appartient à la préhistoire et à la première histoire clunisienne, puisque Bernon la réforme avant de fonder Cluny et qu'Odon y fut prieur, totalement indépendante de l'ordere en 926 et en plein essor à la fin du XIème et au début du XIIème siècle, est soumise de force et réduite à l'état de prieuré en 1147 à la suite de violences perpétrées par les moines contre un chanoine d'Autun qui venait y débattre d'un différend entre son église et le couvent, violences que le Saint-Siège interprète comme le signe d'un profond dérèglement. Cette sanction déclenche chez les religieux une telle animosité que, 'pendant un siècle et demi, un sourd malaise régna dans l'abbaye, que la moindre occasion transformait en rebellion ouverte contre Cluny'.[59]

Aussitôt que l'on sort de France, on contaste que les désirs d'autonomie sont tout aussi forts, au point que Cluny accepte d'accorder quelques libertés. En Italie, après une première période assez faste à l'époque d'Odon et de Mayeul, il y a quelque relachement (des établissements ont quitté l'ordre), mais dans le nord de la péninsule, l'implantation se maintient, autour de St. Benoît du Po particulièrement, sans que l'on connaisse dans le détail les relations avec l'abbaye-mère.[60] En Allemagne, où il y a peu de couvents directement clunisiens, il ne semble pas qu'il y ait des différends. Les monastères anglais, qui dépendent de St.-Martin du Champ dont le couvent pionnier est le prieuré de Lewes, paraissent, sous le contrôle du prieur de cette maison, qui est inamovible, bénéficier d'un statut moins rigide, ce qui n'empêche pas certains d'entre eux, mais beaucoup plus tard (deuxième moitié du XIIIème siècle), de secouer le joug et de manifester leur volonté d'indépendance (Monk Bretton, St. Jacques d'Exeter, Barnstable, Monkhorton, etc.). Dans la péninsule ibérique, le monachisme clunisien cherche à s'introduire avec vigueur sous l'abbatiat de Hugues, mais les liens qui unissent les monastères a l'abbaye bourguignonne ne sont pas toujours très serrés. Sahagun devient en quelque sorte chef d'une congrégation de couvents qui suivent les coutûmes clunisiennes (en Castille et Léon), sans véritable sujétion directe à Cluny.[61] C'est elle qui, dans les années 1080–1085, essaie d'introduire ces usages dans des couvents portugais, jadis aux mains de l'aristocratie laïque, mais où s'est maintenu le plus souvent le droit pour les évêques d'instituer les abbés. Cette tentative aboutit à une assez forte pénétration des règlements clunisiens, mais ne crée pas de rapports étroits de subordination. La réforme clunisienne, de plus, intervient ici un peu tardivement, si bien que les désirs d'une nouvelle

---

[58] G. de Valous, ouv. cité, p. 59; E. H. J. Cowdrey, ouv. cité, p. 85.
[59] R. Locatelli . . ., *L'abbaye de Baume les Messieurs* (Besançon, 1978), p. 48.
[60] G. Penco, *Storia del monachismo in Italia* (Ed. Paoline, 1959), pp. 186 sq.
[61] E. H. J. Cowdrey, ouv. cité, p. 239.

régéneration religieuse seront très tôt captés par les chanoines réguliers et les cisterciens.[62]

Tout cela confirme la leçon essentielle qui se dégage de cette analyse, à savoir qu'à l'intérieur du monachisme l'influence de Cluny s'est exercée d'abord et avant tout en faveur de l'autorité et de l'ordere (respect des règles, refus de tout désordre). Le système clunisien, avec le type de vie régulière qu'il proposait, a même pu jusqu'au milieu du XIème siècle apparaître comme un modèle. Mais, en même temps et surtout à partir de cette époque, les réactions contre l'emprise du chef d'ordre ont été telles que l'histoire clunisienne a sans doute finalement contribué à développer la contestation et les aspirations à l'indépendance et à la liberté plus que tout autre chose. Pierre le Vénérable en prend d'ailleurs pleinement conscience au XIIème siècle, lui qui proteste contre les donations d'abbayes d'obédience qui constituent effectivement des cadeaux empoisonnés. En même temps qu'il tente de régénérer la spiralité dans les monastères repliés sur euxmêmes, il fait fonctionner au mieux le chapitre général, nouvelle institution qui tempère la puissance monocratique de l'abbé et donne à l'organisation un souplesse qui lui avait toujours fait défaut. Les positions trop autoritaristes du régime clunisien favorisent par ailleurs la création et le développement de nouvelles congrégations qui respectent la liberté et le droit de chaque abbaye, et dont Cîteaux – qui a, à sa fondation, posé en principe le refus de l'exemption – représente le meilleur modèle (union entre des abbayes consentie dans la charité, constitutions élaborées et mises en application par le chapitre général, seul Organisme de direction suprême). Peut-être même, à partir des réactions contre l'enterprise clunisienne, dont on relève cependant qu'elle a eu pour avantage de favoriser l'efficacité grâce à la très grande puissance de l'abbé, une réflexion conduira-telle à noter que l'opposition à cette puissance, et donc la déficience du système, ont tenu au regroupement dans un même ensemble de monastères dont chacun avait, qu'on le veuille ou non, abbaye ou prieuré, une personnalité juridique et morale. Si bien que l'on tendra vers des instituts religieux qui n'assemblent plus des maisons, mais seulement des individus, obéissant strictement à leurs supérieurs, cette mutation étant provoquée aussi par un vif désir d'action dans et sur la société, qui avait été d'ailleurs, l'une des caractéristiques de Cluny – au point que c'est peut-être cette volonté d'enterprise 'dans le monde' qui a facilité l'exaltation de la puissance, condition essentielle de la réussite.

Ce rôle de Cluny dans la société, son influence sur la société en faveur de l'ordere ou de la liberté, ont donné lieu ces dernières années à des recherches très savantes et tres fines qui permettent de mieux éclairer un problème dont l'approche est souvent obscure. Les historiens français sont parmi les principaux maîtres d'oeuvre de cette entreprise, au premier rang desquels il

[62] J. Mattoso, *Le monachisme ibérique et Cluny. Les monastères du diocèse de Porto de l'an 1100 à 1200* (Louvain, 1968).

faut citer G. Duby, J.-F. Lemarignier, E. Magnou-Nortier, mais auxquels on doit adjoindre des auteurs d'autres pays.[63] A partir de leurs travaux et en confrontant ceux-ci de façon plus ferme avec l'histoire proprement monastique, on peut dégager le sens général de l'évolution qui montre que Cluny apparaît d'abord comme une force de contestation contre les pouvoirs en place et contre un certain ordre social, puis qu'elle devient au contraire une puissance de conservatisme en faveur d'un autre ordre social qu'elle rêve d'établir.

Parmi les idées qui ont présidé à sa fondation et à d'autres datant de la même époque, il y a évidemment une réflexion sur la société qui conduit à vouloir s'en retirer parce qu'elle est dangereuse et s'organiser en quelque sorte contre elle. La charte de 909 exprime à l'évidence ce souci d'exclure tout intervention des pouvoirs temporels dans l'établissement, non seulement, peut-on penser, parce que ce sont souvent des puissances de fait dont le rôle n'est pas justifié par le droit public ou la nécessité de l'ordere, mais aussi parce que ces pouvoirs sont violents et féroces. La réserve claire à l'encontre des autorités constituées et reconnue légitimes, mais risquant d'être dangereuse (rois, ducs, comtes, évêques), prend, dès les débuts de l'histoire clunisienne la forme d'une contestation fondamentale aussitôt qu'il s'agit des seigneurs et de ce que l'on a appelé l'anarchie féodale.[64] Odon manifeste plusieurs fois cette réprobation,[65] qui conduit à la lutte des clunisiens, dès la seconde moitié du Xème siècle et tout au cours du XIème, pour maintenir et renforcer les temporels des monastères, récupérer les dimes et les paroisses, la réforme grégorienne les aidant grandement dans cette entreprise.[66] De là, résulte finalement un certain renversement de la hiérarchie des pouvoirs. Les pouvoirs constitués, que l'on redoute parfois, sont considérés comme devant être au service des bonnes causes (cela

[63] G. Duby, Les trois ordres . . . ouv. cité; J.-F. Lemarignier, Structures . . . art. cité; id., 'Le monachisme et l'encadrement des campagnes du royaume de France situées au nord de la Loire de la fin du XIème à la fin du XIème siècle, dans Le istituzioni ecclesiastiche nel alto medio evo (Spolète, 1974), pp. 357–405, et bien d'autres articles; E. Magnou-Nortier, 'Les mauvaises coutûmes en Auvergne, Bourgogne méridionale, Languedoc et Provence au XIème, un moyen d'analyse sociale', dans Structures féodales et féodalisme dans l'Occident méditerranean, X⁰–XIII⁰ siècle. (Ec. française de Rome, 1980), pp. 137–172; C. Violante, 'Il monachesimo cluniacense,' art. cité; E. H. J. Cowdrey, 'The peace and the trust of God in the eleventh century', in Past and Present, Fevrier 1970, pp. 42–67; etc. . . .

[64] M. Pacaut, 'Structures monastiques, société et Eglise en Occident aux XIème et XIIème siècles', dans Aspects de la vie conventuelle au XIème et XIIème siècles (Cahiers d'Histoire, 1975), pp. 11–23.

[65] Ainsi dans l'Epitome morialium Gregorii in Job, où il dénonce les méfaits de certains princes (P.L., t. CXXXIII, col. 337).

[66] J. F. Lemarignier, Le monachisme . . ., art. cite; G. Constable, Monastic Tithes from their origins to the twelfth century (Cambridge, 1964), p. 89–93; H. Dienier, 'Das Verhältnis Clunys zu den Bischofen', in Neue Forschunge, pp. 355–426.

transparait dans *la Vie de Saint Géraud, comte d'Aurillac*, par Odon) etc., en conséquence, comme inférieurs aux offices écclesiastiques qui seuls déterminent les objectifs et parmi lesquelles les plus éminents sont les autorités monastiques, et d'abord et avant tout Cluny (on retrouve là l'attitude à l'encontre de l'épiscopat). Cette réflexion a pour conséquence d'exalter encore davantage l'abbé de Cluny, comparé a l'archange supérieur à toutes les puissance humaines, et pour lequel on édifie un palais somptueux.[67]

Cependant s'il y a réserve et contestation, il n'y a pas rejet absolu des pouvoirs laïcs, d'une part parce que, de par son recrutement, Cluny est étroitement lié aux milieux aristocratiques qui exercent ces pouvoirs, d'autre part, parce que, très délibérément, ses grands abbés veulent jouer un rôle dans la société et apporter un message social. Il s'ensuit que, adoptant une position très critique à l'encontre de la description trifonctionnelle des Adalberon de Laon et Gérard de Cambrai, et surtout refusant aux évêques l'office premier, constatant par ailleurs que le pouvoir royal est défaillant (ce qui est éclatant en Mâconnais), Cluny entend diriger spirituellement et moralement la noblesse en la 'monachisant'. Par ailleurs, Odilon prend, à l'égard des guerriers qui sont au service de ces nobles mais forment aussi souvent des groupes de pillards, une attitude originale. D'une part, il les combat et les fait combattre par les armes, car il est nécessaire de lutter contre la violence et le désordre. D'autre part, il tient aussi à les 'monachiser' et à les faire aider aux bonnes causes; il pousse donc à les intégrer davantage à la noblesse en faisant d'eux des chevaliers, cette entreprise constituant l'un des aspects des mouvements de paix.

Probablement aussi, les clunisiens entendent défendre les humbles et les pauvres. Dès le début, Odon insiste là-dessus. Ce qu'il faut d'abord, écrit-il, c'est 'libérer le pauvre qui hurle' en même temps qu'aider les veuves et les orphelins,[68] et il n'hésite pas, à ce propos, à rappeler que, de par la nature, les hommes sont égaux et que c'est Dieu seul qui a confié à certains d'entre eux 'le pouvoir sur leurs égaux'.[69] Mayeul et Odlion pousuivent sur la même voie avec des termes semblables, au point que Raoul Glaber, qui réflète comme un miroir l'idéologie clunisienne, place, dans la description théorique qu'il donne du pélerinage, la plèbe immédiatement après les moines et avant tous les autres.[70] Il y a donc, ici aussi, contestation de l'ordre social et souhait de 'libérer' (le mot est employé) les pauvres de leur misère et des abus dont ils sont les victimes.

Tout cela, cependant, masque quelque peu le véritable objectif qui est d'asseoir la puissance et la liberté de Cluny. Cette contestation, qui existe à certains moments de l'histoire de Cluny et de la part de certains clunisiens,

---

[67] G. Duby, *Les trois ordres* . . ., pp. 248–249.
[68] Epitome . . ., *P.L.*, t. CXXIII, col. 338).
[69] Id., col. 399 ('potestatem super aequales').
[70] *Historia*, IV, 6, 18.

ne se maintient pas en permanence. Tout au contraire même, il semble que la vraie continuité se trouve dans le refus de tout désordre préjudiciable au monachisme, si bien que, dès les années 1030 et peut être même plus tôt, on décèle un comportement de plus en plus conservateur.

La politique en faveur des mouvements de paix, que Cluny favorise et diffuse en Bourgogne dès le début du XIème siècle, dont le but est d'apaiser les appétits de la haute aristocratie et de lutter contre les guerriers pillards (que l'on intègre au groupe dominant), par dessus tout de préserver les patrimoines ecclésiastiques, ne conduit pas à un affaiblissement de la noblesse, car dès l'époque d'Odilon, celle-ci est confortée par le modèle élaboré qui exclut la contestation et justifée par le maintien de l'ordere qui lui est confié, ses pouvoirs et ses droits étant ainsi légitimés. On peut d'ailleurs pousser plus loin l'analyse, ainsi que l'a fait E. Magnou-Nortier[71] et relever qu'à partir des années 1050, les chartres et accords de paix montrent, d'une part, que l'on écarte l'ost des terres monastiques, que Cluny récupère les dîmes et le casuel réservé aux desservants des églises et bénéficie des dépouilles, d'autre part que les contraintes et interdits ne concernent pas les alleux et les fiefs. C'est-à-dire que l'aristocratie peut faire ce qu'elle veut sur ses domaines, sauf de trop pressurer les 'villani', et que les seigneurs moyens ayant les mêmes possibilités, peuvent, entre autre choses, construire des châteaux. Ainsi, plus que jamais, en collaborant avec la haute aristocratie contre laquelle elle avait lutté au début du XIème siècle, mais qui, maintenant, la protège, elle assure l'ordre aristocratique, allant même jusqu'à fortifier les assises de la moyenne noblesse. Certes, peu après 1100, Hugues, puis Pons, cessent de soutenir la chevalerie et en dénoncent les méfaits; mais, cette fois encore, ainsi que l'a souligné G. Duby,[72] ce n'est pas pour contester la société en poussant les pauvres à en refuser l'agencement; c'est au nom des intérêts cluniens et de l'ordere (anti-désordre) tout court. D'ailleurs, il ne semble pas que ces critiques visent la haute aristocratie et on est en droit de se demander si ne profile pas aussi le désir d'un pouvoir suprême qui garantirait pleinement cet ordre et que l'on trouvera dans l'autorité monarchique, dont Cluny perçoit les avantages qu'elle pourrait en retirer dès les années 1070 et plus encore, après la fondation du prieuré de St. Martin des Champs. La société seigneuriale étant par nature encline à l'anarchie, on espère en une puissance plus stable et plus légitime: après l'essai d'entente avec la haute aristocratie et la 'liberté' laissée à la moyenne noblesse, voici venu le temps de l'ordere des monarques, auquel aspire Pierre le Vénérable lorsqu'il déplore, vers 1140, que le Mâconnais soit un pays 'sans roi, sans duc, sans prince'.[73]

Quant au soutien des pauvres, il faut nuancer aussi les appréciations trop souvent avancées. Il est évident que Cluny les assiste et les secourt tout au

---

[71] Art. cité.
[72] Ouv. cité, p. 249.
[73] P.L., t. CLXXXIX, col. 101.

long de son histoire: c'est là obligation de charité selon les termes de la règle de saint Benoît. Mais les clunisiens, pratiquant la pauvreté en esprit, ne vivent pas dans un cadre pauvre, ne vivent pas dans la pauvreté, ne vivent pas la pauvreté.[74] Par ailleurs, s'il est vrai qu'ils défendent les villani contre ces excès de réquisitons des seigneurs et contre leurs abus de pouvoir, s'il est exact qu'ils regrettent à ce propos les 'mauvaises coutûmes', ils pronent à l'inverse le maintien de la puissance seigneuriale et d'un système agraire que seuls contrôlent les grands propriétaires. Ils laissent les paysans être des 'dépendants' et ils ne s'interessent guère aux pauvres des villes et aux marginaux des campagnes. Bref, ils ont un comportement moral chrétien (charité); ils n'ont aucune attention aux problèmes de justice sociale.

Si l'on abandonne l'étude de l'influence de Cluny sur les structures politiques et sur les structures ecclésiastiques pour s'attacher à son ascendant religieux sur la société, on aboutit à des constatations similaires. Certes, il est évident que les clunisiens ont joué un rôle éminent dans la christisation des campagnes auprès des seigneurs et des paysans et qu'ils ont grandement participé a là première édification de la piété et de la culture chrétiennes. Mais, sans entrer dans les détails d'une analyse qui relève d'un autre secteur de l'histoire, force est de noter que la religion clunisienne, proposée aux puissants et aux humbles, est une religion de contrainte. L'accent y est mis sur la liturgie et les obligations cultuelles, sur les pratiques communautaires controlées par le clergé (et d'abord par les moines), sur la préparation à la mort qui est jugement de toute une vie et sur le culte des morts. Comment cela a-t-il été reçu? Dans quelles mesures ces données ont-elles été perçues comme fondamentalement chrétiennes? Ce sont là des interrogations sur lesquelles on ne se penchera pas ici. Mais il est clair, même si l'au-delà est adouci par la foi dans la bonté de Dieu – et peu à peu par la croyance au Purgatoire – que les propos ainsi répandus risquent fort de provoquer la crainte plus que l'amour et la confiance et d'être finalement traumatisants. La piété devient, elle aussi, nonobstant sa valeur propre qui est indéniable, un moyen de puissance.

Elle confirme que, globalement, Cluny apparait comme ayant été un facteur d'order, d'autorité et de conservatisme, et fut peu un foyer de liberté ou de contestation. L'exemption a pour finalité l'indépendance de Cluny pour sa propre grandeur et à la rigueur pour la grandeur de l'Eglise romaine qui, elle aussi, passées quelques formules et écoulés les premiers moments de la réforme grégorienne,[75] tend à l'hégémonie. La congrégation clunisienne est fondée sur l'obéissance au pouvoir quasiment souverain d'un abbé monocrate. L'ordre instauré dans la société, auquel elle coopère, est celui des puissants, et d'abord celui de sa propre puissance. Ces

---

[74] On ne peut suivre là-dessus l'opinion de P. Lamma (*Momenti di storiografia cluniacense*, Rome, 1969).

[75] Voir M. Pacaut, *Les mutations de l'Eglise aux XIème et XIIème siècles* (*Congrès International des Sciences historiques*, Bucarest, 1980, à paraitre).

remarques, cependant, ne doivent pas masquer d'autres réalisations, car il demeure certain que Cluny a exercé par bien d'autres arguments, et justement grâce à sa puissance, des actions bénéfiques. Dans le développement historique chacun, on le sait, apporte à son tour sa pierre à la construction. 'Il y a beaucoup de demeures dans la maison du Père' (Jean, XIV, 2).

THE EARLY CISTERCIANS AND THE OLD
MONASTICISM

A. H. Bredero

An educated Cistercian monk in the first half of the twelfth century, and consequently belonging to the order's first generation, if asked about the Cistercians' relation to the old monasticism, would probably have answered that his order was its continuation: or at any rate that the Cistercians had cut their links with Benedictine monasticism as practised traditionally in those days, because it deviated too much from the old monasticism. An indication for such an answer is already provided by the earliest account of the origin and beginnings of the Cistercian order, the *Exordium parvum*. The monks who left the Molesmes monastery to found 'the new monastery', the original name given to Citeaux, reached their decision as a result of frequent conversations among themselves about the neglect of the Rule of blessed Benedict, the father of monks. They lamented the fact, and were saddened by it, that other monks who in solemn profession had promised to keep this rule, did not observe it at all, and thus were consciously guilty of perjury.[1]

The earliest Cistercians wanted to combat abuses in contemporary monasticism through a return to the old, that is to say original precepts of Saint Benedict, and to forgo all changes, mitigations or extensions which this rule had been subjected to as a result of ensuing customs which had obtained the force of law within traditional Benedictine monasticism. With respect to this they considered themselves reformers, who moreover were especially interested in the last chapter of Benedict's Rule: a chapter considered by some as a later addition.[2] In it the rule is described as a rule for

---

[1] 'De egressu cisterciensium de Molismo', in *Les plus anciens textes de Citeaux*, edited by J. Bouton and J. B. van Damme (Achel, 1974), p. 60.

[2] E. Manning, 'Le chapitre 73 de la règle Bénédictine est-il de S. Benoît?' in *Archivum Latinatatis medii aevi (Bulletin du Cange)*, 30 (1960), pp. 129–141.

beginners and those who are in a hurry to reach the full unfolding of monastic life, are referred to the doctrine of the holy fathers, the exercise of which leads man to the summit of perfection.[3] These holy fathers are the monastic predecessors of St. Benedict and on account of the attention paid by the early Cistercians to those 'desert fathers' their monasteries have at times been described as 'the deserts of the twelfth century'.[4] When founding their monasteries they behaved as Emerites who wanted to flee from the world completely; they sought loneliness under extremely difficult circumstances and made inhospitable regions habitable.

Naturally this representation of things contained a certain element of fantasy. In their own opinion the Cistercians were returning to the old monasticism, but in reality their thoughts and conduct were the product of a contemporary situation which was held to be identical with that of the old monasticism. They stuck to this figment of their imagination even in situations which did not fit the conditions they had proposed themselves with regard to the founding of new monasteries, and which had been incorporated as a precept in their oldest *statuta*, namely that monasteries should not be built in towns, fortified places or existing domains, but only in places far removed from human company.[5] In by no means all cases was this completely true. In spite of this a monastic chronicle related sometimes, as in the case of Silvanes, in what barren waste the respective abbey had been founded.[6] Moreover, the oldest Cistercian *consuetudines*, the *Ecclesiastica Officia*, show that a Cistercian monastery with its material provisions was by no means a primitive community in those early days.[7]

I trust that what has been said so far will have made clear that in this context old monasticism means something different from what the early Cistercians understood by it, at any rate if we wish to discuss historical reality. We must inquire into the relation between the young Cistercian order and the traditional Benedictine monasticism which had developed since the Carolingian era and had taken shape in various monastic associations or orders, like Brogne, la Chaise-Dieu, Gorze, Hirsau and Cluny. All these were monastic associations which themselves had attempted a reform of Benedictine monasticism more or less on the lines of the reformatory measures submitted for approval to the synod of Aachen

---

[3] *Regula S. Benedicti, c.* 73.

[4] E. Gilson, *La théologie mystique de S. Bernard* (Paris, 1934), p. 31.

[5] J-M Canivez, *Statuta capitulorum generalium ordinis cisterciensis*, I. (Louvain 1933), p. 13: 'In civitatibus, castellis, villis, nulla nostra construenda sunt coenobia, sed in locis a conversatione hominum remoti'.

[6] C. H. Berman, 'The Foundation and Early History of the Monastery of Silvanes: the Economic Reality', in *Cistercian Ideals and Reality*, published by J. R. Sommerfeldt (Kalamazoo, 1978), pp. 280–318.

[7] B. K. Lackner, 'Early Cistercian Life as described in the *Ecclesiastica Officia*', in *Cistercian Ideals and Reality*, pp. 62–79.

by Benedict of Aniane.[8] Our information about this relationship is restricted, namely to the relationship between the Cistercians and the Cluniacs. Their monasteries were situated close to each other, certainly in the early days of the Cistercian order, which was then limited in its expansion to France. When both orders extended into Germany, also there rivalry would arise between them, at any rate between the Cistercians and monks of the congregation of Hirsau who were described as Cluniacs because they derived their *consuetudines* from Cluny.[9]

This rivalry, which was an important characteristic of the relationship between Cistercians and Cluniacs, had of course to do with the spectacular growth of the Cistercian order.[10] The main facts of this growth are generally known. In 1098 Cîteaux was founded. In the years 1112–1115 this abbey founded its first four daughter abbeys: La Ferté, Pontigny, Clairvaux and Morimond. Forty years later the order already numbered 335 monasteries for men, that is to say in the year 1153 when Bernard of Clairvaux died. Clairvaux and Morimond had taken the lion's share in this expansion. There were then only twenty monasteries for nuns at the most. The hey-day of this branch of the order does not therefore belong to the period discussed here.

The growth of the Cistercian order was a complex thing in those early days. The credit for this has been largely given to Bernard of Clairvaux. The latter indeed involved himself frequently in the take-over of existing abbeys or the acquisition of donations of land on which a new foundation could be started.[11] But at least equal importance must be attached to the fact that in those days Benedictine monasticism underwent a change, a crisis according to some,[12] because a different observance of the rule forced itself upon the monks as a consequence of changes in contemporary society; an observance different from what was customary in the long established monasteries.

These social changes, which stimulated the desire for a different observance of the rule of Benedict, were partly of an economic nature. The old abbeys got into financial trouble because an important part of their income, the tithes of landed property not belonging to these monasteries, began to decrease. This was partly due to an increase of population on the

---

[8] J. Semmler, 'Die Beschlüsse des Aachner Konzils in Jahre 816', *Zeitschrift für Kirchengeschichte*, 74 (1963), pp. 15–82.

[9] *Herbordi Vita Ottonis episcopi Babenbergensis*, lib. I, c. 12–4; *Monumenta Germ. Hist., Scriptores* XX, p. 708.

[10] Cf. L. Janautschek, *Originum cisterciensium*, I. (Vienne 1877).

[11] A. H. Bredero, *Bernhard von Clairvaux im Widerstreit der Historie*, (Wiesbaden, 1966), pp. 47–53.

[12] J. Leclerq, 'La crise du monachisme aux XIe et XIIe siècles', *Bulletino dell' Istituto storico per il medio evo e Archivio Muratoriano*, 70 (1958), pp. 19–41. Idem, *Aux sources de la spiritualité occidentale* (Paris, 1964), pp. 175–199.

domains, giving rise to a more intensive consumption of agricultural produce. Partly also this decline of income was a result of the advent of a market economy which was made possible through an increase in the circulation of money. It became more attractive to sell surpluses of produce for money than to donate them to monasteries. The decline in income did not automatically result in a reduction in an abbey's costs and expenditure. The circulation of money, moreover, opened the possibility of borrowing money, of which the monks made use too freely, because on the one hand they did not comprehend the structural character of the decline of their income, and on the other because they lacked experience in the paying of interest. On the whole, however, this did not become a serious problem for the Cistercians. Their strict rule of life restored to its pristine place of honour the prescript of manual labour. This manual labour was made productive in the reclamation of land and the cultivation of the fields. Whereas the old Benedictine monasteries were mostly situated on hills (although Cluny was an exception to this rule) the Cistercians consciously chose the valleys, where they harnessed the water courses and adapted them to the needs of their monasteries. This in its turn resulted frequently in secular initiatives for the foundation of Cistercian abbeys. These abbeys were often looked upon as incentives for the development of an agrarian economy.

The Cistercians did not consider tithes to be a legitimate income for monks. For neither the Rule nor the 'life' of Benedict mentioned them.[13] This also means that they rejected the obligation to pay tithes to a third party, an obligation sometimes attached to property donated to them. Moreover, their recruiting methods differed somewhat from those customary in the traditional Benedictine monasteries. No one was allowed admittance to a community under the age of eighteen, and the novitiate of one year's duration prescribed by the Rule, but often ignored in the Cluniac monasteries, was strictly adhered to. The Cistercians also developed the institution of the lay brothers or 'conversi', although the idea for it had not come from them. During the week these lay brothers remained in the country houses, the granges, and were only present in the abbey on Sundays to participate in the liturgy. Thus a distinction developed between choir monks and working brothers, as a result of which the difference between the choir monks of the traditional monasteries and those of Cistercian abbeys was in fact less sharp than was often imagined.

The point on which the differences between Cistercians and Cluniacs were maintained longest and about which no mention was made at all in the polemical writings exchanged between the orders, was the organisation of these orders. Cluny had developed from a monastery into an order because to this monastery had been entrusted other monasteries by their

---

[13] 'Exordium parvum. Instituta monachorum cisterciensium de Molismo venientium', in *Les plus anciens textes* ... (n.1.), p. 77.

then owners, often lay persons, in order that the Cluniac way of life might provide them with the leaven of renewal. On the occasion of such a take-over Cluny had usually sent a number of monks to join such a community. As a result of this such an abbey became, unless older privileges prevented it, a priory belonging to the order of Cluny. Anyone entering that priory made his profession in the presence of the abbot of Cluny. Consequently the latter became abbot of all monasteries affiliated to Cluny and by their bond with him these monasteries formed an order. In his supervisory duties the abbot of Cluny was naturally assisted by others. But he was personally responsible for the policy of the order and of its monasteries. For that reason he would undertake many journeys of visitation and was considered to be the abbot-general.[14]

Things were quite different with the Cistercians. The order did not have an abbot-general, but it did have a general chapter, which was convened once a year and in which in principle all abbots had to participate. True enough, the first four daughter abbeys of Citeaux possessed special rights within the order – rights obtained only later by Morimond, although it had been founded simultaneously with Clairvaux, for which reason it vied with Clairvaux in the founding of daughter abbeys.[15] But even in respect of their behaviour vis-a-vis their daughter abbeys recourse could be had to the general chapter. One of the great advantages of instituting a general chapter was that moral decadence and crises in Cistercian monasteries could be tackled much more efficiently, while on the other hand there was no tendency of individual abbeys towards independence from Citeaux. In Cluny, on the contrary, this tendency towards independence within various monasteries, or the movement towards the restoration of the free election of abbots, was often the cause of internal crises, while the person who had to solve this problem, the abbot of Cluny himself, was at the same time its institutional cause.

Finally the Cistercians and the traditional Benedictines differed from each other in something which to us may appear trivial but which in those days was considered essential, especially because of the symbolic explanation given to it. It was moreover a difference which tended to be conspicuous at all times. For it had to do with dress. From of old the Benedictines used to wear a black habit, while the Cistercians opted for a habit of undyed wool which therefore had a greyish-white colour. It was chosen because the Cistercians wished to dress more soberly than was usual in the existing monasteries. The difference in colour which in the *Exordium parvum* was in fact not mentioned,[16] easily led to animosity between the

---

[14] G. De Valous, *Le Monachisme clunisien des origines au XVe siècle*, II, (Paris, 1970), pp. 26–40.

[15] Bredero, *Études sur la Vita prima de Saint Bernard*, (Rome, 1960), pp. 65–66.

[16] 'Instituta monachorum', in *Les plus anciens textes* . . ., p. 77: 'reicientes a se quidquid regulae refragabatur, froccos videlicet et pellicias ac staminia, caputia

two orders because of the meaning ascribed to it. This is clear, for example, from the argument with which Robert of Deutz, himself a Benedictine abbot, transformed his preference for the black monastic dress into a value judgement, referring to the text of the Canticle of Canticles: *Nigra sum sed formosa* (I am black but beautiful).[17]

Among the Cluniacs this difference of colour was by no means something incidental. Peter the Venerable, abbot of Cluny, in a letter written by him in 1128 to Bernard of Clairvaux, accused the Cistercians of pride because of their choice of a white habit. The ancient fathers, so he assured them, had dressed in black out of humility, but the Cistercians evidently thought themselves better than their fathers. But at the same time he was also willing to give a positive interpretation of this colour. The white habit signified that the Cistercians found their happiness in poverty, their joy in sorrow, and their cheerfulness in grief.[18] In later letters to Bernard of Clairvaux the abbot of Cluny returned to this difference in colour. In doing so he especially drew attention to the fact that it contributed to misunderstanding between both orders.[19] From the side of the Cistercians this difference in colour was discussed only in an anti-Cluniac polemical document which appeared shortly after the death of Bernard of Clairvaux: the *Dialogus duorum monachorum*. In this it was argued that the life of a monk approaches the life of an angel, and that consequently he ought to wear also the dress of an angel, and therefore a white habit.[20]

For the rest there was certainly a lot of negative comment on the Cistercians among the traditional Benedictines, also outside the order of Cluny itself. Orderic Vitalis, a monk of Evroul, an abbey in Normandy, and author of an *Historia Ecclesiastica*, written in about 1135, gave his verdict as follows:

> Many noble soldiers and persons who seek deeper truth, flock to them because of the novelty of their unusual behaviour ... Together with good people there arrive also hypocrites who – dressed in white or motley clothing – mislead people and perform a great comedy for the crows. Most of them wish to emulate the true servants of God, not by their virtue but by their outward behaviour. Their number

quoque et femorialia, pectina et coopertoria ...' For the rest it does not mention clothing.

[17] *Patrologia Latina*, 170, col. 511–12.

[18] Epistola 28, edited by G. Constable, *The letters of Peter the Venerable* (Cambridge [Mass.] 1967). I, p. 58. Concerning the interpretations of these colours, *ibid.*, II, p. 116.

[19] Epistolae 111 and 150. Constable, I, pp. 290 and 367–71.

[20] *Dialogus* III, 46 (r. 931–35), published by R. B. C. Huygens, *Le moine Idung et ses deux ouvrages* (Spoleto, 1980), pp. 180–81.

provokes the disgust of those watching this, while in respect of the insufficient insight of people they make virtuous monks despicable.[21]

This negative reaction to the Cistercians from within traditional Benedictine monasticism was caused by a concrete point of friction which had occurred between Cistercians and Cluniacs and which had inevitably led to rivalry between the two orders; this at least was the obvious explanation of the many writers who commented on it. The point of friction par excellence that could occur between monasteries, namely the arrival of monks wishing to exchange their monastery and order for another, also occurred between Citeaux and Cluny. This problem had already been anticipated in the rule of Benedict. For it lays down that an abbot has to be wary of accepting permanently into his monastery a monk from an abbey that is known to him without permission or letters of recommendation from the monk's abbot.[22] At the same time, however, it was customary for an abbot to consent to the departure of a monk from his abbey, when the latter wished to exchange his way of life for a stricter one.

On this idea at any rate the privilege was founded which in 1097 Cluny had received from Pope Urban II, namely to be allowed to accept monks from another monastery. The abbot of Cluny did not have to take into account the objections or complaints of the abbey from which the monk in question originated, at least if the latter made the change *pro vitae melioratione*. But other abbeys had stayed out of this movement, probably against the wishes of some of their monks. Naturally several of those monks then opted for Cluny on their own account, but they did not always obtain the cooperation of their abbot. Urban II who before his election as pope had been great-prior at Cluny, possessed first-hand knowledge of this problem. This is probably the reason why he granted Cluny this privilege which deviated from the Rule of Benedict.[23]

The Cistercians at first observed this prescript of the Rule; this at least is the impression one gets from the letters of Bernard of Clairvaux dealing with monks joining the Cistercians from other abbeys. Repeatedly Bernard sent back a monk if it appeared that the latter's abbot did not approve.[24] The letters in question belong, admittedly, to the first period of Bernard's abbacy. But according to his treatise *De Praecepto et de dispensatione* (about precepts and dispensations from them) which he wrote after 1142, he had become even more cautious in accepting monks from

---

[21] *Historia ecclesiastica*, lib. VIII, c. 26; published by M. Chibnall, *The Ecclesiastical History of Ordericus Vitalis*, vol. IV (Oxford, 1973), p. 326.

[22] *Regula S. Benedicti*, c. 61.

[23] Jaffé-Loewenfeld, *Regesta Pontificum Romanorum*, nr. 5676; *Patr. Latina*, 151, col. 487.

[24] Bredero, 'Cluny et Citeaux au XIIe siècle', in *Studi medievali*, 3rd series, XII (1971), p. 146, n. 48.

Benedictine abbeys. In answer to questions from some Benedictine monks Bernard had written this treatise, which he sent to them through their abbot. In it he also dealt with the motives which might lead a monk to cease to observe his vow of *stabilitas loci* which the rule demanded of him, and to go to a different abbey.

He naturally maintained that monks could not join another abbey without the consent of their abbot. Besides, the only valid argument for a change of order or abbey was the choice of a stricter way of life than the one customary in the abbey where one was residing. He illustrated his exposé with the example of a Cluniac monk who wished to leave his order because he had chosen the poverty of Citeaux instead of the Cluniac way of life. To the above-mentioned conditions which would allow such a change of monastery to take place, Bernard added some commentary. One should not condemn a person leaving his monastery for this reason, but neither should one condemn some one who in such circumstances decided not to leave his monastery in order not to scandalize his brethren.[25] From the example given and the commentary added to it we may conclude that the abbot of Clairvaux had some experience with Cluniac monks joining the Cistercians. Also in other ways it is clear that here he was dealing with a delicate problem. Of the 335 monasteries of men which in 1153 belonged to the Cistercian order, a number existed already before joining the order. At times monasteries joined the order separately, as was the case specially with canons regular, then again they did so as a group of abbeys, as in the case of the congregation of Savigny. However, the number of Benedictine abbeys or priories taken over by the Cistercians was very small, and among them there wasn't even one Cluniac monastery. In Cluny the monks who opted for the poverty of Citeaux, had to face the problems which Bernard outlined in the above-mentioned treatise.

Bernard's view on the stricter way of life which gave a monk the right to leave a Cluniac monastery for one of the Cistercians – with the proviso already mentioned – also makes clear that in the opinion of the Cistercians the privilege granted to Cluny of accepting monks without the consent of their own abbot, could not possibly apply to monks of their own order. For a Cistercian leaving for Cluny could not have made a choice *pro vitae melioratione*. With this problem, too, Bernard had to deal as a young abbot, and in a rather exceptional way at that. According to what is known about it, Bernard did not want to resign himself to one of his monks leaving for Cluny. The case is generally known and concerns a relative of Bernard's, Robert of Chatillon, who had entered Clairvaux as a young man, but before that had been promised by his parents to Cluny. This state of affairs was not accepted by Cluny. During one of Bernard's absences from his monastery the great-prior of Cluny visited the monk in question and

---

[25] *De Praecepto* XVI, pp. 44–51. Edited by J. Leclerq, *Sancti Bernardi Opera*, III (Rome, 1963), pp. 283–88.

persuaded him to leave Clairvaux for Cluny. Robert's residence at Clairvaux was against the promise made by his parents to Cluny and apparently Cluny was not prepared to tolerate such a breach of promise.

The reaction of the abbot of Clairvaux to this intervention became widely known. He sent Robert a letter in which according to the *Life* of Bernard he dictated in the open air. When a thunderstorm burst he had continued the dictation and the falling rain was supposed to have spared the parchment.[26] About the contents of this 'letter in the rain', however, the *Life* of Bernard remains silent. Nevertheless something can be said about this. Bernard called the prior who lured Robert away a wolf in sheep's clothing, preaching to him a new gospel in which drunkenness was recommended and sobriety condemned; voluntary poverty labelled as misery, while fasting, vigilance and silence were called foolishness. Naturally Bernard also protested against a Cluniac appeal to Rome, where this course of things was supposed to have been legalized. In this letter Bernard compared himself with the woman, whose child was stolen by another woman who had smothered her own child in her sleep. But he could not count on the wisdom of a Solomon to redress this injustice. He also asked himself what kind of love the Cluniacs fostered for the salvation of this monk, if in its cause they had to destroy the salvation of Bernard himself.

The text of the passage following this question deserves to be quoted literally:

> Could they not have saved you without murdering me? But how? Would happiness then consist in a concern for clothing and an abundance of food rather than in frugal fare and modest clothing? If holiness is achieved through soft and warm furs, fine and costly garments, long sleeves and a broad hood, through bed-covers made of animal skins and woollen vests, why then should I procrastinate and why don't I follow you? But all these are soothing remedies for the sick and not weapons for men on the battlefield. Those who are dressed in soft garments dwell in the abodes of princes. Wine and wheat-flour, meat and fat strengthen the body, not the spirit. Pastry does not benefit the soul but the body. Many brethren in Egypt served the Lord for à long time without ever eating fish. Pepper, ginger, cumin, sage and thousands of similar herbs indeed titillate the palate, but they at once excite lust; and do you feel at ease in such a situation?[27]

The brethren in Egypt mentioned here are the ancient desert monks to

---

[26] *Vita prima*, lib. I, *c*. XI, 50; *Patr. Lat.*, 185, col. 255: 'Scripsit ergo epistula in mediu imbre sine imbre'.

[27] Epistola I, *c*. 11; *S. Bern. Opera* VII, (Rome, 1974), p. 9.

whom Bernard considered the Cistercians to be related, and with whom he contrasted the Cluniacs. This shows that Bernard used the incident with Cluny about the monk Robert to attack the Cluniac way of life. The incident was nothing more than the occasion to do this. For if his main purpose had been to get Robert back to Clairvaux such a public indictment of the Cluniac way of life would hardly have been the most appropriate means to achieve it. He made use of the incident for this controversy. This becomes quite clear if one knows that a short time afterwards he repeated the same polemical stand in his *Apologia*. This polemical treatise Bernard wrote at the request of a Benedictine abbot, William of Saint-Thierry, to whom moreover he sent this criticism of the Cluniac way of life officially. In it he repeated the reproaches which he had already uttered in his letter to Robert, but also denounced other matters, like the pomp and splendour with which the Cluniac abbots surrounded themselves during their journeys and also the luxury shown in the building of monasteries and churches.[28] It was especially because of this last point that this *Apologia* continued to be widely read during the later middle ages. In the fourteenth century Geert Grote referred to it when in a pamphlet he attacked the plans to build a tower next to the cathedral at Utrecht.[29]

But the polemical writings of Bernard of Clairvaux mentioned above do raise some questions. Everyone agrees that the letter to Robert was not meant for him personally, but must rather be considered a pamphlet used by Bernard to attack Cluny. Some such outburst by Bernard was understandable as long as it was generally thought that the pamphlet was written before 1122, the year in which the then abbot of Cluny, Pons de Melguiel, was forced by Rome to abdicate. This abdication was explained as a consequence of the abbot's rule which was considered to have been a period of lawlessness which was supposed to have done serious harm to the spiritual life at Cluny.[30] But the letter to Robert cannot be linked with this situation of decadence, at least not as a criticism of the way of life at Cluny as it was supposed to have been under the Abbot Pons. For it has been proved that this letter was written as late as the end of 1124,[31] only a short time before Bernard wrote his *Apologia* in the course of 1125.

Thus we have to conclude that Bernard attacked the way of life at Cluny during the abbacy of its new abbot, Peter the Venerable, who for the rest is known as a reformer of the Cluniac way of life. At the moment when Bernard denounced the abuses at Cluny, this new abbot was meeting a lot of opposition in his monastery and his order from followers of his deposed

---

[28] *Apologia*, c. XII, pp. 18–30; *S. Bern. Opera*, III, pp. 104–7.

[29] *Geert Grootes Tractaat contra turrim traiectensem teruggevonden*, edited by R. R. Post (The Hague 1967), p. 56.

[30] *Petrus Venerabilis, De Miraculis*, lib. II, c. XII, *Patr. Lat.*, 189, col. 922–24.

[31] D. van den Eynde, 'Les premiers écrits de saint Bernard', in J. Leclerq, *Recueil d'Études sur saint Bernard et ses écrits*, III (Rome, 1969), pp. 395–396.

predecessor. The latter had first made a journey to Jerusalem; such a reaction was customary in those days on the occasion of a social impasse, and could be seen as an act of eschatologically determined resignation in respect of problems one could no longer cope with.[32] In 1124 Pons returned from Jerusalem and took up residence in northern Italy in a small monastery of Eremites, belonging to the jurisdiction of Cluny. Subsequently his followers at Cluny took up contact with him once more and in the course of 1126, during an absence of his successor, he returned to Cluny. His followers welcomed him back as their abbot. It is said that this was accompanied with acts of violence committed by the lay population living round Cluny, who had also chosen Pons' side. But there are also indications that violence was only used when followers of Peter the Venerable made an attempt to regain control of the abbey.[33] Anyway, Pons' position at Cluny became untenable, because Rome refused to accept him once more as abbot. A papal legate was sent and subsequently a process was conducted against him in Rome, after which he remained in an ecclesiastical prison in that city until his death which occurred soon afterwards.[34]

Between these events and the anti-Cluniac writings of Bernard we must accept, in my opinion, the existence of a direct link. In his *Apologia* the abbot of Clairvaux made clear among other things that he did not write because the change of monks from one abbey to another was such a tremendous problem for him, and he also made clear that he was intervening in an internal problem of Cluny itself. Concerning the first point he wrote:

> I do know that some people from other monastic communities or institutions came running to our order; they knocked on our door and entered, but by acting like this they caused vexation among their brethren and moreover gave offence to us. For as they exasperated the others through their reckless leave-taking, so they caused commotion in our abbeys by the poor quality of their conversion. As out of pride they despised what they possessed, so they recklessly laid claim to something beyond their power; in a dignified manner God finally saw fit to show up their unsuitability through their departure,

---

[32] Bredero, 'Jérusalem dans l'occident médiévale', in *Mélanges offerts à René Crozet*, edited by P. Gallais and Y-J Riou, I (Poitiers, 1966), pp. 259–271.

[33] H. E. J. Cowdrey, 'Abbot Pontius of Cluny (1109–1122/6), in *Studi Gregoriani*, XI (Rome, 1978), pp. 237–41.

[34] Cf. G. Tellenbach, 'Der Sturz des Abtes Pontius von Cluny und seine geschichtliche Bedeutung', in *Quellen und Forschungen aus italienischen Archiven und Bibliotheken*, 43/3 (1964), pp. 13–55, P. Zerbi, 'Intorno allo scisma di Ponzio abate di Cluny (1122–1126)', in *Studi Storici in Onore Ottorino Bertolini* (Pisa, 1972), pp. 835–91. Reprinted in P. Zerbi, *Tra Milano e Cluny* (Rome, 1978), pp. 309–71.

when they deserted thoughtlessly what they had thoughtlessly undertaken, and returned covered with shame to what they had so rashly abandoned. By seeking our monasteries more out of discontent with their own order than out of a desire for ours, they showed who they were; and while with inconstant rashness they ran to and fro between you and us, they offended both you and us and all well-disposed people.[35]

The difference of opinion implied in these two writings of Bernard must not be interpreted as an expression of rivalry between the two orders. Bernard considered them too different from each other to merit comparison. What he wrote about Cluny was not meant to compare Cluny with Citeaux in order to condemn it; but he wrote because he condemned certain developments in Cluny and wanted to oppose them. This intention he had already made clear in the first part of the *Apologia*. In it Bernard also reprimanded the Cistercians who wanted to belittle the order of Cluny.[36] By way of conclusion to this reprimand of his fellow-Cistercians he observed that at this point his treatise could have been brought to an end. But the attack on Cluny has as yet to start. Its opening words made clear that it was not meant to be an attack by the Cistercians as such against Cluny, but an intervention in the internal affairs of that order. This conclusion becomes all the more cogent if we link up this treatise with what happened at Cluny shortly afterwards and with the reply, later, of Peter the Venerable to the reproaches Bernard had levelled against the way of life at Cluny in his *Apologia*.

The opening words of Bernard's so-called attack on Cluny are as follows:

In order not to create the impression that on the one hand I do not spare the members of my order in the least, while on the other I too readily agree with some of yours in certain matters in which I shouldn't, I deem it necessary to add something concerning certain matters which – I know – are repugnant also to you and which doubtlessly have to be avoided by all well-disposed persons. Although these things occur in your order, this does not mean at all that they proceed from the nature of your order. For there is no order that allows disorder; where disorder rules, there is no longer any order. Consequently I must be considered to speak not against but in favour of your order when I proceed to reprimand in its members not their order, but their human faults. Those who love the order will not consider it harmed by my word in this matter, I have no fear of that. On the contrary, they will accept gratefully that I am going

---

[35] *Apologia*, c. XII, p. 32; *S. Bern. Opera*, III, pp. 107–8.
[36] C. II, 4–III, 5; *S. Bern. Opera*, III, pp. 83–85.

to persecute what they have been loathing for so long. If it should displease some people nevertheless, then these individuals manifest themselves as persons who do not love the order, because they do not want the order's decay – human shortcomings – to be condemned. Allow me to answer them with this word from Gregory (the Great)! It is better for offence to arise than for the truth to be abandoned.[37]

The Latin word for offence, used here by Bernard, is *scandalum*. A literal translation of this word is in place here, because Cluny had indeed to face a scandal, namely when Pons returned to it. The current opinion on this event is mainly dependent on a report on it by Peter the Venerable. But the latter was clearly a party in the conflict. Later on, in 1127 or 1128, he answered Bernard's reproaches with a long letter in which he defended all the existing customs at Cluny, providing them with his commentary. He even defended things that had not been mentioned in the *Apologia*, nor in the letter to Robert.[38] This letter was moreover sent by Peter the Venerable to all Cluniac priors.[39] This makes us presume that this letter was just as much addressed to his own Cluniac order, the more so as Peter the Venerable addressed this very long treatise to someone he did not yet know at the time, but who had interfered in the internal problem within his order.

For if one reads the above-mentioned passage from the *Apologia* against the background of the conflict that subsequently arose at Cluny and which Peter the Venerable afterwards had to settle, one can only understand it as the opening stage of the intervention Bernard addressed himself to an internal controversy at Cluny. This controversy became an open conflict when Abbot Pons returned there and Peter the Venerable was so far involved in this that his leadership was being questioned. This leadership was under attack from the followers of Abbot Pons, but when the latter had lost their cause, Peter the Venerable had to take charge once more. For this purpose he wrote a defense of the existing way of life at Cluny. For his leadership had to do with the maintenance of this way of life, from which many had wished to deviate. Bernard had chosen their side, first in his letter to Robert and subsequently much more clearly in his *Apologia*. This circumstance then provided Peter the Venerable with the opportunity to settle the internal conflict at Cluny, which had led to a scandal through Abbot Pons' return and of doing so in a veiled and discreet manner. For he could pretend not to have to settle conflicts within the order, but simply to answer objections that had been brought against Cluny from outside.

This interpretation of what happened at Cluny in the years 1124–1126/27 also calls for a revision of the reason why Pons de Melgueil

---

[37] C. VII, 15; 94.
[38] Epistola 28; Constable, *The Letters*, I, pp. 52–101.
[39] Constable, II, p. 206 (note added to Letter, 161).

abdicated as abbot of Cluny. Generally the cause of this is sought outside Cluny, though the pope acted on complaints against Pons from within the order. Even more surprising is the supposition that the general crisis experienced by monasticism in the transition from the eleventh to the twelfth century could have left Cluny completely untouched. This crisis led to new interpretations of the Rule of Benedict which people wished to observe once more in an authentic way, stripped of the customs which had gradually overgrown it. It is just unthinkable that in Cluny, where these customs had developed to such a degree, no discussion should have taken place about this problem. Such a discussion must have undoubtedly taken place at Cluny and the letter which Peter the Venerable addressed to Bernard of Clairvaux in 1127 or 1128, and in addition to all priors of his order, fulfilled the role of a final chapter.

The aforesaid crisis at Cluny was a result of this discussion and the manner in which it was conducted between champions and opponents of change in the monastic way of life, resulted in the two camps ending up diametrically and implacably opposed to each other. Abbot Pons, too, took sides in this discussion and he did so in favour of those who advocated change. His choice was probably partly determined by the fact that the current way of life at Cluny had resulted in economic problems. But he did not allow himself to be led exclusively by economic considerations. For, while during the later years of his abbacy his community lived in poverty, no cuts were made in the daily distributions of food to the poor; a situation which later on was denounced by Peter the Venerable as mismanagement.[40]

The latter was at first not mixed up in the controversy about the way of life, at least not directly. He was chosen as abbot by Abbot Pons' opponents after the premature death of the latter's successor. Only then did Peter the Venerable come to Cluny, where as a young abbot he embarked on the course advocated by Pons' opponents, namely the return to the traditional way of life. This task the young abbot adhered to religiously during the first years of his abbacy. So much is clear from the letter he addressed to Bernard of Clairvaux ostensibly in answer to the latter's letter to Robert and to the *Apologia*. For in it he made clear to the priors of the Cluniac monasteries that all existing customs remained in force. The arguments he used to buttress this statement amounted principally to this; that these customs had to remain unaltered because they had originated during the time of Abbot Hugo, Pons' predecessor (who meanwhile had been canonized). Gradually, however, it must have dawned on Peter the Venerable that also at Cluny some changes were necessary, and that reforms in the way of life were needed. From a report by Orderic Vitalis it appears that his efforts to achieve this, which he started in 1132, met with opposition. Moreover the *Statuta* which he promulgated in connection

---

[40] *Dispositio rei familiaris; Patr. Lat.*, 189, col. 1047–8.

with these changes, began with an elaborate defence of the changing and adjusting of customs as such.[41] The reforms he introduced were carefully formulated. He limited himself mainly to the shortening of liturgical usages and acts. But in addition he emphasized existing precepts concerning the abstention from meat, fasting, silence, and the use of furs and cloaks: precepts taken from the rule, by which current customs were pushed into the background. Thus there is quite a distance between the point of view held by Peter the Venerable in the above-mentioned letter to Bernard and his later *Statuta*, however carefully he formulated them. What really aroused his indignation in later days appears quite clearly in a letter which he sent to all Cluniac priors. In it he wrote, in addition to other reproaches, the following:

> and our brethren, belonging to a holy order and predestined for heaven, monks bearing the name of Cluny, continue the whole year round in God-forsaken and shameless manner with the consumption of meat. They do not do so secretly, but openly and publicly, and thus proclaim, according to a word of the prophet, their sins which emulate those of Sodom.[42]

For a more accurate assessment of the relation of Citeaux to the old monasticism it is important to know what happened at Cluny when Pons was forced to abdicate and Peter the Venerable began his abbacy; because with his letter to Robert and his *Apologia* Bernard intervened in this internal conflict about conservatism and renewal. It is not easy to bring those events to light because we depend on nothing more than indirect information. For Peter the Venerable tried meticulously to wipe out all traces of these events for posterity. Though later on he embarked to a certain degree on the same course that Pons had wished to follow, he always made it appear as if his task as a reformer consisted in restoring order after the lawlessness during the regime of his predecessor, Pons. In this he ignored the fact that slowly he had had to change his own abbatial policy considerably, and this was probably so because the customs, from which he, too, had deviated, were more dear to him than they had been to the reformers who earlier on had received Abbot Pons' support. Thus the contradiction, contained in his policy does not become too conspicuous. But it does show itself quite clearly if one compares the attitude taken up by Mathieu d'Albano, Pons' strongest opponent within Cluny and at first a

---

[41] *Statuta Petri Venerabilis abbatis Cluniacensis*: Apologetica, hoc est satisfactionalis praefatio Domini Petri Cluniacensis abbatis de quibusdam suo tempore mutatis consuetudinibus. Edited by G. Constable in *Corpus consuetudinum monasticarum*, VI, (1975) pp. 39–40.

[42] Epistola 161; written between 1144–1156. Constable, *The Letters*, I, pp. 388–89 and II, p. 206.

collaborator of Peter the Venerable, in respect of efforts at reform by
Benedictine abbots at Reims;[43] if one compares this attitude with the efforts
then being made by Peter the Venerable at Cluny to achieve reforms in
spite of everything. Nevertheless the latter later on wrote Mathieu
d'Albano's hagiography, in which Mathieu's implacable opposition to
Pons de Melguiel is reckoned among his greatest merits.[44]

It seems to be equally hard to recover clear data with regard to the
intention Bernard of Clairvaux had with his polemical writings in respect
of Cluny. Was he indeed involved in the internal conflict there? An
indication that he was is offered by two letters which in the summer of 1126
the abbot of Clairvaux sent to the Cardinal-legate Peter. The latter had
been sent by Rome to start an investigation into the events of Cluny, in
other words into the drama that took place following the return of Abbot
Pons. From the first letter it appears that the cardinal-legate would have
liked to speak to him, but the abbot declined the request. He thought that
he should stay as much as possible in his monastery; a somewhat
remarkable argument if one looks at his constant travelling. The cardinal-
legate then seems to have inquired about what Bernard had written. Also
this time the abbot must have evaded the issue. At the end of a long treatise
he wrote that his writings were not very important and did not deserve the
cardinal's attention. He then summarized them and concluded this
summary as follows: '. . . and then one more piece of writing: the *Apologia*,
addressed to a friend, in which I deal with the monastic observances of the
Cluniacs and those of us, Cistercians. Besides I have written some letters to
various persons'.[45] On the basis of these letters, in which Bernard gives
evasive answers to the person who had to investigate the events of Cluny, is
it hazardous to conclude that the abbot of Clairvaux thought it advisable,
after the fact, to draw a veil also over the way he had intervened in the
internal controversy at Cluny through these polemical writings?

Bernard's intention in composing these writings becomes clearer if we
consider what induced him to start on them. It was a daring thing at that
moment for Cistercians to pit their strength against Cluny. From Bernard's
own declarations it appears that he did not want to make propaganda for
Citeaux; moreover the text of these writings shows that his main
preoccupation was to contrast the life which the Cluniacs should lead with
the way of life which was in fact customary at Cluny when Peter the
Venerable started his abbacy. An explanation for Bernard's intervention in
this matter is offered by his relation to the Benedictine abbot William of
Saint-Thierry, a man who had a deep influence on him. He asked Bernard
to write the *Apologia*, which the latter considered as *scriptitare*, and

---

[43] U. Berlière, *Documents inédits pour servir á l'histoire ecclésiastique de la Belgique*, I.
(Maredsous, 1894), pp. 94–102.

[44] *De Miraculis*, lib. II, *c*. IV–XXIII; *Patr. Lat.* 189, col. 913–36.

[45] Epistola 17 and 18; *S. Bern. Opera*, VII. pp. 65–69.

therefore as re-writing.[46] Consequently William asked Bernard to do his work again, namely to replace the letter to Robert with another text, because it had not become sufficiently clear that the objections against Cluny, voiced in the letter, only concerned those who had abandoned the life which should ideally be lived there.

Abbot William is someone of whom more is known from his writings than from his life, which on the whole has been insufficiently studied. We cannot fill up this lacuna on this occasion either, but we can safely maintain, that he devoted himself for a long period of time to the introduction of reforms within the old Benedictine monasticism. By this he caused a good deal of annoyance to the Cluniacs. While Peter the Venerable later on reached a relationship with Bernard of Clairvaux which he described as friendship, he consistently ignored William of Saint-Thierry and even avoided him explicitly. Cluny entered into a communion of prayer with Saint-Thierry only when William had abdicated as abbot of Saint-Thierry and retired to a Cistercian monastery.[47] Apparently they were not willing to forgive him the influence he had had on Bernard of Clairvaux with regard to the latter's intervention at Cluny. How great William's influence on Bernard was is clear, for that matter, also from other things: for example the fact that Bernard later on, at the instigation of his friend, also attacked the opinions of Peter Abelard.[48] It appears moreover from the first book of the *Vita prima Bernardi*, which the former abbot of Saint-Thierry wrote during Bernard's lifetime, that William knew Bernard well.[49] But it is striking that in a later conflict between traditional Cluniac opinions and reformatory tendencies within the old monasticism, led by abbots in the archdiocese of Reims and headed by William of Saint-Thierry, Bernard took no sides. He let William fight this battle all by himself; a battle against the then most implacable opponent of Pons de Melgueil, namely Mathieu d'Albano.[50]

This brings us finally to the question of what Bernard's intervention in the controversy at Cluny meant in relation to the Cistercians' attitude vis-a-vis the old monasticism. What Bernard tried to achieve, under orders

---

[46] 'Usque modo si qua me scriptitare iussistis'. *S. Bern. Opera*, VII, p. 81.

[47] Reims, City Library, hs. 349 (obituary martyrology of Saint-Thierry), folio 19 verso.

[48] Epistola 326; *Patr. Lat.* 182; col. 531–35 and *Revue Bénédictine*, 79 (1969), pp. 376–87. The negative feelings of Peter the Venerable in respect of William of Saint-Thierry probably contributed to the fact that Abelard, after his condemnation at the Council of Sens, could find a refuge at Cluny.

[49] Bredero, *Études sur la Vita prima*, pp. 100–109.

[50] Berlière, *Documents inédits* (n. 43), pp. 102–110. Cf. S. Ceglar, *William of Saint-Thierry: The Chronology of his Life with a study of his treatise on the Nature of Love, his Authorship of the 'Brevis Commentatio', the 'In Lacu', and the Reply to Cardinal Matthew*, (Ann Arbor, 1973), pp. 400–13.

from William of Saint-Thierry, was not accomplished. The reform-minded camp at Cluny suffered a definitive defeat through the events accompanying the return of Pons, and Bernard himself, too suffered a loss of his good name. In general his intentions were probably badly understood both among the Cluniacs and elsewhere, at least that is the impression one gets from the 'answer of the old monasticism to the manifesto of Bernard of Clairvaux', written in England.[51] Its probable author, Hugo of Amiens, may have written his answer in consultation with Mathieu d'Albano, with whom at any rate he was in contact.[52]

But it is remarkable that Bernard afterwards abstained from all criticism of Cluny, also on the occasion of some conflicts that arose between the two orders about business interests.[53] He did not intervene either in connection with the reform movement of the Benedictine abbots in the archdiocese of Reims. He expressed his approval of their efforts in general terms, but did not assist at their meeting to which he had been invited,[54] leaving William of Saint-Thierry, as was mentioned before, to reply on his own to Mathieu d'Albano's attacks on these reform projects. More important in this connection is probably the fact that Bernard in his letters to Peter the Venerable nowhere acceded to the latter's repeated request to collaborate in reducing the animosity between Cluniacs and Cistercians which according to the abbot of Cluny manifested itself at every meeting between monks of both orders.[55]

In addition to this it is quite remarkable that from the side of the Cistercians nothing more was written against Cluny after Bernard had written the letter to Robert and the *Apologia*. Only after the death of the abbot of Clairvaux did the *Dialogus duorum monachorum* appear in 1155. Also from this document one can conclude that the Cistercians had developed a strong aversion for Cluny, which, however during Bernard's life time was no longer being expressed in writing. One could comment that the region where this *Dialogus* originated, contained at the time an explanation for this, because there the rapid growth of the Cistercian order had come to a standstill, whereas the number of abbeys belonging to Hirsau was rapidly increasing; and these abbeys were there considered as

---

[51] A. Wilmart, 'Une riposte de l'ancien monachisme au manifeste de Saint Bernard,' *Revue Bénédictine*, 46 (1934), pp. 296–344. Cf. C. H. Talbot, 'The date and the author of the "Risposte",' in *Petrus Venerabilis, 1156–1956*, edited by G. Constable and J. Kritzeck (Rome, 1956), pp. 72–80. [Studia Anselmiana, 40].

[52] Hugo dedicated his *Dialogorum seu quaestionum theologicarum libri septem* to Cardinal Mathieu d'Albano; *Patr. Lat.*, 192, col. 1141–42.

[53] Cf. G. Constable, 'The disputed Election at Langres in 1138', in *Traditio*, 13 (1957), pp. 119–152. Id., 'Cluniac Tithes and the Controversy between Gigny and Le Miroir', *Revue Bénédictine*, 70 (1960), pp. 591–624.

[54] Epistola 91; *S. Bern. Opera*, VII, p. 239.

[55] Epistolae 111 and 150; Constable, *The Letters*, I, pp. 274–99 and 367–71.

belonging to Cluny.[56] Consequently we probably cannot take this text as completely representative of the Cistercian order. But what it unjustly states, namely that Molesmes (where at the time the foundation of Citeaux was being prepared) was a Cluniac abbey, which therefore rebelled against its order, agrees to a certain extent with what is said about it in the *Exordium magnum*. For this Cistercian text, written at Clairvaux at the end of the twelfth century and dealing among other things with the beginning of this order, also links the rise of Citeaux with the decline of Cluny.[57] This representation of things clearly deviates from what earlier on had been narrated by the *Exordium parvum* and the *Exordium Cisterciense*. There we read only this: that the founders of Citeaux had separated themselves from the community of Molesmes because of the decay of traditional monasticism, which nonetheless continued to show itself in this young community.

In this animosity, which apparently developed gradually among Cistercians against Cluniac monasticism, which was considered to be representative of the old monasticism and which indeed fulfilled this role to an important degree, the polemical writings of Bernard, with which the latter had intervened in a controversy at Cluny, came to perform an important function. From the manuscript tradition we know that specially the *Apologia* spread very widely. On the contrary a work like the *Dialogus duorum monachorum* hardly spread at all. True enough it contained many quotations from Bernard's polemics with Cluny,[58] but from a literary point of view it bore no comparison with what had been written by the abbot of Clairvaux. The reproaches he had uttered against the traditional Cluny were contained in a text that could not be equalled. This probably explains partly why further polemical writings from the Cistercians against Cluny did not appear, not to mention the fact that Bernard did not want a continuation of this polemic. But in the opinion of the Cistercians themselves what could be said against the Cluniacs had already been said by Bernard in such a way that nothing needed to be added to it. It was sufficient to read these texts. But in all this they did not realise that the abbot of Clairvaux had written his polemic with evidently a different intention from the one with which people used to read it afterwards.[59]

[56] B. Albers, 'Hirsau und seine Grundungen vom Jahre 1073 an', in *Festschrift zur 1100 jährigen Jubiläum des deutschen Campo Santo im Rom* (Freiburg i B 1897), pp. 115–129.

[57] *Exordium magnum sive narratio de initio cisterciensis ordinis*, dist II, c. IX. Edited by B. Grieser (Rome 1961), pp. 59–60.

[58] *Les plus anciens Textes* ... (n. 1), pp. 59–60 and 111.

[59] This article is a summary of a number of detailed studies about the relations between Cluny and Citeaux in the twelfth century, already published by the author or soon to be published. They are the following studies:
'Cluny et Citeaux au XIIe siècles: les origines de la controverse', in *Studi Medievali*, 3rd series, XII (1971), pp. 135–175.

'Encore sur Pons de Cluny et Pierre le Vénérable' (in collaboration with J. Leclercq and P. Zerbi), in *Aevum*, XLVIII (1974), pp. 135–149.

'A propos de l'autorité abbatiale de Pons de Melgueil et de Pierre le Vénérable dans l'Ordre de Cluny', in *Études de civilisation médiévale*. Mélanges offerts à Edmond-René Labande (Poitiers, 1975), pp. 63–75.

'Pierre le Vénérable: les commencements de son abbatiat à Cluny', in *Pierre Abelard – Pierre le Vénérable: les courants philosophiques, littéraires et artistiques en occident au milieu du XIIe siècle*. (Paris, 1975), pp. 99–116.

'Guillaume de Saint-Thierry au carrefour des courants monastiques de son temps', in *Saint-Thierry, une abbaye de VIe au XX, siècle*, actes du colloque international d'Histoire monastique, réunis par M. Bur (Saint-Thierry, 1979), pp. 279–97.

'Comment les institutions de l'ordre de Cluny se sont rapprochées de Citeaux', in *Institutioni monastiche e istitutioni canoniche in occidente (1123–1215)*. Atti della Settima Settimane internationale di Studi medioevali, Mendola, 28 August–3 September 1977. (Milan, 1980), pp. 164–202.

'Le Dialogus duorum monachorum. Un rebondissement de la polémique entre Cisterciens et Clunisiens', *Studi Medievali*, 1981. pp. 501–85.

'Une controverse sur Cluny', *Revue d'Histoire Ecclésiastique*, 1981, pp. 48–72.

'Cluny et le monachisme carolingien: continuité et discontinuité, in *Benedictine Culture*. Proceedings of the International Conference at Louvain, May 18–21, 1980.

ART AND SPIRITUALITY IN CHAPEL ARCHITECTURE: F. W. LAWRENCE (1882–1948) AND HIS CHURCHES

Clyde Binfield

To begin at a tangent. Hannah Elizabeth Pipe was the foundress, proprietress and principal of a girls' boarding school in Clapham Park, south London, one of those women to whom 'good-breeding is the polished surface of Christianity'.[1] 'She kept beauty before our eyes . . . in the house, by dainty morris papers and carpets . . . in the study, by copies of the antique and reminders of Italy framed on the walls. Her own sitting-room was a sanctuary of beauty, and contrasted almost reproachfully with the middle-Victorian drawing-rooms to which most of us were accustomed . . .'[2] John Ruskin had written to her in 1879 after they had brushed over a fashionable sculptor: 'The best thing you could do to teach your girls what sculpture means, would be to put a photograph from Luca della Robbia in every room in the house. There are enough different ones to be had now to be endlessly delightful.' Miss Pipe responded by putting a cast of della Robbia's 'Singing Boys' on to her music room wall.[3] When she retired in the early 1890s it was to Limpsfield's 'blue and silver distances'.[4] There she worshipped at the parish church, planned a convalescent home in the neighbouring village of Oxted, persuaded its squire to build a village hall, and promoted health lectures, Dante lectures

---

[1] Anna M. Stoddard, *Life and Letters of Hannah E. Pipe* (1908), pp. 236–7.
[2] Thus a pupil recalling the late 1870s, *ibid.*, p. 234.
[3] *Ibid.*, p. 264. The gospel of Della Robbia was contagious. Two churches attended by families who sent daughters to Miss Pipe's school had casts of Italian mural sculpture at their pulpit end, in each instance given by the families concerned: Rake Lane congregational church Liscard, and Bowdon Downs congregational church Altrincham.
[4] *Ibid.*, p. 362.

(Oxted's rector was a Dante scholar), mothers' meetings and meetings of the National Reading Union. 'She yearned for the salvation of "the people", in health, rectitude, capacity for fine work, whether in agriculture, handicraft, or service, and believed that their recall to the land by means of decent homes, gardens, good schools, and social recreation, was one of the intelligent instruments of that salvation'.[5]

Some of the meetings were held in Hookwood Cottage, where Miss Pipe lived with Miss Pope. The cottage had a work-room for writing and flower arranging, with the figure of Christ high on a bracket, arms outstretched in welcome. In the sitting room, with Miss Pipe's piano, Miss Pope's organ, 'the sofa in its ingle-neuk' and bridge or whist or patience in the evenings, there was more carving, designed and worked by an old friend, the legend of the Poverello's laud for Brother Fire from his Canticle of the Sun.[6] For Miss Pipe and Miss Pope had moved insensibly from Morris carpets and Ruskinian advice to St. Francis. Miss Pipe read Paul Sabatier's life of the saint and the closing years of her life found her sharing in the Franciscan revival.[7] She attended the International Association for Franciscan Study's inaugural meetings in 1902 and got to know the Sabatiers. And she fell in love with Assisi, the 'Galilee of Italy', its atmosphere 'a glorious blue'. She wrote about it to the Oxted rector's wife:

> The nightingales, the fireflies, the bugloss and the snapdragon on the walls, the clouds of love-in-a-mist in the hedges, the sword lilies among the corn, the bells of St. Stefano and Sta Maria Maggiore, which are as when St. Francis blessed them and all things beautiful and musical around him . . . But what would he have thought of the great church, not to say three churches, built over his ashes, with their glorious cycle of painted legend and splendid glass and sumptuous services, – all raised to the honour of the poverello?[8]

That questioning note is significant. So is the influence of the Sabatiers, for the Sabatiers were protestants and Miss Pipe, although so obviously a churchwoman, was not an anglican but a Wesleyan. The nuances of her Wesleyan churchmanship are worth examination.

[5] *Ibid.*, p. 370, also pp. 366 ff.
[6] *Ibid.*, pp. 363–4.
[7] 'The remarkable revival of interest in St. Francis, consonant doubtless with the growing philanthropy of the last quarter of the nineteenth century, had reached her at its initiation, through Monsieur Paul Sabatier's great Biography of the Saint'. *Ibid.*, p. 397. Sabatier's *Vie de St. François* appeared in 1893, a year after the completion of Hookwood Cottage but in the same year as the completion of its sitting-room, and its first English edition was in 1894. Anna Stoddart was herself the authoress of *Francis of Assisi*, 1903.
[8] *Ibid.*, pp. 398–9.

In the autumn of 1882 Miss Pipe, Miss Pope, and a third friend, visited a cathedral. An incident during their visit provoked this letter:

> After this morning's service we went round your beautiful cathedral, and soon found ourselves in a chapel at the end of which, against the wall, is a mosaic not easily seen from beyond the red cord stretched in front of it. As we looked towards it, the cord was withdrawn and two gentlemen stepped up to examine the mosaic. Three ladies, of whom I was one, followed, but the clergyman, with a fine tenor voice, who had just been intoning the service, checked us and called us back, with the curt warning, 'We do not allow women in there'. Will you kindly allow me to ask whether this clergyman acted under any rubric so sacred that it might not lawfully be waived even by courtesy in favour of strangers who had been accidentally misled? and, further, does this distinction between men and women with which one is familiar in the ecclesiastical foundations of Italy really obtain in the Established Church of England? With the asceticism of the Roman tradition it is in honest keeping; but could our clerical censor lay down any principle openly acknowledged in his own Church on which the distinction he drew could be argued and defended? One of the 'fopperies of Romanism', to use a phrase of Mr. Shorthouse's, this kind of distinction cannot be called. It is a sincere, symbolical rendering of that view of life and society which the Roman Church openly professes to take and has consistently maintained through all the ages since Hildebrand, and indeed long before him. But imported into the Church of England, this sign 'signifying nothing' seems to me – I speak ignorantly and under your kind correction – an affectation, a 'foppery' strictly so called. I myself am a dissenter (a friend indeed of that dissenting family who had the honour in one and another of its members to lend a hand in the carving of your restored choir and to present the olive wood of the altar), but one of my two companions was a loyal churchwoman, and the other the sister of no fewer than five clergymen (two in Catholic orders and three in Anglican), and they were not less surprised than I at the manner of our exclusion from the pavement behind the red cord. We had left your noble choir grateful to God and man; refreshed, soothed, and cheered by every word and note of the morning psalms and all the rest of the glorious service, and were more painfully jarred, perhaps, than in a lower key of feeling we might have been by the sudden discord of this accident.[9]

[9] *Ibid.*, pp. 294–6. The letter was addressed to its 'leading cleric'. Anna Stoddart suggests that it was a southern cathedral, but the evidence suggests Chester: certainly in the 1870s G. G. Scott's restorations there included the rearrangement of the choir, and this included, at Dean Howson's instigation, an olive and cedar wood

There writes the great headmistress whose standards of courtesy and accuracy have been equally affronted, but there also writes the free church woman whose catholicity had been caught off guard. In the following summer she wrote about her Wesleyanism to the friend who later designed the Franciscan panels of her cottage sitting-room:

> I am a Wesleyan not on conviction, but by birth . . . I am proud of my Methodism, but then I think I should have been proud of any other *ism* . . . The thing I dislike is *d*issent (not *D*issent). I dislike the dissenting temper . . . I dislike the disposition which cannot find rest in its appointed surroundings and go in heartily for what lies nearest. I love Methodism, because one has room to breathe in it: it is the largest of all the Protestant Churches. I love it because better than any other religious organisation it has known how to deal with the poor. I love and honour it because it is believed by many to have saved us from a French Revolution . . . I love it for its hymns and liturgy, and its good and great men . . . I think I love it also a little because it is unfashionable and accidentally, poor thing! though by no means necessarily, a little vulgar . . . The only Church that I *in the full and high sense of the word believe in*, is the Holy Catholic church, which follows from belief in the Holy Ghost, and leads on to belief in the Communion of Saints.[10]

Hannah Elizabeth Pipe was a remarkable woman, but there was nothing remarkable in this confluence of education, prosperity and womanliness, of sensitivity to the past, or to the countryside, or to craftsmanship. Miss Pipe expressed sentiments common to many thoughtful people in the last quarter of the nineteenth century and such sentiments were naturally reflected in their homes and their churches. Where these thoughtful people were nonconformists it was no less to be expected that their churches too should reflect the rediscovery of a common Christian heritage. Late Victorian and Edwardian nonconformity was not solely a matter of central halls and passive resisters.

table carved by G. F. Armitage, who also carved three choir stalls. Armitage was an active congregationalist; Armitage family tradition has it that one of the family gave the altar wood – and several of Armitage's sisters were the pupils of Miss Pipe. But the conclusive point would be that at the end of Chester's south quire aisle there is a chapel dedicated to Erasmus, with mosaics (by Clayton, executed by Salviati), representing women's ministry in the church, and introduced in 1879. G. W. O. Addleshaw, 'Architects, sculptors, designers and craftsmen 1770–1970 whose work is to be seen in Chester Cathedral', *Architectural History*, XIV, 1971, p. 97; the Very Revd. T. W. Ingram Cleasby to the author; private information; for Armitage (1848–1937) see C. Binfield, *So Down to Prayers* (1977), pp. 172–7.

[10] Hannah E. Pipe to Lady Huggins, 4 July 1883, Stoddart, op. cit., pp. 308–311.

Oxted and Limpsfield is a case in point. When Miss Pipe retired there in the early 1890s she made her peace with the parish church, but there were the seeds of a small local dissenting community which in the next forty years found its characteristics naturally expressed in a building in which she could only have found delight. The development of this community and its ultimate architectural expression is an interesting outworking of the climate which nurtured Miss Pipe.

The congregational church at Oxted was a suburban graft on to a village cause. There had been congregational services – indeed, a church – locally since the early 1800s, but these had flickered to a close in the early 1870s. In 1887, however, the railways reached Oxted. That altered the situation without transforming it. Oxted was ten miles south east of Croydon, close to the Kent border; it was on a cross country route, with the North Downs impenetrable between it and higher Pooterland.[11]

Consequently, the railway brought quality rather than quantity. As the *Congregational Year Book* put it nearly twenty years after the arrival of the railway, 'the land is being opened up for the building of houses of a superior nature and a high–class residential neighbourhood is in the process of making'.[12] So the Oxted congregationalists – or rather their fellows from Croydon and Caterham – built unpretentiously, but suitably, in Station Road. The design, by Rowland Hooper of Redhill, was copied from Redhill's primitive methodist chapel: £1,500 worth of red brick, with the *Year Book* making the best of the obvious: 'the circumscribed site limited the principal features of design to the front, which is in early decorated English gothic'.[13] That was in 1900, two years before the church was formed and one year before Limpsfield saw its first motor car.

The cause, however, promised more than the building. With Silvester Horne[14] of Whitefield's Tabernacle preaching at the opening, flanked by dissenting MPs, it was clear that significant things were intended, and within four years there were plans for £5,000 worth of new building on a better site: Blue House Lane as opposed to Station Road, 500 sittings as opposed to 250. This time the architects were Crouch and Butler.

The choice was apt. Joseph Crouch and Edmund Butler were successful Birmingham architects whose *Apartments of the House* (1900) beckoned their clients back to days when 'every village workman had his lathe, and

---

[11] E. E. Cleal, *The Story of Congregationalism in Surrey* (1908), pp. 82–5; C. Pritchard, '*The Church is People*' *A History of the Congregational Church in Oxted 1900–1975* (Tunbridge Wells 1975), p. 6.

[12] *Congregational Year Book* (1905), p. 133. Even in 1960 the population of Oxted was only 6,000.

[13] *CYB* (1902), p. 148. Minutes of the Building Committee of the Oxted Congregational Church.

[14] Mrs. Silvester Horne was one of Miss Pipe's old pupils: but there is no evidence that Miss Pipe took an interest in the doings of the Oxted congregationalists.

knew how to use it with taste and spirit'.[15] Crouch and Butler houses were ingle-nooked and casemented, their quaintly shaped windows affording dim, cosy peeps within. For purists they must mark the descent from Arts and Crafts to stockbroker's Tudor.[16] Yet in 1901 their *Churches, Schools and Mission Halls for Nonconformists* also appeared, displaying a dignity far removed from the starved gothic of previous decades. Their Oxted design may have been gothic for Christian stockbrokers, but it was more than mere whimsy.[17] The bricks had become local rich yellow limestone; the primitive methodist rectangle had turned into nave, aisles, transepts and choir; there was to be a tower. 'The interior will be particularly interesting, the perspective effect of the nave, columns and open timber roof giving size and impressiveness'. The intention was to strike a truly architectural note: 'No attempt has been made at over elaboration, but the designs have been prepared with the idea of obtaining character in the work by sound design and a sober use of good materials.'[18]

As it happened Crouch and Butler never built their church and the Oxted congregationalists worshipped in Station Road for thirty five years.

It was a curious community, more of a free church than a congregational church.[19] In part it was a genuine village church. Could it be anything else with Harry Coldbreath as organ blower or Hetty Forehead in the League of Young Worshippers? Some of its adherents were villagers who came in reaction to parish church presumption, as when the rector of Limpsfield would catechise only the village school children, while the gentry's children sat at the back, never questioned lest the rector embarrass them and their families. Or there were the girls from the local National Children's Home, accompanied by the sisters in their navy blue uniform

---

[15] J. Crouch and E. Butler, *The Apartments of the House* (1900), p. 4; criticised as 'arty and silly in a peculiarly meretricious way . . .' in N. Cooper, *The Opulent Eye: Late Victorian and Edwardian Taste in Interior Design* (1976), p. 19.

[16] 'morality . . . degenerating into sentiment, functionalism and constructive honesty . . . becoming mere chunkiness'. Cooper, op. cit., p. 39. With illustrations of The Anchorage, and Navarino, Sutton Coldfield, plates 188–121.

[17] The judicious Martin Briggs, writing in 1946, however, felt that as representing 'The state of enlightened Free Church opinion on architectural style at the close of the nineteenth century . . . their views on practical questions are eminently sane.' M. S. Briggs, *Puritan Architecture and its Future* (1946), p. 50. Joseph Crouch later wrote *Puritanism and Art: An Inquiry into a Popular Fallacy* (1910). With a preface by Silvester Horne.

[18] *Congregational Year Book* (1905), p. 133.

[19] The following account is based on these sources: conversations with Miss E. Dowell and Revd. S. Jackman; Oxted Church Meeting Minute Book 1902–20; Minutes of the Building Committee of the Oxted Congregational Church, 1899–1902; Book of Photographs of the New Building 1934–5; Oxted Congregational Church Committee Minutes Book 1902–1921; Deacons' Minutes 1921–1936; Church Meeting Minutes 1920–1937; C. Pritchard, op. cit.

Oxted exterior

and streamered bonnets. Church membership was small, never above
eighty, and so were congregations; fifty in the morning, twenty in the
evening, when the maids went.

It is the maids who provide the clue, for Oxted was a divided
community. The village proper was ineradicably rural. 'The morality of
these picturesque innocent looking villages is incredibly low', Hannah Pipe
found in the 1890s; but Miss Pipe was part of the problem. It was her sort,
with their modish demand for weekend cottages, who made good
accommodation for labourers and outdoor servants harder to find.[20] From
its earliest days the chapel in Station Road housed a larger smattering of
'quality' than most congregational villages churches: not just retired city
men, but senior civil servants, even politicians, or at least political
journalists and publishers. The cause had begun at Mrs. Jefford's Oxted
House. From 1904 there were the Paishes of Glebe House, with their sons at
Winchester. George Paish, the Liberal economist and publisher, became a
deacon and church treasurer almost at once, and his knighthood in 1912
was a delightful jab in the arm for any village chapel. Rather later there

---

[20] Stoddart, op. cit., pp. 372, 394.

were the Benns – Miss Benn of Wayside; Sir John, retired from London progressive politics; Sir Ernest, the publisher, at Blunt House (where the young Wedgie was recalled by a gardener as being 'a boisterous young bugger then too'). For a while, between 1908 and 1911, the organist Miss Cholditch Smith, was a professionally trained organist, and the original American organ rapidly gave way to a second-hand Willis.

It was a daunting community with too many masterful personalities, by no means free of tensions, not least when it came to individual communion cups or a sung 'Amen' or responsive prayer, let alone any more formal liturgical order. Yet it managed to convey in its halfway house between stockbrokerdom and 'our village' more than a hint of the puritan alternative. It is recalled that one of its Caterham benefactors, Garfield Soper, drove to the Caterham chapel in his carriage, whence he would proceed to the deacons' vestry with his coachman, who happened to be a fellow deacon; so, fifty years later, Oxted was served by a retired gentleman's gentleman who, dressed in his Sunday wing collar, tendered the offertory plate as if he were still handing round the cigars. And if the congregation in the late 1970s included the local Labour parliamentary candidate, so in the early 1900s it provided a meeting place for Oxted's radical alternative. The Oxted Women's Liberal Association met in its schoolroom in 1911 and a Working Men's Institute had been started there. Ten years later Mrs. Pease, the Quaker Fabian, wanted to use it for a Labour women's meeting and though her request was declined, 'owing to the unsafe condition of the floor', Mrs. Pease's Labour women were allowed in two years later, and by 1927 the Cooperative Women's Guild were holding whist drives there, while throughout these years there was a clear concern for the unemployed.

No doubt Oxted's was not a typical Labour party and its unemployment less obtrusive than elsewhere, but it is this lively concern with wider issues which marks out this small church and which was perhaps the mark of that vital element in any local church, its ministers.

From 1900 Oxted was never without a resident minister. The stipend was never high (£100 in 1900; £150 in 1911; £250 in 1922) and therefore it tended to attract men on the verge of an important career. There was the temptation for its minister to become chaplain to a group of select families, and between the wars there developed an Oxted temperament, very cultivated, rather delicate, suited to Oxford (or Cambridge) graduates trained at Mansfield College. Vaughan Pryce, its first minister, came from a bristling ministerial dynasty; so did Sidney Berry, his successor but one, who later went on to Carr's Lane, Birmingham, and a national influence in the free churches; the pedigree of Wilton Rix, Berry's successor, was stiff with ejected puritan divines – he went on to Ealing to expound the puritan virtues of costume drama in liturgy.

It was in 1920, during Wilton Rix's term at Oxted, that serious attention was once more given to a new building. Rix, however, left for Ealing in

1922 and the scheme hung fire during the ministry of his successor, A. G. Matthews: but Matthews, who had private means, retired in 1927 to devote his life to puritan scholarship and *Calamy Revised*. He remained in Oxted, attending his old church – of which he became secretary – on Sunday mornings, with evensong at the parish church, a reincarnation of an ejected divine, in complete accord with his minister (with whom he holidayed annually in Paris for a week) and rector alike, and in remarkable accord with the catholic priest; all of them, after all, Oxford men.[21]

It was Matthews's successor, Geoffrey Edmonds, who finally built the new church. The opening, in September 1935, was a friendly affair. The builders were congregationalists – indeed the firm's founder was one of the chapel's founders; there were messages from Ernest Benn and Wedgwood Benn (who had lectured the previous year in aid of church funds), from George Paish who was in Geneva, and Vaughan Pryce. Sidney Berry was there; Wilton Rix's people at Ealing contributed £200; the rector spoke, the catholic priest stood by and the local county councillor, a baptist minister's son, made an ambiguous speech: 'today the civil authorities know only too well that those districts where the religious life was strongest were those which were most easy to govern, and whose needs it was most easy to provide for'. The architect was not there. His motor car had broken down *en route* from Wales, so he sent a telegram: 'I am grateful indeed that another lamp has been lighted in a dark and troubled world'.

Oxted's was a church for the motor age. Oxted houses were garage houses now, and although the church grew slowly yet, its future lay with the garage society. There remained the question of its name. All its officers lived in houses with names, unmarked by numbers or even roads. The church was no longer to be Oxted – or even Oxted-and-Limpsfield – congregational church. Christ Church was suggested, and Church of the Pilgrim Way, but Church of the Peace of God was chosen. The name was agreed on 3 July 1935. On 24 July Church Meeting noted: '*Peace*, expression was given to our deep concern at the resumption of the armaments race in Europe and the threat thus given to Peace: that we give

[21] When Matthews died in 1962 he left a bequest to the parish church; his house is now (1981) the Oxted Friends Meeting. 'If his manner sometimes suggested an Olympian uncommittedness more natural in an undergraduate or a country gentleman than in a Christian minister, at other times the flame shot forth from his blue eyes or in his gentle but decisive voice, revealing an affectionateness, severity, a fury for truth and decency, which self-protection and good manners normally veiled'. His books (including Proust) were 'tastefully bound but not for show'; his enthusiasms were for gothic architecture, music and birds; postcard views of French cathedrals lined his summerhouse walls, but family portraits, a portrait of Cromwell, and modern art took pride of place indoors. G. F. Nuttall, 'A. G. Matthews', *Transactions Congregational Historical Society*, Vol. XIX, No. 4, May 1963, pp. 176–7.

Oxted interior

special thought to this matter at a Sunday service and continually in our prayers'.

To its members the Church of Peace of God became simply 'The Peace', its minute book noting prosaically as year succeeded year through the international pressures of the 1930s, 'Anniversary of opening of The Peace'.

So the community of the Peace, its corporate fellowship of gathered believers, unfolded in the four and a half decades since Hannah Pipe and the other select city folk settled in the neighbourhood. What of the building itself, and F. W. Lawrence, its architect?

Inspiration for the design came to the architect some years before he received the commission. He was in Switzerland 'evolving a new church in a rather casual way, but gradually it assumed quite new and, as I thought, interesting lines'.[22]

So they were. The brief was for a chapel suited to 'a neighbourhood which demands the picturesque',[23] to seat four hundred and to cost £4,200.

---

[22] L. Temple, *The Shining Brother*, n.d. [*c.* 1940–41], pp. 27–28. Oxted appears disguised as Inglewell: the attribution is borne out by Lawrence's secretary, Mrs. B. Tiller, in correspondence to the author.

[23] *Congregational Year Book* (1939), p. 736.

Ewell exterior

In the event it sat more and cost considerably more:

> ... As one looks, on entering, towards the Lord's table, a screen of light falls from the twenty windows (invisible from the rear) of the central tower. Round this screen of light are the four great arches of the church. Through this light one perceives the rather darker chancel. Beyond this is the golden light about the table from hidden windows of amber. In this glow will be the blue curtains and the embroidered gold. This effect will be silent and powerful. As one sits in the nave there is no window in the direct line of sight. This is important in helping meditation, a point not always taken into account... Leaving the Communion Table and looking towards the arch by which one entered, one will see a marble paved lobby and three ribbons of light; these three windows are very narrow and tall, having low sills, and although leaded they will have clear glass. Through this is seen the water with the lilies and reeds.[24]

[24] *Ibid.* (1934), pp. 244–5.

Ewell interior

That was the intention. In the event, windows behind the communion table replaced the blue and gold draperies; the table, pulpit and desk were of oak rather than Columbian pine, stained warm sepia, with arabesques of gold and colour; the floor was to be covered with purple matting, the walls distempered in ivory white and stone. Outside, the concern was with the grouping of masses, with proportion rather than ornament, with the union of man and nature. 'Two terraces with a small fountain, bird sanctuary, and lily-pond complete the exterior. The water and the lilies are visible from any point in the central aisle through delicately leaded windows'.[25] Here surely, in this consciousness of colour, of atmosphere, of texture, this manipulation of sight, silence and drama, is both Calvinist aesthetic and occasion, the setting for what the poet Donald Davie has memorably described as 'sensuous pleasure deployed with an unusually frugal, and therefore exquisite fastidiousness'.[26]

Frederic William Lawrence, who composed this pleasure, was born in

[25] *Ibid.*, and 1936, p. 682.
[26] D. Davie, *A Gathered Church: The Literature of the English Dissenting Interest 1700–1930* (1978), p. 26.

1882, the year of Miss Pipe's brush with the cathedral canon, and died in
1948. His origins were Nottinghamshire Wesleyan, and the rest of his life
might be interpreted as a reaction against them; at the end of it he described
his first church design as 'essentially ... a reaction against the not-too-
happy days spent about sixty years ago in one or two of the smaller Free
Churches of the Midlands.'[27] The reaction of one of his sisters to their
upbringing was to join an anglo-catholic order; his own was to join no
church, but rather to develop an intensely personal theology which
allowed him to remain loosely free church, worshipping most often with
the congregationalists opposite his house, whose church he had designed
and with whose members and ministers he developed close friendships.

Frederic Lawrence was a charmer. He was a bachelor ('a huge man – 6 ft
3 or 4 ins') with a dry sense of humour. He suffered from prolonged bouts
of ill health and became very deaf, a disability which he turned to good
account when conferences with chapel building committees became
tiresome.[28] In fact they seldom became tiresome; the charm which he first
exerted through his beguiling conversation and watercolour perspectives
survived the transformation of wash and words into bricks and mortar. 'I
am glad to hear you are having Lawrence as your architect', wrote
Geoffrey Edmonds, having just emerged from three years of the Lawrence
treatment, to a fellow minister about to undergo it:

> He's an awfully nice chap. Like all architects he has his pet ideas and
> sticks to them: but we found him most pleasant to work with and
> amenable to our suggestions. He is a little deaf ...
> He told us our Church would be very light, but it isn't – don't tell
> him I said so: it is light enough, but only just.
> If he wants you to have a bird bath etc. remember that ours cost
> quite £80 ...
> Best wishes to you! You will soon have the second best church in
> Surrey! ...[29]

That stated the situation exactly. Lawrence's plan for Surrey's 'second
best church' (to seat 300 and cost £5,000) had arrived two weeks earlier,
typed on the blue writing paper which was a Lawrence trademark:

> I am not sure whether this is a proper place to state the fact that I have
> quite definite ideals regarding church design. One is that the whole

[27] N. A. Turner-Smith, *Living Stones: The Building of Immanuel Congregational Church Southbourne 1910–1965*, n.d. (*c.* 1965), p. 19.

[28] Information from Miss Doris M. Lawrence, 1 June 1977; Mrs. Gwen Watson, May 1977; Mrs. B. Tiller, 8 November 1978; Rev. J. Norman Beard, 6 October 1978.

[29] Revd. G. Edmonds, Oxted, to Revd. E. Parkes Perry, Ewell, 8 December 1936, Ewell United Reformed Church MSS.

building should be sound and good behind and before with no noticable [sic] inferior back. This can be achieved when cost is of vital importance only by discarding all superficial ornament and modelling the whole building so that its various masses have beauty in themselves and in their relation to one another.

Good shape costs nothing.

With regard to the interior, this I have endeavoured to design to assist meditation and worship.

Height in a church immediately suggests spiritual aspiration but it is impossible to design very high roofs where money is necessarily limited.

I have therefore contented myself with making the one section of the roof which all face, unusually high. Chancel, Nave and Transepts are comparitively [sic] low. The central portion is suddenly higher and the roof which would be before the eye of each worshipper rises to over 31 ft. The ridge of the Nave and Transepts is about 21 ft . . .

One other point. The Apse is lit with four amber windows; these are high above the apse arch, and are designed to give a golden glow onto the Lord's table.

This golden light together with the light from the sixteen high windows in the central portion would have an effect of beauty which would be permanently impressive . . .[30]

The similarities between Oxted and Ewell, Surrey's best and second best in outer suburban churches, will be apparent. So it was with all Lawrence's churches, both from design (divine design, Lawrence felt) and because they were all commissioned within a distinct period of his professional career, the 1930s, when he devoted himself solely to church work. Distinctive though that work was, however, it fitted naturally into the development of his career.

Despite his midland origins, Lawrence was really both product and beneficiary of that middle-class explosion of seaside and suburban property which enveloped the Edwardian and Georgian home counties. His father became a Southbourne estate agent and his own career was a sensibly inevitable extension of this. He became an architect.[31] His master, Arthur Marshall, was a solid Nottingham practitioner, with a Wesleyan background and a large workhouse practice; but there was also an Arts and Crafts side to Marshall, who was a watercolourist, an advanced photographer and the author of a standard monograph, *Specimens of*

---

[30] Lawrence's *Plan*, November 1936, Ewell MSS. The present minister writes '. . . the secretary commented on how the golden light spoils the effect of the pastel shades illuminated by fluorescent strips in the apse. So the vision fades . . .' Revd. R. Church, 26 April 1981.

[31] The outline of his career depends on the R.I.B.A. Biographical Record.

Antique Carved Furniture and Woodwork (1888): 'I admire these old examples as records of the honest work and skilful hand of the old English workman'.[32] This was the world of Crouch and Butler but Frederic Lawrence's own artistic tendencies were further disciplined by periods of study under Solomon Solomon, whose contribution to war art was the perfection of *camouflage*,[33] and Frank Brangwyn, whose once famous murals in muddy brown and fading golds await their renaissance.[34] For a while Lawrence's architectural and artistic training was fused in a design consultancy at Liberty's, but for most of his life he practiced in Southbourne, building shops and innumerable houses. It was only in the late 1920s that he started in personal practice and his specialism in churches really began in 1932, two years before his F.R.I.B.A. In the eight years before May 1940 he designed seventeen churches and added to or altered another fifteen; and in May 1940 he was discussing plans for a further eighteen churches and seven halls.[35]

Frank Brangwyn, Liberty's of London, and the pines and rhododendrons of south coast real estate – the perfect foil for thoughtful and gently prosperous free churchmen, pillars of the distributors' civilisation that is suburbia: as a survey of his other churches, besides Oxted and Ewell, might suggest.

All Lawrence churches exerted the threefold appeal of reverence, relevance and practicality. The Ewell church was cruciform, but that, felt the *Year Book*, had 'the effect of gathering the congregation about the pulpit', while Lawrence wrote reassuringly, 'I feel that it is a practical church on sound lines that will not be expensive'.[36] Lawrence's first church, and perhaps his best known, was Immanuel, Southbourne; 'A good example of its date (1927–1930); blocky brickwork with round-headed windows and a square tower. Churchy interior with tripartite 'Venetian' arches to both choir and sanctuary. Byzantine capitals.'[37] The official description was naturally more expansive:

[32] Marshall's contract for Nottingham Workhouse, suspected by some of being a rigged job, was massive – it used up to seventeen million bricks. For Marshall (1858–1914) see Pauline F. Heathcote, 'Arthur Marshall Architect and Photographer', *Nottinghamshire Topic*, October 1976, pp. 12–13; I am grateful to Mrs. Heathcote for further information. Also Pike and Briscoe, *Nottinghamshire and Derbyshire at the Opening of the Century; Contemporary Biographies*, p. 162.

[33] Solomon J. Solomon (1860–1927) was a fashionable portrait and subject painter, a pupil of Leighton and Alma Tadema whose 'Echo and Narcissus' (1895), a 'notable exercise in flesh painting', remains notable. See *D.N.B.*

[34] For Sir Frank Brangwyn (1867–1956) see *D.N.B.*

[35] C. D. Thomas, 'Introduction', L. Temple, *The Shining Brother*, n.d. [1940–41], p. 10.

[36] *Congregational Year Book* (1938), p. 690; F. W. Lawrence to Revd. H. Kenward, 10 December 1936, Ewell MSS.

[37] N. Pevsner and D. Lloyd, *The Buildings of England: Hampshire* (1967), p. 600.

Financial considerations [it cost £8,000 and was to hold 550]
exercised some influence upon the choice of style: extreme simplicity
was enjoined.

It represents an attempt to achieve dignity by mass rather than by
ornament. The exterior lines of the structure, for which the bricks
were specially burnt under the architect's direction, would be of
classical severity were they not relieved by a tendency towards
Byzantine freedom. With such catholicity of fancy the formation of
a lily-pond and bird sanctuary in the forecourt, over which the figure
of St. Francis of Assisi presides, is in full accord.

Within, impressions proper to a sacred building are bound up with
the sensation of height produced by the deep coloured glass window
in the memorial tower, and the lofty arch connecting the tower to
the church, and with the sensation of mystery produced by the
golden lighting of the apse. Indeed, this golden note plays an
important part in softening and enriching the interior.

There was a practical touch too: the first eight pews contained 'earphones
connected to microphones, for deaf worshippers'.[38]

1934 and 1935 saw the building of the church at Oxted; in these years
Lawrence was first overwhelmed by church commissions. 1937 and 1938
saw the building of the church at Ewell. By now Lawrence was responsible
for a cluster of churches, mostly small, some tiny, all in brick, acoustically
difficult. Danbury, in Essex, seating 100 for £1,180, relied for its appeal 'on
simple proportions and good brickwork' so that 'a certain charm could be
obtained at little cost'.[39] In the suburbs of Nottingham there were two
churches: Arnold, opened in 1938, and Sherwood a year later, larger and
with drawbacks, for sermons tended to disappear into the wide and lofty
tower at the crossing.[40] There were also renovations. Middlegate,
Yarmouth, a puritan cause in dissenting gothic dress, managed to combine
Lawrentian softness with blatant gentrification: central aisle, raised
communion table set back in its apse, reredos behind, pulpit to right and
lectern to left, Hammond electric organ. 'The impression that the building
makes upon entering it is that it combines the richly prized intimacy of our
Free Church worship with the reverence and dignity associated with
Anglican buildings. The appearance of the choir in their simple black
gowns enhances this impression.'[41] There were more congenial alterations

[38] *Congregational Year Book* (1932), pp. 209–10; *Ibid.* (1929), p. 203.

[39] *Congregational Year Book* (1938), p. 689.

[40] 'The nave roof is at the same level as that of the chancel, and when I am in the
pulpit I feel that the congregation is seated in a kind of tunnel at the far side of the
great space of the tower. But the building is much appreciated by the members . . .'
Revd. R. R. Turner, 4 April 1977; *Congregational Year Book*, (1938), p. 688; *Ibid.*,
(1939), p. 737.

[41] *Congregational Year Book*, (1938), p. 695. The black gowns are now blue.

for Paton College. Paton, named after J. B. Paton, its most remarkable principal, was the Nottingham congregational theological college intended for students who were older than the normal run, or less academically oriented. In the 1930s, in a curious moment of aberration, Paton moved house to a castellated manor house, 'too prim to be truly picturesque', next to a parish church dismissed by Pevsner as 'archaeologically highly incorrect'.[42] Lawrence's part in this, in 1937, was to turn two brick storage sheds by the mansion's side door into a chapel, to seat fifty, to cost £300:

> One of the rooms was made to form a large apse, containing the communion table, flooded with golden light from an unseen window ... Above the communion table, in the light panelling to the apse, is an arabesque in gold and green, cream and ruby, in the form of a cross. The room is panelled with dark oak. The floor has old stone flags. The exterior door is painted royal blue and has black iron studs ... The architect describes the chapel as 'Franciscan – in that it is little and among trees, and curiously like the houses of prayer in Assisi – in that it is part of a mass of other buildings, and under an arch, and only to be found by search'.[43]

Congregationalists were not alone in warming to Lawrence's churches. For the Worthing presbyterians there was a replica, smoothed and improved, of Immanuel Southbourne.[44] At Worthing as at Southbourne due attention was paid to the requirements of a rapidly growing, comfortably circumstanced congregation. A 'carriage way' round the church gave parking space for motor cars; and there were hearing aids in selected pews. The building was to be an object lesson, its cruciform shape a sharp contrast to an age 'where secularism is so strong', its style, with Roman arches and lofty tower, 'mass in bold outline', witness that 'man's progress must be upwards rather than along a horizontal plane ... aspiration rather than acceleration'. Though there was here to be no modern 'stream-lining, suggestive of speed', there was to be that other modern spirit of simplicity and sincerity: the organ invisible, marked only by an oak grille, 'through which the sound enters the Chancel'; the lighting indirect, suggestive, with no windows in the people's line of vision. 'Amber windows light the apse, and steel-blue windows light the chancel. This has the effect of creating a golden glow about the Communion Table

---

[42] For Rollaveston Manor see N. Pevsner, *The Buildings of England: Nottinghamshire* (1951), p. 188.

[43] Information from Revd. R. R. Turner; *Congregational Year Book*, (1938), p. 693.

[44] The following account is based on St. Columba's building *Brochure* of 1936, for which I am indebted to Mrs. J. L. Armour.

Alverstoke exterior

. . .' Lawrence took pains to be explicitly reformed at Worthing. His apse, dignified with carved stone arcading, touches of Byzantium shading into the Celtic fringe, was large, 'to give architectural expression to what is distinctive in our Church government, namely the Session'. During communion the elders were to sit there rather than make do in the choir stalls. In the apse's centre was the focal point, the table, giving 'due emphasis to the end of all our worship, namely fellowship with our Risen Lord', but the pulpit too was shaped and placed to draw the mind to 'that vital necessity, the prophetic Ministry of the Word'.[45]

[45] The building was to seat 450 and cost, inclusive of furnishings, £11,000 of which £4,000 was still required by late 1936. The cause had started in 1927. By March 1931 a building, later to serve as hall and schools, had been opened. By February 1935 a building fund for a new church had been launched, encouraged by two gifts of £3,500: and the congregation was 300 strong. The builder, A. W. Clements (Grigg, Immanuel's builder, had submitted too high a tender), was currently building three other local churches (Christian Science, baptist and anglican) but St. Columba's was his preferred commission, useful, attractive and easy in its builder–architect relationship: 'a happy combination which few architects achieve!' Indeed, thanks to a capable assistant, architect and builder rarely met after the initial meeting. A. W. Clements, 9 September 1979.

Lawrence's methodist commissions included the small churches at Sway and Barton-on-Sea, both in Hampshire, and Little Church, the chapel for the National Children's Homes' Alverstoke branch:

> . . . there stood the Little Church its doors invitingly open. And in the shelter of the trees that surrounded the Church was a beautiful little figure of Francis of Assisi with a bird in his hand, the water trickling round him into a pool where water lilies grow.[46]

Its walls were of stone and cream cement trowelled 'to a special texture suggesting Italian masonry'; its roof was of dull red cloister tiles; inside 'golden light from hidden sources' played upon the apse:

> In the planning of the building there have been incorporated provisions for a type of worship which it is hoped 'Little Church' will be able to develop fully and beautifully. In the Form of Service used there will be co-operation by responses in Orders of Worship, simple and direct, which make full use of the words of Scripture, of prayer and of devotional music. In this way there will be opportunities for sharing such parts of the service as can be used to help young people to realize that the service is their own and not merely for them . . .[47]

For the anglicans there was St. Saviour's, Iford, in a cherry-blossomed area of bright semi-detacheds, not one of them suitable for a vicarage; 'new houses are rushing up and new people are pouring in', people with 'absolutely no money to spare. They bought their house, their furniture, and their car — if they had one — on hire purchase and their future was mortgaged for a number of years'.[48] Iford edged on to the no man's land between Bournemouth and Christchurch, north of Southbourne and a step or so down the middle class ladder. Such a district needed a church within its first five years lest the opportunity be lost for ever. For Pevsner St. Saviour's is 'decent brick Romanesque'.[49] Its site was presented by the maiden ladies who had presented the site for the congregational church nearby, a recreation in lawns of a southern meeting house barn.[50] Its

[46] Alice Campling, *The Little Church*, (Alverstoke, n.d.), pp. 4–5.

[47] *The Opening of 'The Little Church' Alverstoke Wednesday, June 23rd 1937, Order of Proceedings*; J. W. Bromwich, 'Opening of "Little Church", Alverstoke,' *Children*, June 1937, p. 237.

[48] *Scrapbook of Cuttings 1932–1973*, unpaginated, compiled by Revd. C. W. E. Caulfield Browne and in the possession of the Revd. D. E. C. Jardine.

[49] Pevsner, *Hampshire*, op. cit., p. 125.

[50] For Iford congregational church, by P. Hardy, F.R.I.B.A., seating 275, costing under £6,000 and originally intended as the first stage in a grander complex, see *Congregational Year Book*, (1935) p. 254; *Ibid.*, (1939), p. 732. As M. G. J. Payne, the

builders were the firm of congregationalists who had built Immanuel Southbourne. It was Lawrence's first anglican church and it bore all his marks – dull red Roman tiles on the roof, and an interior 'light with hope', its woodwork carefully understated, plaster walls finished 'in the style of old Italian masonry', east window shaped like a Latin cross, a 'perpetual sunshine' of amber and blue, all of it modelled on the Upper Church of San Francesco in Assisi, to hold under 500, to cost between £8,000 and £10,000. And at least one of its parish workers responded to its architect's Franciscanism, as she described its consecration in the swirling mists of a late September evening by Bishop Garbett of Winchester:

> ... We at last heard the sound of chanting. We saw dim shadows out of the past. Next three loud knocks at the west door – the Bishop was demanding entrance in the name of the King of Glory . . . And after the Bishop's secret prayer the procession led by the Cross . . .
> White walls for His white life, and hangings blue
> As Mary's robe. His Table whitely spread,
> Meet for an honoured Guest; silver and lace,
> And flowers in rich profusion graced the board
> In this Divine abode
> . . . .
> An evening came
> Of light and colour, music, praise and prayer
> On which they gave to Him His House . . .[51]

There were more prosaic, almost semi-detached, facets to such mystery. In the belfry there were Marconiphone loudspeakers 'to which recorded peals of bells can be relayed and amplified from a gramophone inside the church', while the equipment would allow Bishop Garbett, for example, 'sitting in his study at Wolvesey, to address the St. Saviour's parishioners, assembled in their church, by means of a land-line from Winchester'.[52]

There is nothing mysterious about Lawrence's clients. The bush telegraph of the trade and denominational press, the wide contacts of suburban and seaside-retired families, his reputation for easy efficiency, are explanation enough. The experience of the Worthing presbyterians'

Vicar of St. James Pokesdown put it, St. Saviour's was 'right on top of the Congregational Church, and they got in first; and we know that wherever they are there is always a certain influence around them'. St. Saviour's was consecrated in September 1936; by January 1937 its electoral roll was 547, with 165 on its free will offering list [*Scrapbook*, op. cit.]: in contrast by 1938 the congregational church had 130 members.

[51] N. D. Jacob, *The Story of the Parish Church of St. Saviours, Iford.* (Bournemouth, 1976), unpaginated.

[52] *Scrapbook*, op. cit.

building sub-committee is instructive here. They were presented with seven designs, three from architects suggested by the denomination's central home church committee, four from men whose names were submitted 'by various friends'. Lawrence was one of these. The seven quickly became a short list of three, and 700 miles of travelling in five days at the sub-committee's own expense did the rest. Southbourne, Oxted and the rapidly building Iford exerted their charm and the sub-committee, swayed by these expressions of simplicity and dignity, these sensations of worship and spirituality, opted for Lawrence.[53]

Often, however, there were suggestive personal links. The Nottingham commission resulted from a chance holiday encounter ending in close friendship with Hartley Holloway, who was an architect *manqué*, or at least atmospheric buildings were his hobby.[54] At the time Holloway was minister of Castle Gate, Nottingham, a church which liked to see itself as the east Midlands' answer to Carr's Lane, Birmingham, but which some saw as a ministers' graveyard; Holloway shortly moved on to Immanuel Southbourne. Similarly with Chetwode Caulfield-Browne of St. Saviour's. He was a retired naval man who had taken up architectural and land work in the 1920s. St. Saviour's was his first parish and he created it single handed with a freedom denied to the chapel building committees of congregational churches. He too had firm ideas, among them a dislike of memorial tablets. 'Always put your foot down against any proposal to spoil that simplicity and beauty . . .'[55]

Lawrence's methodist friendships, however, were the most suggestive of all. These were with a group of successful, yet not entirely conventional

[53] The architects sumbitted by the Home Church Committee were Thompson of Edinburgh, Rieve of Manchester, Brightliff of London: to these were added Parkinson of Blackburn, Ayrton of London, Meredith of London, and Lawrence. Ayrton's gymnasium-like St. Andrew's, a Wembley of a place, was the newest glory of Cheam; and Lawrence had already taken the Ewell commission from Meredith, who believed he had the prior claim. Meredith failed to submit designs; Thompson, Parkinson and Rieve were not impressive enough to attract the Worthing folk to 'the far north' to view their work; that left Brightliff, Ayrton and Lawrence. The sub-committee's unanimous commendation was strengthened by a testimonial from Sir Bannister Fletcher, P.R.I.B.A., and, unsolicited, from a minister who described Lawrence as 'an architect of originality and vision who evidently gives a most meticulous attention to detail'. Report of the Building Sub-Committee to the Committee of Management, Wednesday, 8 March 1936. Typescript in St. Columba's Worthing Minute Book, 1929–1940.
[54] Mrs. B. Tiller, 11 October 1978. For George Hartley Holloway (1889–1945) see *Congregational Year Book*, (1946), pp. 443–4.
[55] Caulfield-Browne lived from 1895 to 1973. See *Scrap Book.*, op. cit. St. Columba's Worthing Committee of Management confirmed in October 1937 that 'no stained glass windows, or mural memorial tablets affixed to or upon the fabric of the Church be accepted'. Minute Book, op. cit. 19 October 1937.

St. Columba's, interior

ministers who combined evangelism, culture and mysticism in generous measure: J. H. Litten, the principal of the National Children's Homes, for whom the building of the Little Church and the reconstruction of the Alverstoke branch completed the Homes' Jubilee, liked to use music in worship as behaviour therapy.[56] T. H. Kirkham befriended the New Forest gypsies, while R. M. Pope was a Cambridge classicist and hymnologist of the early church who superintended the little Sway circuit which developed from the New Forest Mission.[57] But the choicest spirit of them all was the 'Jesus mystic', A. E. Whitham. Whitham was Bournemouth's dominant methodist personality. He was superintendent of its Punshon memorial circuit for nearly seven years, chairman of the Bournemouth district thereafter. He had never ventured beyond Wesleyan bounds, for he

[56] I am grateful to Mrs. Audrey O'Dell for information about Litten (b. 1878).

[57] Pope had lectured in Hellenistic Greek at Southampton University, and, in 1914–18 to the troops in Salonika. He was superintendent at Sway to 1935 and remained for some time after; Lawrence's church there was completed in 1936. I am indebted for information about the Revd. R. M. Pope (1865–1944) and the Revd. T. J. Kirkman (1880–1973) to the Revd. C. E. Belfield.

was a son of the methodist manse, his education had been in methodist schools, and he had been a methodist minister since the age of twenty-three. Those constraints liberated him into what can only be called Wesleyan catholicism. Throughout his career Whitham attracted (the word is deliberately used) people from all denominations. An Essex farmer's son who became a congregational minister, more modernist than catholic, would cycle before the first world war into Southend or Shoeburyness to hear the young Whitham. 'He was brilliant, daring in his modernism and had a strong face with piercing eyes. We sat almost in rapture drinking in every word'.[58] A dozen or so years later an Edinburgh undergraduate in training for the congregational ministry found himself drawn to the Wesleyan Nicholson Square rather than to the congregational Augustine church by this same power with words. But the modernism had gone. Here, with a practical sense given a literary turn, was a 'wonderful pastoral occasion', here now was 'orthodox preaching at its very best', set in an extraordinary depth of public prayer.[59]

There had always been this side to Whitham. When the fascinating congregationalist turned catholic, W. E. Orchard, was still in his first, presbyterian, pastorate at Enfield, before the First World War, he and Whitham would meet each monday to think over and refashion their prayers of the previous day.[60] It was the great war, however, which focused these abilities. Whitham was convinced that as a minister of reconciliation he must dedicate himself to his enemies: and those whom he found that he most feared were not Germans but Roman catholics. Armed with a reading list provided by the principal of Cliff College, the nerve centre of methodist evangelism, Whitham immersed himself in Roman catholic spirituality. He took to it 'as to his native air'.[61] This was the Bournemouth Whitham, first president of the Methodist Sacramental Fellowship, and leader, if there were one, for Whitham was no ecclesiastical statesman, of methodism's 'high church' party.[62]

A close friendship developed between Whitham and Frederic Lawrence, and given Lawrence's profession and Whitham's public standing this had visible results. The suggestion is that the nature of those results depended at

[58] P. Bentall, *Days That Were*, typescript reminiscence, n.d.c. 1971, p. 26, in possession of Mrs. M. Bentall.

[59] The Revd. Dr. John Marsh to the author, 9 October and 13 November 1979. For Whitham at Edinburgh see too A. Gammie, *Preachers I Have Heard*, (1945), pp. 192–121.

[60] Orchard's book of prayers, *The Temple*, issued from these meetings. Dr. Marsh to the author, 13 November 1979.

[61] Revd. Gordon S. Wakefield to author, 13 September 1979.

[62] *Ibid.* For Whitham, 1879–1938, see too Fiona Mary Whitham, 'My Father', in A. E. Whitham, *The Discipline and Culture of the Spiritual Life: A Memorial Volume* (1938). I am also grateful to Revd. C. E. Belfield, Rt. Revd. Gordon Arthur and Miss Violet Cragg for describing the impact of Whitham.

least in part on the powerful personality of a man like Whitham.

Such a clientèle led to larger commissions, but we have no means of judging a large Lawrence church for the two which came his way remained at the colour wash stage. Lawrence died before his commission to rebuild Bournemouth's Punshon Memorial Church, where Whitham had ministered in the earlier 1930s, could be started. The present Punshon Memorial (1964–8), although by Lawrence's pupil Ronald Sims, is a very different sort of building.[63] The friendship with Whitham and the design for Punshon Memorial were perhaps factors in Lawrence's selection to rebuild the bombed City Temple, London's leading congregational preaching centre, for the methodist Leslie Weatherhead; but Lawrence died before his plans for this too were completed, and the commission went to Seely and Paget.[64] The largest of all remained a dream. In 1932 Lawrence competed for Guildford cathedral, but of course the commission for that went to Edward Maufe.[65]

Lawrence's surviving churches[66] are, without exception, greatly liked by those who worship in them, who tolerate the acoustics, healthily sceptical about the amber holiness.[67] But all of them share one curiously uncongregational characteristic. As Lawrence's secretary has put it: 'each of these Churches is endowed with an atmosphere of power and peace, obvious especially when the Church is empty of humanity . . .'[68] The mark perhaps of the lonely artistry of a deaf man, unable to commit himself to membership of a gathered Christian fellowship.

What special gifts, then, did Lawrence the architect bring to bear on the uneasy coalition of corporate fellowship, building committee and pastor?

[63] Mrs. B. Tiller to author, 11 October 1978; Pevsner describes it, with its 'tall spike' as 'spiky . . . in other ways typical of church designing today'. Pevsner, *Hampshire*, op. cit., p. 127.

[64] A. E. Whitham had been Weatherhead's immediate, and successful, predecessor at Brunswick Wesleyan church, Leeds, in 1929, the setting of Weatherhead's first widely known ministry. Mrs. Dorothy Butler to author, 13 June 1977; Revd. J. N. Beard to author, 6 October 1978; B. Hammond, J. Dewey, L. D. Weatherhead, *The City Temple in the City of London: Past, Present and Future*, (1968), pp. 35–8.

[65] Lawrence was one of 183 competitors. Maufe (1882–1974) was known in free church circles for his methodist Clubland Church, Walworth. Mrs. B. Tiller to author, 11 October 1978.

[66] The chapel at Tollerton has been dismantled, the church at Barton-on-Sea has been replaced by a larger building, that at Sway is no longer used for methodist worship.

[67] Thus Ewell: 'Two small windows to the apse have been thought to have provided very impressive lighting. I do not know that otherwise there is any special effect of mystery or reverence . . . [its acoustics] have always been thought poor'. P. Jeffrey to author, 9 December 1978.

[68] Mrs. B. Tiller to author, 14 October 1978.

Ministers with an artistic sense could see easily enough the psychological benefits in recovering a lost churchmanship. Hartley Holloway of Nottingham and Southbourne was such a minister. Impressed by the symbolism of the blood-red cross cut into the lantern above Leslie Weatherhead's pulpit at Brunswick Leeds (the light of the cross burning its way into men's minds, healing their physical and moral ills), he introduced such a lamp to Castle Gate, Nottingham, whose members were at once worried lest the psychological power of the symbol should dull their God-given critical faculties. Holloway responded vigorously: 'Has the Cross on all the walls round the Church been a hindrance to your worship ...? When Castle Gate refuses to use freedom to adapt its worship then the Church must look for a Minister who does not value the 'glory of heritage' as much as I do ...'[69]

This was the spirit to which Lawrence responded and it is with Immanuel, Southbourne, Lawrence's first church, to which Hartley Holloway came as second minister, that one can best follow Lawrence's *personal* response to a chapel community.

Immanuel was not a suburban graft, like Oxted or Ewell. It was a completely new cause founded at a time (1910) when a free church was not just desirable but necessary for a successful residential development. Lawrence's connexion began with the ministry of Harold Brierley (1919–36). Since the late 1890s Brierley's pastorates had been at 'thoughtful' churches – Queen Street Sheffield, Clarendon Park Leicester, Highbury Quadrant. Brierley's recreations were cricket, football and golf; his sermons were essays in psychology; his health was not good.[70]

Brierley's sense of congregational church order was lax, but his independency was undoubted: 'I must be in the position of an independent minister and be perfectly free from any semblance of subordination'. Immanuel was his creation.[71]

His building schemes began in 1922. By 1927 there was a building committee and a building fund, but there was no architect. Lawrence's name, apparently, came up when Brierley and the building committee secretary, E. J. Marsh, had demolished drawings submitted by a local man.

[69] This was in 1932. A transformation of Castle Gate's ancillary premises planned in 1945–8 was yet another scheme thwarted by Lawrence's death. R. Duce, *Castle Gate Church in the Twentieth Century*, (Nottingham, 1977), pp. 51, 70, 72. Castle Gate, like Middlegate Yarmouth, was a 'robed choir' congregational church. The City Temple led the way, in purple, in 1904. By the 1930s the move was common – black at Yarmouth, but purple, with tricorne hats, frilly long sleeves and cravats for the ladies, not women here surely, at Nottingham.

[70] For Harold Brierley (1873–1954) see *Congregational Year Book*, (1955).

[71] The chief source for the following account is N. A. Turner-Smith, *Living Stones: The Building of Immanuel Congregational Church Southbourne 1910–1965*, (n.d., c. 1965).

'Go to Frederic Lawrence', Marsh urged. 'He has never built a church before, but I believe he has the genius'.

So Brierley went to Frederic Lawrence, whose response, by his own account, was much as if he had been asked to build a cinema.[72] Towards the end of his life Lawrence wrote down his memories of Immanuel's inception:

> The design of the church was an endeavour to . . . express in ordinary bricks the simple Matterhorn rock of Christianity.
>
> The genius of Mr. Brierley made Immanuel possible and the enthusiasm of a little well-defined group of people made an atmosphere magical to work in. The word 'magical' is exactly right, for in that atmosphere ideas grew of themselves and became winged.

And Lawrence recalled the building committee and Marsh its secretary; Griggs the builder, his sons and his workmen; everybody from Colonel Cox to Mr. Sims the scaffolder.

But magic did not bring ease. The shape of the church only evolved some weeks later, one summer evening, during a drive home from Reading. 'The air was still and waiting, the sun was going down between two long islands of gold and the last birds were homing'.

That was in June 1927. In July came the formal competition for the church, which Lawrence won. Building began early in 1929. Meanwhile Lawrence had spent long periods in Switzerland, seriously ill, and he became convinced that while the exterior of the proposed church was entirely right, its interior should be changed. His recollection sheds a rare light on the harmony sometimes possible, but seldom achieved, between builder, client and architect. It was now early spring 1929.

> About six one morning I woke all fresh and well and strolled down in my evening gown. I made myself a cup of tea and put on the gramophone. The music was the Londonderry Air, not in any sense great music but sweet.
>
> In the middle of that I suddenly saw the whole of Immanuel as it is now. It literally was instantaneous. The plans were handy so I spread them out and saw that this extraordinary flash was possible as a design. It *fitted*.
>
> I nearly went off my head and quickly put it on paper. There was, just as there was with the outside, a queer sense of *certainty*.
>
> When the drawings were made I showed them to Mr. Brierley . . .: 'Magnificent, Lawrence! How much extra is it going to cost?' At this point Griggs the builder came to the rescue: 'Just you do the

[72] L. Temple, *The Shining Brother*, op. cit., p. 25.

working drawings. We won't bother about the committee and I
guarantee it won't show as an extra'.

So it was done. Lawrence was deprecating about the result: 'The inside,
architects don't think so much of. Now, *architecturally*, the inside isn't a
patch on the outside; but I personally think that there is a kindliness, a kind
of mercy about it which is honest and good'.

The nature of that kindliness and mercy needs to be probed; and the
story's end, as far as Immanuel and the present study are concerned,
provides the point of departure for this quest. It concerns the question of
the forecourt statue to St. Francis, and the acquiescence in the 1920s of a free
church to such a thing. Lawrence wanted it, rather as a personal memorial
to the saint: 'a pool of water-lilies with running water and a small island-
bath for birds in the centre. Presiding over all was to be a statue of Francis
himself '[73]. So personal a scheme could not easily be communicated to a
client. From the building committee's side there would be the fear of cost;
from the denominational side there would be cries of 'Rome'. In fact the
cries of Rome came chiefly from outsiders and the question of cost solved
itself. So did the question of sculptor. In July 1929 Lawrence went to
Haslemere for the Poetry Society's garden party at Aldworth, Tennyson's
old home. There he met the widow of G. F. Watts. From their
conversation came a promise that she would sculpt St. Francis. 'Half an
hour later I was driving home through the mellow evening without a care
in the world, for I had begun to feel that Immanuel was coming alive'.

St. Francis arrived at Immanuel in March 1930 and the church was
opened on 3 June with the singing of 'Onward Christian Soldiers' and
'Light up this House with Glory, Lord'. The new building's first Sunday
was Whit Sunday with R. J. Campbell, once of the City Temple but a
canon of Chichester now, preaching in the morning and Sir Dan Godfrey
conducting the Hallelujah Chorus in the evening. Twenty-eight years after
Hannah Elizabeth Pipe's enraptured discovery of Assisi from the cool
rooms of the Hotel Subasio, Frederic Lawrence's Matterhorn Rock of
Christianity, as Immanuel's historian has put it, softened without by the
merciful simplicity of St. Francis' lily pond and within by the apse's golden
light, exploded into praise:[74] a south coast recreation, if only for a moment,
of Lawrence's experiences in the Upper Church at Assisi, its candles of
golden fire in the vast darkness, with music and incense streaming about
them, and 'the transparent gleam of something other than candlelight'.[75]

---

[73] *Ibid.*, p. 26.

[74] Turner-Smith, op. cit., p. 29.

[75] *Ibid.*, pp. 25–6; *Shining Brother*, p. 163. An account, continuing the story
further, of what Lawrence believed to be the implications, for himself and for his
work, of his Franciscan experiences can be found in C. Binfield ' "Shining
Brother": F. W. Lawrence (1882–1948) and his churches', *The Christian
Parapsychologist*, Vol. 4, No. 5. March 1982, pp. 151–158.

INDEX